A LIFETIME OF MEMORIES

To Lady Saltoun,

With my best wishes and happy memories

[signature] 27th February 2004.

Coat of Arms of Sir Albert McQuarrie Kt

A LIFETIME OF MEMORIES

by

Sir Albert McQuarrie Kt

The Memoir Club

© Sir Albert McQuarrie 2013

First published in 2013 by
The Memoir Club
Arya House
Langley Park
Durham
DH7 9XE
Tel: 0191 3731739
Tel: 0191 3735660
Email: memoirclub@msn.com

All rights reserved.
Unauthorised duplication
contravenes existing laws.
British Library Cataloguing in
Publication Data.
A catalogue record for this book
is available from the
British Library.

ISBN: 978-1-84104-541-2

*In memory of Roseleen
and
with fondest love and gratitude to Rhoda*

*I thank my son Dermot for the love and affection
shown to his Mother before her sudden death
and for his continued love and devotion
to me at all times*

*My grandchildren –
Catherine, Jonathan, Louise, Roseleen,
Robert, Stephanie, Elizabeth and Dermot*

*My great-grandchildren –
Caitlin. Holly, JJ-Albert and Madison
Elli, Constance, Lottie and Felix
Jak and Josh
Poppy*

All are a great joy to me.

Contents

List of Illustrations ix
Acknowledgements xiii
Foreword xv
Chapter 1 The Early Years 1
Chapter 2 The War Years 16
Chapter 3 Return to Civilian Life 37
Chapter 4 The Great Storm of 1968 51
Chapter 5 Answering the Call to help the People of Gibraltar ... 63
Chapter 6 A Lighter Side of Life 82
Chapter 7 Entering into National Politics 92
Chapter 8 Entering the House of Commons as a Member
 of Parliament 110
Chapter 9 Down to Work as an MP 119
Chapter 10 Mr Fish and the Buchan Bulldog 131
Chapter 11 The British Nationality Bill, 1981 140
Chapter 12 The 1981 Budget Fuel Price Crisis 161
Chapter 13 Parliamentary Delegation to Australia 171
Chapter 14 Common Fisheries Policy, 1983 180
Chapter 15 St Fergus Gas Terminal 187
Chapter 16 A Holiday in South Africa 198
Chapter 17 Peterhead Harbours (South Bay Development) Order
 Confirmation Bill, 1986 205
Chapter 18 Safety at Sea Bill, 1986 216
Chapter 19 The Sudden Passing of Roseleen 227
Chapter 20 Visiting the Homeless in the Streets of London 233
Chapter 21 The Chairman's Panel 238
Chapter 22 Margaret Thatcher 245
Chapter 23 Special Events, 1986 252
Chapter 24 General Election, 1987 257
Chapter 25 Elections! 265
Chapter 26 The Conclusion 272
Index 276

List of Illustrations

1. The McQuarrie family, 1925 1
2. My brother Robert 4
3. My brother Algernon 4
4. My sister Margaret 4
5. My brother Charles 4
6. Granny with my parents, Margaret and Charles on holiday in Yarmouth 6
7. Playing the bagpipes with the Scouts 9
8. In our Scout and Cub Uniforms 10
9. In Air Cadet Officers' Uniform 11
10. At Crookham Camp Fleet, 1940 18
11. The *Arandora Star* sunk by Germans 21
12. With Major Clark and Lieut Robson, 1941 25
13. Greenock Blitz damage by Germans in Dalrymple Street 27
14. Greenock Blitz damage by Germans at Westburn Sugar Refinery ... 27
15. Greenock Blitz damage by Germans in Waverly Street 28
16. Copy of oil painting of me by soldier, 1942 30
17. Our Wedding photograph, 1945 34
18. Alice McPhail hands a Good Luck Horse Shoe to Roseleen 35
19. Roseleen with Parents, Dermot and 'Dirk' the favourite dog 36
20. Presentation of the Royal Horticulture Society Medal for 50 years service 45
21. Great Storm damage Glasgow City, 1968 55
22. Great Storm damage Glasgow City, 1968 56
23. Great Storm damage Glasgow City, 1968 56
24. Great Storm damage Glasgow City, 1968 59
25. Group of workers off to Gibraltar, 1969 66
26. Our family at Dermot and Libby's Wedding 71
27. McQuarrie and McCaffery families in Paisley 72
28. Bronze Head and Shoulders of Her Majesty The Queen 74
29. Gibraltar Health Centre under Construction 76

ix

30. The Health Centre completed and in action 77
31. Gibraltar £10 note showing Health Centre 77
32. Standing beside the stone Tablet, 1974 78
33. The Tablet at the Health Centre entrance 78
34. With Roseleen and Dermot on the *Orsova*, 1970 82
35. The Party on the *Orsova* with Fijian friends 83
36. At a House Party in Fiji with friends, 1970 85
37. Prince Charles handing over Independence Documents in Fiji October, 1970 85
38. Albert Park Fiji Independence Celebrations 86
39. Raffles Hotel Singapore 88
40. At Burns Society Dinner in Hong Kong 90
41. Teuchar Lodge my Constituency Home 98
42. At No. 10 Downing Street with Fishing Petition 99
43. With Party Supporters at Downing Street 100
44. With Edward Heath in the Constituency 101
45. With Alan Chisholm and Sandy Cook of Bredero 102
46. The Capsule at Paisley Shopping Mall 104
47. George Younger MP receives a lobster from Jimmy Lovie on a visit to the Constituency 106
48. Margaret Thatcher visits Peterhead, 1978 107
49. Celebrating election as a Member of Parliament at Aberdeen Beach Ballroom with Roseleen 108
50. House of Commons Chamber showing the Red Lines and White Line Bar at the House 115
51. On the Terrace for Members Only section 116
52. The Terrace with Bill Waker MP and friends 117
53. At the Pyramids in Cairo 124
54. In Jerusalem at the Menorah 125
55. Back on board the *Daphne* 126
56. The Buchan Bulldog canvassing 132
57. The Buchan Bulldog and Dog 137
58. Ariel view of Gibraltar 140
59. Changing the Guard at Governor's House 142
60. Gibraltar's New Marina 147
61. The New Gibraltar 152
62. Signing the Freedom Register 156
63. Spanish officials opening the border gates 158
64. Print of Gibraltar presented to me after the Commons victory 159
65. Standing beside the bronze figure of Governor Macquarie 172
66. Sitting in Chancellor's Chair at Macquarie University 174

LIST OF ILLUSTRATIONS

67. Laying Wreath at Cenotaph 175
68. At Fish Processing Factory in Fraserburgh 182
69. Prime Minister surrounded by supporters in Strichen 185
70. Prime Minister signs Visitors book at Party HQ in Mintlaw 187
71. St Fergus Gas Terminal 189
72. Burnt out roof of 'A' Hall after Peterhead Prison Riot 193
73. A Helicopter trip to the Gold Mines 197
74. Drilling for Gold at the Nibe 198
75. With children at the Mine School 199
76. Unveiling of South Bay Development Peterhead 212
77. Unveiling of the Sir Albert Quay Peterhead 213
78. Citation presented to me by the Board of Directors at Peterhead Harbour Authority 214
79. Emergency Position Indicator Radio Beacon. EPIRB 219
80. The Safety at Sea Act 1986 promoted by me 226
81. Roseleen at our Teuchar Lodge Home, 1985 227
82. Roseleen and me with the grandchildren at Teuchar Lodge Cuminestown in summer, 1985 230
83. The homeless in London's Cardboard City 234
84. Chairman of Scottish MPs meeting in Edinburgh, 1986 239
85. Margaret Thatcher in Dundee, 1978 246
86. Margaret Thatcher in East Aberdeenshire, 1979 247
87. With Lord and Lady Boothby signing Fishing Petition 252
88. Prime Minister's letter, 17th July 1987 261
89. At Buckingham Palace with Knight Bachelor Insignia 262
90. With my Son Dermot at Buckingham Palace, 1987 266
91. Election Campaign House at Ballindalloch 268
92. On the campaign by helicopter - European Election, 1989 267
93. Rhoda and me in Order of St John of Jerusalem Robes 271
94. Rhoda and me attending Grandson Robert's Wedding 273
95. Rhoda and me attending Prime Minister's Reception 274

Acknowledgements

I wish to express my sincere thanks and deep appreciation to the organisations and many people who provided information enabling me to obtain extracts for my book from Media articles, Hansard and other Official reports. I am grateful for copies of photographs from a number of sources. I am pleased to print names of those who have assisted me. Sadly a number have passed away. If I have omitted anyone I apologise.

The support I have received from Miss Lynn Davidson and her staff at The Memoir Club, Publishers of my book, has been exceptional.

Media

Press & Journal, Aberdeen; *Evening Express*, Aberdeen; *Buchan Observer*; *Fraserburgh Herald*; *The Scotsman*; Thomson Publications Ltd; *The Herald*; *The Times*; *Daily Telegraph*; *Turriff Advertiser*; *Ellon Advertiser*; *Knock News*; The Official Report (Hansard); *Greenock Telegraph*; *Banffshire Journal*, *Gibraltar Chronicle*; *Gibraltar Democrat*.

Journalists and Organisations

William Raynor; James Naughtie; Bill Doult; Alastair Bisset; Peter Woodifield; John Dron; Peter Strachan for their journalistic skill in reporting my activities in the House of Commons and the Constituency. To Albert Poggio CBE of the Gibraltar London office for copies of photographs. To David Gordon Editor of *Knock News* for his help and photographs, especially the outer cover of the Book Jacket; House of Commons Image Department for photograph; Total Oil E&P UK for photograph and help; Norman Burniston for photographs of Greenock Blitz; *The Herald* for photographs of 1968 Glasgow Big Storm damage.

Friends whom I wish to thank

Bill Mackie, John Wallace, David Buchan and all Directors of Peterhead Bay Authority; Ken Duncan Editor *Buchan Observer*; Louis Peralta and

Dominique Searle in Gibraltar; W.L. Ramsay Shaw for help and photographs; Lady (Sally) Grocott; David W. Shaw; Michael Watt; Alan Buchan and John Anderson of North East Weekly for computer advice and assistance. There are also those whom I have thanked within the Chapters of the book.

There are two people whom I wish to give a special mention
First of all my friend and colleague of many years the Rt Hon Sir Malcolm Rifkind KCMG, PC, QC, MP who accepted my invitation to write the Foreword, I extend my appreciation and grateful thanks.

Secondly to my dear wife Rhoda who assiduously worked daily for ten months, rectifying and setting out in meticulous manner my writings of each Chapter. I much admired her patience and determination to ensure the completion of *A Lifetime of Memories*. Rhoda has played a big part in my life for many years particularly the last twenty-four when we have enjoyed a happy married life. I cannot thank her enough for all the care and attention lovingly given to me.

Foreword

Albert McQuarrie the 'Buchan Bulldog', was a splendid colleague of mine in the House of Commons, during the Thatcher years.

At the age of 95 he has published his memoirs and they demonstrate what an extraordinarily varied and interesting life he has led.

His public service began two-thirds of a century ago when in 1949, he became a Councillor on Gourock Town Council where he remained until 1955. A Parliamentary candidate in 1966, he was an MP from 1979-87 and was always at the centre of debate and controversy.

He was a fine campaigner. To have lost his seat to Alex Salmond, the future First Minister of Scotland, was no disgrace. It is worth remembering that, eight years earlier Albert McQuarrie had entered Parliament by defeating the incumbent SNP MP by 558 votes, and held it again four years later.

He was formidable in his campaigning methods. It is said that at a meeting of parliamentary candidates, before he was an MP, one of his colleagues was complaining about the difficulties of getting reported in the local paper which tended to report only the speeches of his opponent, the elected MP. Albert rejected this criticism allegedly saying that the best way to get coverage in your local paper was to own it! He did and, as a result, his activities and speeches were reported regularly. I do not know whether this story is true but we all were happy to believe it and admire his resourcefulness.

As an MP he was a great champion of the fishing industry of the North-East of Scotland and this, rightly, led to him being referred to as the 'Buchan Bulldog'. It was a reference both to his physical appearance and to his tenacity. He was as happy with the title as Margaret Thatcher was with being known as the 'Iron Lady'.

His energy and enthusiasm was not confined to his own constituency. He championed the people of Gibraltar and their entitlement to remain British, for many years; chaired Parliamentary scrutiny committees at the

Speaker's request, and has done valuable charitable work. His knighthood was a well-deserved recognition of his public service.

Writing your memoirs at the age of 95 is no mean achievement. Given that his health is impressive and his energy and character seem undimmed, perhaps he should follow Churchill and entitle this book 'My Early Years.'

We could then look forward to the next volume!

Rt. Hon. Sir Malcolm Rifkind KCMG, PC, QC, MP

CHAPTER ONE

The Early Years

I WAS BORN AS THE SECOND CHILD OF Algernon Stewart McQuarrie and Alice Maude Sharman, on the 1st January 1918 in our home at 14 Murdieston Street, Greenock, Renfrewshire, which was a stone built property in a nice area of the town.

1. The McQuarrie family, 1925

Greenock originated as a small fishing village giving employment to its people in the prolific herring industry. It also had a shipyard building which was the forerunner of a massive shipbuilding industry employing thousands of people over the years. After the Act of Union in 1707 Greenock was the main hub in Scotland for trade with American ocean going steamers and the importation of raw sugar from the Caribbean. Wool garments were produced from the Merino Mill which employed hundreds of people, mainly women. The Sugar Industry was vital to Greenock. At one time there were fourteen sugar refineries and a sugar beet factory in the town providing

1

employment to many. My brother Algernon was Chief Engineer at the Westburn Sugar refinery in Drumfrochar Road. I well remember when I was about 12 years of age running behind the horse drawn carts full of sugar for the refineries and plucking a handful of sugar before the driver would dismount and 'whipping' us away!! Fortunately for Greenock, when, the shipyards experienced a downward trend in employment the American firm of IBM in 1951 set up a business on the outskirts of Greenock on land at Scott's Farm on the road to Inverkip. Initially thousands of people were employed at the business which local people referred to as 'the valley of opportunity'.

Greenock has its own newspaper called the *Greenock Telegraph*. When I was young it was a custom of mine to go down to the bottom of Sugarhouse Lane where a paper vendor was to be found every day crying out in a strong distinct voice '*Telegraph*, 5 o'clock *Telegraph*, come and buy it here'. He did a good job in keeping up the name of the *Greenock Telegraph* which was first issued in 1857 and is still going strong today.

It is said the name of Greenock came from an oak tree which in the old days stood in the centre of Cathcart Square near the Municipal Buildings. Today a large ornamental fountain stands where the oak tree used to be. One of the theories about the name lives on in a little ditty which has existed for many years and is sung regularly at home and by ex-patriots wherever they may be. I have enjoyed meeting up with ex-Greenockians all over the world and singing *The Green Oak Tree* with the words:

> I'll sing about a wee toon that stands doon by the Clyde,
> It's the toon whaur I was born and it fills my heart with pride
> My mother often telt me as she crooned me on her knee,
> That Greenock took its name from the Green Oak Tree.
>
> **Chorus:** So here's tae the Green Oak that stood upon the square,
> And here's tae its roots that are still slumbering there,
> And here's tae its townsfolk wherever they may be,
> For I'm proud that I'm a branch of the Green Oak Tree.
>
> May Greenock, like the Green Oak Tree, still flourish 'neath the sun.
> Her trade and commerce still increase for a thousand years to come
> And may each son o' Greenock, as he battles through life's storm
> Be honest, true and ne'er disgrace the town where I was born.
> Now Greenock's no' a bonny place, I've heard some folks complain,
> That when you go to Greenock you'll get nothing there but rain
> But let them say whate'er they may, with them I'll no agree,
> For aye the name o' Greenock toon will aye be dear tae me.

THE EARLY YEARS

I am proud to have been born a citizen of Greenock Town and to be one of only four Greenock born people elected to the United Kingdom Parliament and to serve in the House of Commons, albeit my constituency was not Greenock but East Aberdeenshire. The *Greenock Telegraph* frequently refers to me as 'one of Greenock's most famous sons'. I am humbled to be so honoured by this worthy newspaper.

My parents did not start married life in Greenock. They were married at the Holy Trinity Church in London as my father was serving in the 2nd Battalion Scots Guards and stationed at that time in London. At the battle of Ypres on 20th March 1915 my father was severely wounded and also suffered from gas contamination. A bayonet had been pushed through his stomach by a German soldier, the result of which was he had to wear a support bandage around his stomach for the rest of his life. As the Germans retreated from the onslaught of the Scots Guards they released poisonous gas which affected my father's face resulting in him having to paint a special lotion on his face daily. For his bravery in this battle my father was Mentioned in Despatches. In my young days I often wondered why he painted his face with this white liquid. It was only when I was old enough to understand that I learned the reason for his war wounds. I was very proud of him. After a period of hospitalisation my father was discharged from the Army on account of his injuries and returned to Gatehouse of Fleet in Kirkcudbrightshire, the place of his birth. At this time, as the First World War had not ended there was very little employment in the village. My father and mother who was born in Ranworth near Norwich decided to take up residence in Greenock where work in the Engineering companies was available. He found employment and remained with the firm of Rankin and Blackmore until 1946 when he decided to join me in the business I was to set up on my return from service in the Second World War.

My father and mother had three more children to follow my eldest brother Robert and myself. Algernon Stewart, known as Algy, was followed by our sister Margaret Hastings who was the first female McQuarrie to be born to a member of our section of the Clan McQuarrie for six generations. The youngest of the family, Charles, was born in 1922. He served in the Royal Air Force during the Second World War and was posted to South Africa.

My elder brother Robert Sharman McQuarrie, a non-commissioned Officer in the 77th Highland Field Brigade (TA), was killed in action at Dunkirk in 1940 aged 24 years. Algernon Stewart McQuarrie married Janet Boyle – both now deceased. He served as an Officer in the Renfrewshire Special Constabulary as he was in a Reserved Occupation and not allowed to

A LIFETIME OF MEMORIES

2. My brother Robert

3. My brother Algernon

4. My sister Margaret

5. My brother Charles

THE EARLY YEARS

take up Military Service. My sister Margaret Hastings McQuarrie served in the Womens Royal Naval Service (WRNS) during the Second World War. Margaret married Samuel Forbes McPhail, now deceased, who was a renowned player of the bagpipes. My brother Charles took up youth work on his return from the Royal Air Force. He married Rachel McCloy, a local girl. They moved to England spending their lives working for young people in difficulties and latterly in social work in the City of Norwich where they now enjoy their retirement.

As children we enjoyed the freedom to play around a former garden allotment, a short distance from our home and away from what traffic there was at that time. It was in the old huts we met and played with our friends knowing that mother knew where we were. The Murdieston Dam (pond) was quite close by and we were warned not to go near it. On one occasion I disobeyed my mother taking myself off to the Dam. Wandering around the edge I saw a small sailing boat. Being adventurous I headed to retrieve the boat and had barely set foot in the water when I fell over. The water was shallow, fortunately, at that point so I got myself out and dripping wet headed home fearful of what my mother would say, or what my father would do when he was given the news. I have vivid recollections of what my mother said and remember the pain from the 'walloping' I received from my father. No sympathy was afforded to me but I did learn the lesson and did not repeat my misdemeanour ever again.

During my school years the family travelled to Great Yarmouth for the summer holiday to stay with Granny Sharman, my mother's mother at 26 Stone Road, Great Yarmouth. All five of us were dressed in kilts. I remember how we visited the harbour area where the women from the north east of Scotland were gutting and filleting the herring. As we were wearing our kilts the women took a liking to us and provided us with a 'fry' of herring each day to take home to Granny who was an excellent cook.

Every morning when we were on holiday with Granny in Great Yarmouth, Uncle Bob raised the Union Flag at the bottom of the garden. He was a real royalist, never failing to raise the flag each day, taking it down as darkness fell. We as children were greatly moved by his routine.

I was sad not to have known my Grandfather Sharman. He was a fishing skipper along with his four brothers. In his spare time Grandfather Sharman was a lay preacher and according to all accounts a very fine one too. He died at a young age leaving Granny Sharman to bring up their thirteen children. I have the fondest of memories of these holidays in Great Yarmouth where oddly enough I was posted for a short time during my service in the Second World War.

6. Granny with my parents, Margaret and Charles on holiday in Yarmouth

At the age of five I was enrolled at the Highlanders Academy. This school had been built to cater for the large number of families from the Highlands and Islands of Scotland who had come to Greenock for employment. The original school in Roxburgh Street was demolished and a new school constructed in 1887 between Dempster and Wellington Streets, only a short distance from our home. Sadly, due to the need to integrate schools on the account of falling rolls, the Highlanders Academy closed its doors on the 27th June 2012. A new school has been built a short distance away but not named the Highlanders Academy which I find sad as I have such high regard my first ever school.

My education at the Highlanders Academy was sound. My teacher was Miss McKirdy who had a wonderful capacity to earn the respect of her pupils. Her pleasant but firm manner instilled in us the need to learn the three R's if we were to achieve anything in life. I have fond memories of the years I attended the Highlanders Academy. To digress, in 1938 when I attended the Centenary and Jubilee Reunion of Highlanders Academy in the Greenock Town Hall, we enjoyed whist, tea and dancing until 2.00 a.m. – all for *five shillings*. During the celebrations for the 150th Anniversary of the Highlanders Academy, I was invited to give an address to the staff and pupils at a church ceremony. I am proud to have been a pupil of the Highlanders Academy, and if I may be a little boastful the school was proud of me and called me its 'most famous pupil'.

At the age of eleven I received a good result in the Qualifying Examination which allowed me to be accepted as a pupil in the Greenock High School, the only senior secondary school in the area. As there were no mixed classes in the school the boys entered at one side and the girls at the other side of the High School building from Dunlop Street. I recall the dining hall where we could buy lunch and the playing field attached within the precincts of the school. The Janitor was Sandy Pearson who I got to know well. In those days most of the pupils were well behaved but Sandy was not afraid to report to the Rector when pupils were caught misbehaving. Discipline was maintained. Sandy had applied for a transfer to the newly built High School as there was a new bungalow at the school entrance built specifically for the Janitor.

I enjoyed my years at Greenock High School, applying myself to the learning of subjects which would be of value once my school days were over. I gained a number of Certificates which have been to my benefit when my business life took off.

One sad event happened, which has never left me, during my time at Greenock High School was the tragic death of my chum Sandy Park who lived opposite the school. Sandy was cycling just outside the 'girls' gate when the wheel of his bicycle caught in a manhole in the road. Sandy was thrown from his cycle striking his head on the ground as he fell. He was taken to hospital but never recovered. To this day whenever I pass the manhole the memory of Sandy comes flooding back to me.

In my earlier days there were organisations attached to the local churches for young people. In my case there was a Band of Hope which met on a Thursday evening in the Mount Pleasant Church just round the corner from our home. It was great fun singing and listening to talks by prominent local Evangelists. On a Friday evening I attended the Christian Endeavour organised by the Orangefield Baptist Church in Nelson Street, Greenock. The Superintendent was a Miss Brown who was an outstanding leader for young people. At the Christian Endeavour weekly meeting, the topic for the following week was selected. Everyone had to take their turn and stand up to make a speech on the topic which was invariably of a biblical nature. As I did this perhaps it was then the seeds were sown enabling me to make many speeches during my political career. I rehearsed my prepared speeches for the Christian Endeavour to such an extent that I could speak without notes, something which proved so useful to me in later life.

I well remember at the end of each Christian Endeavour meeting we sang *God be with you till we meet again*. The words of the verses deeply impressed me and for many years I found myself when driving along the road humming the tune or singing out loud the first verse which I hope readers of my book will also enjoy.

> God be with you till we meet again,
> By His counsels guide, uphold you,
> With His sheep securely fold you;
> God be with you till we meet again.
>
> **Chorus:**
> Till we meet, till we meet,
> Till we meet at Jesus feet,
> Till we meet, till we meet,
> God be with you till we meet again.

Oh, those happy days when we hadn't a care in the world, all thanks to wonderful parents.

The family worshipped at the Church of Scotland West Kirk in Nelson Street, an imposing building with a large clock in the tower. It was called McCulloch's Clock. I think this was the name of a former Minister of the Kirk. Every Sunday we trooped down the aisle into the pew for which my parents paid an annual fee to have our name on the brass plate. In the afternoon each Sunday after lunch we were taken on a walk through the Greenock Cemetery, weather permitting. At that time we had no one buried there, but it certainly became a place of great interest to us reading the names. We could connect to some of the well known local Shipping and Engineering businesses in the town. Perhaps there was method in our parents taking us on these walks as it taught us so much about the town of our birth and of its people.

We also attended Sunday School where the Superintendent was Mr William Hutchison, a very kind gentleman who was Headmaster of the Highlanders Academy.

I have never forgotten one very interesting thing I discovered about attending the Morning Service in the Church. The Minister, the Reverend W.J. Nicol Service was an excellent preacher and his sermons were driven home to the congregation with clarity and persuasion. However, having listened to the Sermons for one year I began to realise I had heard the same sermon before. I began to carefully note in a little book the date and the subject of the sermon. Sure enough, it was in fact the case that the Minister had a book of sermons which he used for the year, starting again at the beginning of a new year. I was so pleased at my discovery but it did not diminish the pleasure I had each week listening to the delivery of the Minister's sermons with enthusiasm as if it was the first time I had heard them.

On reaching the age of 16 I joined the Bible Class. These classes were taken by the Assistant Minister, the Reverend Alan Bowie. He was a very kindly person who gained the confidence of us all in the Bible Class especially during our outdoor activities in the summer months as our leader. Sadly he is now deceased. It was at the time of joining the Bible Class that I also joined the Church Choir as a tenor singer. Until I left Greenock in 1939 to serve in the War, I was part of the choir under its Choirmaster Mr Arthur Hudson. One of the outstanding voices in the choir was that of Mitchell Hodge who I sat beside. I enjoyed singing along with him. My tenor voice was improved even more when I joined the Philharmonic Society where I took lessons from Conductor Robert Constable who certainly brought out the best in my voice. I have been blessed with a good voice which gives me, and others, pleasure even now.

7. *Playing the bagpipes with the Scouts. I am on the right side*

My brother Robert and I joined the 5th Renfrewshire (West Kirk's Own) Boy Scouts which had a Pipe Band. Algy and Charles joined the Cubs and my sister Margaret joined the Brownies. Not only were the weekly Scout meetings and the Pipe Band practice entertaining, there was the weekend camp to look forward to at Everton Farm in Inverkip – some six miles from Greenock. Each time we walked there with our gear strapped to our backs.

The 5th Renfrewshire had their own hut just off site at Everton which had the capacity to sleep at least fifteen Scouts, with a little room at the end of the hut for the Scoutmaster or whoever was in charge of the camp that weekend. I took part in all the daytime activities at the camp which ended each day with a sing-song round the camp fire – the wood for which we gathered from the woodland adjacent to the camp site.

The Camp Warden was a Scoutmaster affectionately known as 'Pa Daley' of the Martyrs and North Church Scout Group in Greenock. He was a terrific enthusiast for scouting and much respected by us all for his organisational capabilities and friendship. It is hard to find people today willing to dedicate themselves to the youth as 'Pa Daley' did.

8. In our Scout and Cub Uniforms

As a Scout member I learned to play the bagpipes under the tutorship of Pipe Major Richardson, a former Army Pipe Major. The band had won the World Championships in London in 1926 and I felt proud to belong to this band with brother Robert as Drum Major. In 1938 just before he was called up to the Territorial Unit of the Royal Artillery he was runner-up in the World Championships Drum Major contest at Dunoon. By that time he was

Drum Major in the Greenock Wellington Pipe Band.

One member of our Troop was Sammy Wren who worked as a paper boy for the *Greenock Telegraph*. When we were at the camp he used to wake up shouting 'Ten bob a week and six buckshee *Telegraphs*'. We thought he was boasting about his pay or he may have been encouraging his fellow Scouts to work as a paper boy to earn a bit more. No one ever took him on.

It was while I was a member of the 5th Renfrewshire Scouts I won my first trophy for swimming. My mother knitted my costume. The swimming competitions took place in the West End Baths (not swimming pools in those days) in Campbell Street, Greenock. Today this is the building where the Greenock Arts Guild hold their events and it no longer has a swimming pool.

Service in the Air Cadet Corps

9. In Air Cadet Officers' Uniform

When I was 19 years of age I was invited to join the Air Defence Cadet Corps (later the Air Training Corps) as a Commissioned Officer in the 49(F) Squadron which had its headquarters at Seafield House on the Esplanade in Greenock. The Squadron was commanded by Hector G Russell a local businessman who held the rank of Wing Commander (later promoted to Group Captain). Mr Russell had previously been very active in the Boy Scouts and with the problems gathering in Europe and Germany in particular he decided to put his efforts into training young men in a military atmosphere and formed the 49(F) Squadron. He was able to recruit a large number of young men to such an extent he formed another Squadron under the title of 75th Squadron Air Defence Cadet Corps. This Squadron was under the command of Mr James Hart another local businessman who was extremely popular with all members of the Squadron.

Hector Russell never missed an opportunity to be involved in or connected with an organisation which had the potential for financial gain. During the Battle of Britain many young pilots were killed in action, a good number from Scotland. Amongst those killed were three brothers called MacRobert whose home was the House of Cromar at Douneside in Aberdeenshire. Their father, Sir Alexander MacRobert, had taken over the house from Lord Aberdeen in 1927. Lady MacRobert lived there at the outbreak of the Second World War.

Lady MacRobert was devastated at the death of her three sons killed during the Battle of Britain. As a reprisal against the German enemy Lady MacRobert offered to supply a new Bomber Aircraft which would be funded by her and presented to the Royal Air Force in memory of her three sons. At Lady MacRobert's request the Bomber was to be named 'The MacRobert's Reply'. This most generous offer was accepted by the Government and shortly afterwards the aircraft was operating against the Germans, destroying military bases in Europe which had been taken over by the Germans.

This was when Hector Russell used his ingenuity. He contacted Lady MacRobert and requested her agreement for the 49th (F) Squadron of the Air Defence Corps to be called the MacRobert's Reply Squadron. Lady MacRobert readily agreed. Hector Russell quickly arranged for Lady MacRobert to visit Greenock and formally name the Squadron with its new title of 49th (F) (MacRobert's Reply) Squadron and to present the Squadron with new colours embracing the MacRobert Coat of Arms. It was a most impressive ceremony and Lady MacRobert was praised for her determination to help defeat the Germans with her gift of the Bomber Aircraft.

During the visit Lady MacRobert made a handsome donation to the funds of the Squadron to purchase a large house called Bellaire in the West End of Greenock for the purpose of creating an administration centre for the Squadron. It also allowed several rooms in the house to be used for

THE EARLY YEARS

recreational areas for the cadets. Lady MacRobert continued to generously support the 49th (F) (MacRobert's Reply) Squadron for a number of years after the war and appointed Hector Russell as one of her Trustees.

It is interesting to record another generous gift Lady MacRobert made at that time. After the death of her three sons she renamed the House of Cromar and called it Alastrean House. The name was derived from a composite Latin phrase meaning 'a place of honour by the hearth of winged heroes of the stars'. The home was used as a rest and recuperation centre for the RAF and Commonwealth airmen on active service. Lady MacRobert set up the MacRobert Trust to operate the house after the war as a leave centre for RAF Officers. One of the most notable who used the centre when on leave was Flight Lieutenant 'Willie' Reid VC, one of Scotland's service-men awarded the Victoria Cross for gallantry in action. He was a Trustee for many years after the war ended.

The house was destroyed by fire in 1952. It was rebuilt and opened in an impressive Ceremony in 1958. Alastrean House continues to be operated by the Trustees as a residential Care Home with respite facilities. It is a wonderful memorial not only to the three brothers who gave their lives in the defence of their country, but also to an exceptional Lady who was determined to retaliate against the enemy. MacRobert's Reply Squadron still exists today thanks to the foresight of its first Commanding Officer Group Captain Hector Russell.

My duty as a Flying Officer was the responsibility to arrange all training and sporting activities for both Squadrons. It included the planning of all manners of exercises, night patrols and gliding training at Newcastle. My brother Charles who had joined the 75th Squadron under Flight Lieutenant James Hart was one to benefit from Gliding Training gaining a Certificate of Competency after a number of visits to the training area. Charles joined the Royal Air Force in the Second World War and for a time was stationed in South Africa. His training in Gliding was beneficial to him during his time in that country as flying by glider was used extensively.

I was also responsible for organising the summer training at various military establishments in the UK where intensive training exercises were carried out day and night. It gave the cadets a sound insight into what real military life would be like. It certainly encouraged members to join the Royal Air Force when there was a lack of employment in the west of Scotland from time to time. At that time there were no girls in the Squadron, but today girls and boys are integrated into the units with the girls on a number of occasions promoted to Officer Rank and Non-Commissioned Officers - in some instances even commanding their own Squadron of male and female cadets.

It is interesting to record that Group Captain Hector Russell set up a Kilt Making business in Inverness. He left Greenock for Inverness where he remained for the rest of his life. He was Chairman and Managing Director of the company, Hector Russell Highland Industries Ltd. He established branches of the company in Edinburgh, Glasgow, Greenock and in the Borders, and became the most widely known firm of kilt makers in Scotland. Although Hector has long departed this life, the company bearing his name still exists.

My first job

At the age of 15 my father had a serious illness due to his war wounds resulting in him being hospitalised for several months. On discharge from hospital he was unable to work. In order to help with the family income, I left school and took up employment with the local Co-operative. I had the offer of two apprenticeships – one was in the Funeral Undertaking Department and the other in the Plumbing and Heating Engineering Department. Needless to say I had little difficulty in deciding to take the latter and so started my working life.

For the next six years I served under some very fine plumbers led by Mr William Stratton, the Foreman. Men like Hugh McAusland, William Callander, James Bolton and Jimmy Mathie (a fellow apprentice) all taught me the trade, making me a credible operator on my own without further supervision. I remember on one occasion while I was on the roof of a building doing lead-work with Willie Callander, he complimented me on the standard of workmanship I produced then said to me:

> No work is worth doing badly;
> and he who puts the best into every task that comes to him
> will surely outstrip the man who waits for a great opportunity
> before he condescends to exert himself

I took this to heart and seventy-seven years later still implement it in all I do.

In order to become more efficient at my trade I enrolled at the Greenock Technical School and attended classes three evenings each week. The instruction was intensive but productive for me as I learned many of the more difficult areas in Plumbing and Heating Engineering which would have taken months to achieve as an employee in a business learning the trade.

As I had a great desire to gain qualifications in the building industry, I reduced my nights at the Greenock Technical School and enrolled in the Royal Technical College of Science and Technology in Glasgow for three

THE EARLY YEARS

nights a week (now the University of Strathclyde). I had to strip off my overalls from work at 5 o'clock, rush to catch a train for Glasgow in order to attend the classes which were intensive. My fellow students were mainly from Local Authority Offices in the west of Scotland not manual workers like me. This did not handicap me in any way as I had the determination to get ahead in life and improve my job opportunities. Most important of all was to secure a Pass in all the subjects I opted to study. As I look back, it seems fate had decreed I would reach my goal in the future far beyond what I had in mind in the early days of my first job as a plumber.

While attending classes in Glasgow there were a number of occasions when I fell asleep due to tiredness on the train journey home, resulting in my arriving at the Gourock terminus late in the evening with no train back to Greenock. The only way I could reach my home and family was to walk the four miles. I can honestly say all my efforts to obtain knowledge and qualifications in the building industry were of a great help to me in later life, and the walks from Gourock to Greenock did me no harm. I continued travelling to Glasgow with the aim of gaining Diplomas in my subjects which I did, until I volunteered for service at the outset of the Second World War in 1939. My wish to obtain further degrees had to be put off as I was determined to serve my country.

CHAPTER TWO

The War Years

ON 3RD SEPTEMBER 1939 MY STUDIES AT the two Technical Colleges came to an abrupt end. On that day the Prime Minister declared war on Germany. How well I remember it. I was attending the Sunday morning Service in the West Kirk Church when at 11.00 a.m. the Minister made a statement that the Prime Minister had announced a Declaration of War between Great Britain and Germany. There was a hushed silence within the congregation. The Reverend W.J. Nicol Service said a lengthy prayer asking for God's protection from the enemy and the safety of all in the United Kingdom. He then closed the service. Everyone left church stunned at the news.

On returning home I immediately changed into my Flying Officers Uniform and set off for the Headquarters as I was sure there would be an Assembly. There was a deep feeling of apprehension. No one could imagine what lay before us. There was much talk of joining the Armed Forces. I spoke up and said I would be enlisting at the first opportunity. I was instructed by the Commanding Officer to report to the Glasgow University Training Unit for an interview as to my suitability for being granted a Commission as an Officer in H.M. Armed Forces. The following day I travelled to Glasgow and found that there was an Interview Board sitting that afternoon and I would be included for interview along with others. The Chairman of the Board was a Colonel Hinchcliffe who was accompanied by Officers from the three Services – the Army, Navy and Air Force.

On appearing in front of the Board I was questioned on the work I undertook as a Flying Officer in the Air Defence Cadet Corps and how I handled leadership. Many of the questions were related to how I saw myself, if selected, as a Commissioned Officer. My answers to the questions were straightforward and in a manner which would find favour with the members of the Interview Board. I was asked what references I could produce on my character and my scholastic abilities. The Board also wanted a reference on my ability and experience in leading others, which I had been doing in the

Air Defence Cadet Corps. I assured the Board I could secure references from a number of people who, while knowing me, would give an honest and impartial reference. I was invited to obtain the references as quickly as possible and to deliver them to Colonel Hinchcliffe after which a decision would be made as to my suitability to serve as a Commissioned Officer.

On returning home from the interview I contacted my doctor who was a Major in the Royal Army Medical Corps serving in Glasgow and living at home in Greenock. He told me to call at his home that evening and he would give me a reference for the Interview Board. I then contacted the Rector of the Greenock High School, the Reverend W.J. Nicol Service and Group Captain Hector G. Russell, the Commanding Officer of the 49(F) Squadron of the Air Defence Cadet Corps. Within a few days I obtained the references and was delighted with the positive comments made about my character and of my leadership abilities. All spoke of their confidence I would make a good Officer whichever service I was placed with. As I was anxious to know of the result of my interview as soon as possible I took the train to Glasgow and handed the references to Colonel Hinchcliffe.

Within a few days I received word of my interview at Glasgow University Training Centre. I had been recommended for a Commission. It was suggested I should enlist in the Army as my qualifications in Building Construction and Legislation in Sanitary Inspection would be of considerable value to units billeted in camp sites throughout the country. I was ordered to report to the Glasgow Headquarters of the Army in Scotland for formal enlisting and Posting.

After the initial interview I returned to my job having advised the Foreman earlier of my intention to enlist into the Armed Forces. He accepted my decision and wished me good luck. I took my departure from the firm a few days later wondering when I would be able to continue my aim of setting up my own building business and completing my degree course at the Royal Technical College in Glasgow. I could only dream of doing so once the war was over.

Suddenly I realised my life was going to change dramatically. I had never really been away from home before and here I was, with the full support of my parents, volunteering to serve my country in the war against Germany.

Active service

After all my preparations were completed for leaving home, I set off to the Army Recruiting Office in Glasgow and was sworn into Military Service. I was given a Travel Warrant to take me to London and then to Fleet in Hampshire by rail from where I caught a bus to Crookham, one of many

Military Training Camps in England. The journey from Glasgow to Crookham was filled with anticipation and excitement.

10. At Crookham Camp Fleet, 1940

It was a frightening experience to arrive at this huge camp knowing nobody and be put into a very bare barrack room with thirty other soldiers none of whom I knew. There were iron beds with a sheet and blanket. There was little privacy with a communal toilet block at the end of the room. As this was the first time I had been away from home without my parents, I felt very lonely. I recall vividly the day I received the first letter from my mother when I had to escape to the toilet as the tears came pouring out. There were no telephones in ordinary houses so it was impossible to make any contact other than writing a letter.

All this changed as we embarked on the intensive training to make us efficient soldiers. The Sergeants who trained us were very severe. The only consolation was we were all together and ready to help one another in a difficult situation. It was during this time I experienced great camaraderie with other soldiers in the barrack room. This made life bearable and helped to take away the loneliness at being separated from my family.

Every morning we had to be up washed and dressed, beds made and the billet tidy before the Orderly Officer came in to inspect at 6.30 a.m. If the bed was not properly made, or the bed area untidy, extra duties were given, and an evening off denied. The soldiers called it 'jankers'! One of the routine things we had to do was have our boots polished with a very high shine. This was done by 'spit and polish'. The boots were coated with black polish then spat on and polished with the back of an old toothbrush. This took some time but there was great satisfaction on going on parade with shining boots.

The food was not anything like as good as my mother made at home. Food was rationed so there was little to choose from. Breakfast was some form of cereal followed by toast with a scraping of butter, or on occasions marmalade or honey but not both. Lunch was often minced beef and potatoes or corned beef with potatoes. An evening meal would regularly consist of corned beef in some form or other, depending if the cook was imaginative or not, and occasionally we were treated to a steak pie with potatoes and vegetables. There was always tea served with our meals but it tasted more like hot water. Eggs were rationed so we rarely had them in any form.

After a very short time we all blended together in the barrack room. Even the Sergeants became more friendly as the weeks of the course passed by. In the evenings and weekends when off duty, a number from the barracks including myself would go to the canteen at the Baptist Church in Fleet where we had home-baked cakes. The ladies from the church were pleased to entertain us and would sometimes invite a soldier home for a meal which was a treat indeed. I became friendly with a couple called Gifford who were leading members of the church. He was the Manager of Barclays Bank in Fleet and they had two grown up daughters Audrey and Lorna. I had a very enjoyable time with the family and kept up the connection for years after the war ended.

It was always good to get letters and 'goodies' from home which were shared with others in the barrack room. This helped to cement the friendship built up during the eight week training course.

The eight weeks were a test of concentration as we sat through lectures for a large part of the day and daily drill exercises on the parade ground at regular intervals to instil discipline in us, if it was not already there. We all knew at the end of the course we would be posted to an active unit within the United Kingdom where intensive training was being carried out for an onslaught on the German Army. We also had regular night exercises all over the county.

At weekends we were free to do whatever we wanted. I loved to roam the countryside. On one occasion I sat by a stream and found watercress growing profusely on the banks. I was reminded of the watercress I had enjoyed so much when on holiday with Granny Sharman in Norfolk. I returned every week to the stream where I picked and ate the best watercress I have ever tasted!

The first real Posting

I received notice of my first Posting. I packed my bags, said my farewells to the men with whom I had spent the first weeks as a soldier and took the train to London and on to Glasgow overnight. My instructions were to report to the Deputy Director of Medical Services for Health whose office was in Park Circus in Glasgow. When I did so he advised me I would be stationed at the office of the Military Camp Commandant in Johnstone, Renfrewshire where I would carry out the duties allocated to me. I took the train to Johnstone and on arriving at the camp was greeted by the Camp Commandant Major Anderson who told me he was overloaded with work and pleased to have my assistance. He was a retired businessman who had fought in the First World War having reached the rank of Major. Many 'old soldiers' like him volunteered to take on these duties until other trained Commissioned Officers were posted to take over the administration of the Camp.

It was difficult to find accommodation as the entire camp had been taken over by Free French Forces who had escaped to Scotland while serving under General de Gaulle. Johnstone Castle had been occupied by Officers and troops of the Free French Forces. I was required to find accommodation, so I toured the area around the town and found the Scottish Episcopal Church in Floors Street where I understood there may be a room in the Church Hall. I contacted the Rector and explained my position. He took me to the Church Hall and showed me a room with toilet facilities which he said I could have. I thanked him and for the next few months, I had the 'luxury' of my own living quarters away from the mass of soldiers who were under canvas in Johnstone Castle grounds.

My work in Johnstone initially was to ensure the standard of cleanliness in the living quarters, kitchens and dining rooms was maintained at a high level. This might seem to be a trivial job but it was not easy as many of the soldiers' habits left much to be desired. This was also a time when I had to assist in training operations being carried out day and night by the French Troops. They were keen to learn the English language and it was fortunate I remembered some of my French from schooldays. I set up English classes for the Officers and soldiers. Many of them took advantage of this and soon were conversing in English.

It was while I was based in Johnstone I was instructed to include the Transit Camp in Greenock as part of my duties. It was very opportune as my parents were glad to have me near them as they were still grieving over the death in action of my brother Robert. It also gave me an opportunity to see Granny Sharman who had been evacuated from Great Yarmouth due to the bombing. My Aunt Dora and Uncle Bob accompanied Granny and the three stayed with my parents at our home in Greenock.

The *Arandora Star*

On the 3rd July 1940 I received an instruction from Scottish Command Headquarters to proceed to the Transit Camp in Greenock to help with the preparations to receive the survivors from a Cruise Liner the *Arandora Star* which had been torpedoed by the German Navy U-Boats off the coast of Ireland on 2nd July with the loss of 486 lives. The liner was on its way to Canada with Internees. On arrival at Greenock Harbour from a British naval warship, the men were to be taken to the Transit Camp until a decision was arrived at on where they were to be located.

11. The Arandora Star *sunk by Germans*

The Transit Camp was a large building formally used as a Bonded Warehouse for Whisky. It looked like a prison with its small barbed wire windows and would not have been of great comfort to the survivors. The media had learned the survivors were being brought to Greenock by sea and in no time a large number of journalists and photographers gathered at the Transit Camp to await the arrival of the survivors, who would be driven by military transport and off-loaded at a secure area so no photographs could be taken of them.

Soldiers from the Highland Light Infantry who had been stationed at the camp on military duties helped to organise bedding, food, medical equipment and clothes as the men had nothing other than the clothes they were wearing.

It was a pitiful sight to see these men, worn out and desperately in need of sleep. They had been treated well on the warship which rescued them and were loud in their praise for all the kindness shown to them by the Officers and Navy men. I did my best to ensure all the men had a change of clothing. The Army Clothing Depot had been alerted and had sent denim clothing for the survivors who were to remain at the Transit Camp while arrangements were made for them to be transferred to another location. After details of each man were recorded a meal was provided before retiring to bed for a much needed rest and sleep.

The following day I arrived at the Transit Camp to find a large crowd of people, young and old, with the local Police controlling them. The Police Inspector told me they were mostly relatives of the survivors, many having travelled from all parts of Scotland after they heard the survivors were being taken to Greenock. As I made my way through the crowd there were many cries 'Sir let me see my dad' or 'let me see my son'. My heart ached for them.

I was particularly struck by one young woman holding a little girl both crying copiously. I approached them and asked who they were and which relative had they hoped to see. The mother told me the name was Da Prato and her husband was the girl's father and one of the survivors. I told the child to stop crying while I would see what could be done about being able to speak with her father.

I was so touched by the young girl's distress I immediately sought out Mr Da Prato, took him to one of the quieter areas of the Transit Camp before asking for the mother and child to be brought there. The joy with which they greeted one another brought tears to my eyes as I looked on. After a little time together I came back and told them I would have to take Mr Da Prato back to the main area where the survivors had been housed. The mother thanked me for providing these few precious minutes together. I then spent hours doing the same for other survivors and their families but found it impossible to meet all the requests. After the war ended whenever I passed the Da Prato shop in Glasgow, I hoped the family had been happily reunited and the *Arandora Star* tragedy remained only a memory. I never made any attempt to make contact with the Da Prato family nor did they make any contact with me. They probably were unaware I lived in Greenock only some seventeen miles away.

I was deeply mindful I was breaking King's Regulations concerning Internees in allowing them to see their relatives and certainly did not want to bring trouble on my shoulders from my superiors. In fact I considered it was a worthwhile humanitarian act and for the short time brought happiness to these unfortunate people. Fortunately none of my senior Officers learned of what I had done, or I would have been in serious trouble.

THE WAR YEARS

During the days the survivors were detained at the Transit Camp they received large quantities of letters. In accordance with King's Regulations all mail had to be censored. This was one of the most unenviable tasks I had to do during my military service, as it was heart rending reading the human cries of hope and a wish for the war to be over so families could be together again. Fortunately I was not required to do so much censoring and all letters were safely handed over to the survivors.

After a few days the survivors were moved to an undisclosed location prior to being sent overseas again. As I saw the last of them on to the military transport, I hoped the days spent in Greenock gave them some consolation from the terrible experience they suffered when the *Arandora Star* was sunk by a torpedo. Little did I realise then that sixty-five years later I would be reading about the *Arandora Star* to find some of the Scottish Italians who had been on board the ship came from Peterhead, the town and people I was proud to serve in later years as Member of Parliament for the East Aberdeenshire Constituency in the House of Commons at Westminster. I share with them this never to be forgotten experience of the Second World War.

Having completed the memorable assignment I returned to Johnstone Castle from Greenock to find the Free French Troops had been transferred to another location in England and a Corps of the Polish Army had taken over the camp under General Sikorski having escaped from Poland when the Germans invaded that country. I had been doing well with my French but now had to learn the Polish language – never a dull moment!

The Polish soldiers were quite different from the Free French. They were smart and kept the camp in an immaculate condition. The Officers carried out daily inspections. Strict military training was carried out as it was anticipated the soldiers would continue the war against the Germans when the invasion of the continent by the Allies took place. In the early days at the camp I discovered many of the Polish soldiers were musical and had good singing voices, so I formed a choir and set about rehearsing Scottish songs. The first was called *Bobby Shaftoe* – a child's song in Scotland, and from then on they built up a repertoire of well known Scottish songs. It was wonderful to listen to these strong good voices performing, particularly the singing of the Polish National Anthem at the end of each evening by which time I had mastered the words to join in. The next step was to take over the local cinema for an evening's performance. It was packed full and not only were the Polish soldiers proud to be singing in Scotland, the people of Johnstone were thrilled at the performance. Is it any wonder I had a job keeping the young Johnstone girls away from the camp where they wanted to be with the 'singing soldiers'.

It was during this period I was to meet the young lady who later in 1945 was to become my wife. One day I called at the Newsagent and Tobacconist in the Johnstone High Street for a newspaper and was served by a nice assistant who I found charming. I was immediately taken by her and decided I would ask her to have a game of tennis with me. The next day I called in, there was a gentleman serving at the counter. I said to him 'Is your assistant not in today?' He replied 'She is not my assistant, she is my daughter. She works in the bank across the road and comes in for a few hours each day on finishing her day's work.' From then on I made sure my visits were in the late afternoon once the bank had closed!

I had been enjoying my time in Johnstone but knew it would come to end sometime. It was on 9th January 1941 the Colonel sent for me to advise I was being posted to Bristol to take over a detachment of the Royal Pioneer Corps who were engaged on bomb disposal work as the German aircraft had inflicted serious damage in that city. Another chapter was about to commence in serving my country at war. I left Johnstone satisfied I had done my duty to the best of my ability. It was not easy leaving Johnstone and to be parted from my beloved Roseleen with whom I had spent some wonderful times. We knew I could not remain in Johnstone when my work there was completed. I hoped I would be able to obtain leave at some time and spend it with Roseleen in Johnstone and at my home in Greenock.

A new experience

I travelled by trains to London and Swindon to my new posting where the Regiment had its Headquarters. On arrival I was met by the Commanding Officer Major Clark who was a very friendly Scotsman. He explained in detail the duties I would undertake when I took over the command of the Detachment in Bristol. I remained in Swindon for a few days gaining information on the work the unit had been doing in the Bristol area since the Germans started the bombing attack on the city. On my first Sunday with the Regiment the soldiers attended Church Service. Major Clark asked me to take the Parade and inspect the ranks of soldiers. As I walked past each one I saw a face which seemed familiar to me. I said to the soldier 'Are you Stuart Miller?' He replied 'Yes, Sir. We were at school together.' It was a remarkable coincidence.

After the Church Service he and I had a long conversation about our years at the Greenock High School. It was a pleasure to meet my old school friend. I never saw him again as next day I departed for Bristol to take over the Detachment there.

12. With Major Clark and Lieut. Robson, 1941

By agreement with Headquarters at Swindon, I was met at Temple Meads Station in Bristol and driven to the Unit Office at 33 Downlease. I was introduced to the other Officers and Non-Commissioned Officers who would serve under me before being taken to my quarters in the Officers Mess which was a magnificent mansion on the Bristol Downs. The owner, a retired Admiral of the Fleet and a Director of the Wills Tobacco Company moved to his country home having handed over the Bristol one to the Army. There were three other Officers in the Detachment and a Sergeant Major by the name of Peters. The Unit comprised 200 soldiers in the Non-Combatant Corps (NCC) and other soldiers who were serving with the Unit on Operational Duties dealing with the bomb disposal work. The NCC men were not prepared to go into action but still wanted to play a part in defending Britain. I found this difficult to understand but after a few months of having them under my command I fully accepted their situation as I found them more willing to take on any task allotted to them so long as it was not a combatant role. The NCC soldiers worked well with the other soldiers and there was no friction between them. All the troops were billeted in houses which had been taken over by the Army.

On my first night in Bristol I soon knew this was vastly different from the tranquil surroundings of my last posting in Johnstone. At 2.00 a.m. the sirens were sounding all over the city. I jumped out of bed, put on my battle dress uniform and headed for the office. I found the troops assembled and the vehicles with the red painted wings and the letters BDU printed on each side (Bomb Disposal Unit). I could hear the enemy planes in the distance. It was obvious the soldiers had been well trained and ready for action as the unit had been split into sections with each one given a particular area within the city. There was a feeling of excitement in me as this was my first taste of seeing the damage the Germans were doing to our cities. I joined one of the units in their designated area of the city and took cover with the soldiers. Every so often there was a heavy thud as the bombs rained down followed by flashes of fire as the bombs exploded.

Once the German bombers had been forced away by our fighter aircraft and the 'all clear' sounded on the sirens it was our job to go into the city and begin a search and rescue operation where properties had been damaged and people injured. In some cases others had been killed in their homes as a result of the damage caused by the bombs. We also had to establish if there were any unexploded bombs. If any were found, we immediately closed off the area and evacuated any people living nearby. We carried notices which indicated 'unexploded bomb' so there was never any trouble in getting the people to come out of their home and be taken to a place of safety.

Demolishing a massive number of damaged properties was not an easy task. It took several months to do this and it was sad to see the survivors of the properties standing by knowing they had lost their homes and all their belongings. The City of Bristol was well organised together with Civil Defence Services to house the people in other parts of the city and make them comfortable.

Little did I think when dealing with the Blitz in Bristol that I was to learn from my mother how my home town of Greenock had been blitzed on 6th and 7th May 1941 by the Nazi German Luffwaffe. In obtaining the information from the media, I learned that around fifty bombers had carried out the attack on the East End of Greenock setting alight the Whisky Distillery in Ingleston Street and the Sugar Refinery in Drumfrochar Road. Because the whisky caught fire it allowed the German Bombers to select targets using high explosive bombs and parachute landmines causing massive destruction and the deaths of around 280 people with thousands severely injured. Severe damage was done to thousands of homes, many of which were totally destroyed. I was glad to learn there were no further attacks on Greenock but the same could not be said for Bristol where the

THE WAR YEARS

13. Greenock Blitz - damage by Germans in Dalrymple Street

14. Greenock Blitz - damage by Germans at Westburn Sugar Refinery

15. Greenock Blitz - damage by Germans in Waverly Street

bombing continued for some time.

Many unusual incidents took place but there are two in particular which happened during the time I spent in Bristol and are part of the memories of my time spent there.

It was a practice to have a Church Parade on each Sunday when the soldiers would march from the Headquarters to a local church. They had been attending several churches but as I wished to keep them as a single unit I sought out the Methodist Church not too far from the Bristol Downs and the nearest to our HQ. The system was the soldiers would parade to the church, attend the service after which they were marched back to HQ and were off duty for the rest of the day. On my first Sunday there I attended the church service. On arriving at the door of the church I was surprised to observe a number of the soldiers stepping out of the ranks and standing aside. On my return to the office, I questioned the Orderly Sergeant who had led the parade on why some of the NCC soldiers had stood aside and not attended the service. He told me it was due to the fact the Methodist Church was not of their religious persuasion and they were not prepared to take part in the service. As this was the first time I have come across an incident like this I found it strange.

A week later I received a telephone call from the Brigadier at Area Headquarters telling me a soldier had complained to his Member of

THE WAR YEARS

Parliament that he was compelled to attend a service in a church not of his denomination. I was advised to allow all soldiers to attend the church of their own choosing. With a large number of soldiers who were serving as Non-Combatant Corps it turned out there were nineteen different religious persuasions to which soldiers were attached. I was annoyed at this interference with the Church Parade. However I had to obey the instructions received from the Brigadier. I then did what I later realised was a nasty and unbecoming thing to do in my position.

I instructed the Sergeant Major to parade the men in full battle kit after lunch and take them on a two hour training session on the Bristol Downs. To be fair the men accepted this but having done it I certainly was sorry for my haste in getting my own back. It was a strange coincidence the soldier who had complained to his Member of Parliament came from Aberdeen and was a roofer to trade. At the hurricane storm in 1968 which hit the west of Scotland – I write about it in a later Chapter – this man was one of the roofers I secured from Aberdeen to repair the roofs. We had a good laugh about the incident. I may say he was an excellent tradesman and stayed with the company until the final stage of the repairs.

The other incident related to an unexploded bomb which had been dropped into the grounds of the Badminton Estate. It was decided by the Army Authority it should be dug out as it had been established the fuse was not live. I was instructed to send soldiers to the Estate to carry out the work. I sent eighteen men under the supervision of Sergeant Major Peters. He arranged to have the men billeted in local homes and the owners would be paid two 'old' pence per day! He was to pay them each week from funds given to him by the Unit's Chief Clerk.

After two weeks the soldiers were still excavating the ground most carefully. I decided to pay a visit to see the progress myself. All was well and the bomb would soon be exposed for lifting out and taken away to be blown up a long way from the Bristol Channel area. I thought it would be a good idea for me to thank the people who had taken the soldiers into their homes. With the receipt book for the payments of the two pence per night in my pocket I started my rounds. It did not strike me at the time that while there was a record of the payment, there was no record of the recipient's name. I was soon to learn why. Some ladies took the money and made no comment but two did, saying this was the first payment they had received. Then I arrived at the door of an elderly gentleman with a white military type moustache – all hairs bristling! In his case there were signatures acknowledging earlier payments. When I handed over the money to him, like the other two ladies, he said this was the first money he had received. I showed him the receipt book and he shouted at me 'I am a Barrister and that is not my signature'. I told him the matter would be investigated and any payments due would be made promptly.

I was extremely concerned at the set of circumstances and on my return I contacted my Superior Officer at Headquarters acquainting him of what I had discovered. He immediately delegated a legal Officer at Area HQ to interview Sergeant Major Peters. I ordered his withdrawal from the work at Badminton Estate and suspended him from duties with the Detachment in Bristol.

After a full investigation it transpired the Sergeant Major had deductions from his pay for a Compulsory Allotment to his wife. He was also having a Voluntary Allotment deducted to pay a woman he was living with. The result was he only had one shilling a day left out of his army pay. He admitted his guilt to the Law Officer and was put before a Court Martial. He was found guilty and reduced to the rank of Private. The episode was a sad one at a time when I had been enjoying working with this Sergeant Major.

They were a great bunch of men who enjoyed my bagpipe playing in the evenings. Even although times were difficult as the Germans were continually bombing Bristol causing terrible destruction the soldiers stood up to it magnificently. I was proud of them and had no hesitation in telling them so. I don't know if they stood up magnificently to the bombing or to my bagpipe playing in England!

The Painting and the Two Walking Sticks

16. Copy of oil painting of me by soldier, 1942

THE WAR YEARS

Before I move on from the Bristol days there are two other incidents of note. When I was sitting in my office one day a soldier came in and said 'Sir, I am an artist and the other men want me to paint a portrait of you'. I said 'Be off with you I am too busy'. He replied 'Sir they will be disappointed if I don't do the painting'. I relented and sat for several hours over the following weeks. I was pleased with the result which was presented to me in the soldiers' dining room with the majority of them present. Sadly I have no record of the soldier's name as all my war papers which I had kept at my home in Scotland were destroyed by an intruder some years later. The painting hangs in the hallway of our home and is a constant reminder of the days I spent in Bristol.

The other one was of a more severe nature but I am glad to say ended on a happy note. It is the story of the two walking sticks. While I was serving in Bristol I had a most unfortunate experience of which I have been reminded throughout my years.

Late in 1941 in Bristol I was at a badly damaged site. As I walked inside the building I found the soles of my boots burning. My feet were uncomfortable and painful to such an extent I reported to the Hospital Emergency Action Unit. When the doctor took my boots off the skin on both soles and heels of my feet were badly burned. In view of this I was told it would be necessary to transfer me to a military section of the Bradford Hospital in Yorkshire. I was transported by ambulance.

For the next few weeks I was confined to the hospital where the treatment was superb. I was anxious to return to the unit in Bristol but was not allowed to do so until the pressure on my feet was no longer painful. While I was in the hospital I was given two sticks to help me walk and to reduce the pressure on my feet. I was grateful to have them. When I was discharged from hospital still having to use the sticks I returned to the unit in Bristol. The hospital authorities told me to take the sticks with me and to retain them. These walking sticks were of a high quality. One had a bone handle with a brass band around it. The other had an ivory handle also with a brass band around it. The most interesting thing about the one with the ivory handle is the inscription, which on the brass band there are the words 'Wheatley Jackson' and the date of May 17th 1897.

The inscription intrigued me. After returning from the war I tried to establish who this gentleman was. Following much research it appeared the stick had been owned by Mr Wheatley Jackson, a Yorkshire Woollen Miller. It transpires there was a shortage of walking sticks for use by patients in the hospital during their period of recovery. There was an appeal made by the hospital authorities and Mr Wheatley Jackson's family responded with the gift of two walking sticks. These sticks are still used by me and are amongst my most treasured war souvenirs, particularly the one formerly belonging to Mr Wheatley Jackson. The stick I received seventy-one years ago is still being used 115 years since it was presented to Mr Wheatley Jackson on 17th May 1897. They both look as good today as they did when they were given to me in 1941.

A Posting to the Royal Engineers

Once the blitz was over in Bristol things eased off for a time but another area was experiencing the same problem. The bombing was taking place in Plymouth where the destruction was severely disrupting the military establishments, in addition to the residential and business area of the city. Within days I received notice of another Posting. I was to join the 724 Artisan Works Company of the Royal Engineers based in Plymstock on the outskirts of Plymouth.

So ended my stay in Bristol – the first place where I had seen the activities of the German enemy. I had learned much and gained a great amount of confidence in leading the soldiers who had been under my command. In respecting them they in turn gave me their loyalty. Saying farewell to them made me sad as I wondered just what would happen when I joined the Royal Engineers to continue carrying out action to relieve the people whose homes had been destroyed by the bombs. The bombing was intense and there was great destruction of properties and roads.

Serving with the Sappers

On arriving by train in Plymouth, transport awaited me to take me to Plymstock. The Officers Mess was again a large house but this time with more Officers in the Regiment. The unit had been formed from the labour force of the Brighton and Hastings Corporation Direct Labour Department with many of the Sappers working alongside men they knew. All the former foremen had been promoted to Non-Commissioned Rank and some of the Managers were Officers. One of them, Captain McLaren, had been Manager at the Parks and Gardens Department of Brighton and Hastings Corporation. He told a story about the day there was a large Civic Reception in the Town Hall. It was a time of year when there were few flowers in bloom to decorate the platform. Captain McLaren found an abundant supply of leeks with lovely large purple flowers and hit on the idea of using them to decorate the platform. All went well until the hall filled with people and the temperature rose, causing the leeks to give off their not-so-pleasant smell. As soon as the speeches were over the platform 'floral' decoration was

THE WAR YEARS

removed by the gardeners and the hall was fumigated. Captain McLaren said he would never experiment again without checking on potential problems!

I settled in very easily with my fellow Officers and was allocated a Detachment of the soldiers to carry out the same kind of work I had done in Bristol. A day after my arrival I was introduced to one of the soldiers who was to be my Batman. His name was Sapper James Hooker who came from Hastings. He was a bricklayer in the Direct Labour Department. 'Hooker' as he was known from then on was an exceptional soldier. He attended to my every want and kept my uniforms in splendid condition. At the time I wore breeches and knee high leather riding leggings. Hooker spent hours cleaning and polishing the leggings after I had worn them. We formed a very good relationship – I managed to retain Hooker as my Batman for the rest of my military service by having him posted to the same location where I was serving.

The Army used the 724 Artisan Works Company as one of the units which could be mobilised at short notice to undertake works at a number of military establishments. One of these was at Thetford in Norfolk where the Company constructed the first live Ammunition Training Centre called Didlington Hard Standings. Roads were built with whatever suitable materials the Army could find in preparation for the invasion of the Continent. I was present when the first tank arrived into the Training Ground firing live ammunition and destroying buildings which had been erected to train the soldiers in methods of attacking enemy positions.

The Company then moved to Barton Stacey for an intense training period to improve the soldiers' skills in all sorts of difficult and taxing tasks in order to reach a high standard in all situations. The thought of war was always in our minds as each night we heard Air Force bombers from their base in Norfolk heading out for Germany to destroy further targets.

When the training was complete we continued to build projects for all manner of military requirements. Work was undertaken at Luton Hoo for a large army training area followed by Clacton-on-Sea and Great Yarmouth where I visited Granny Sharman, Kings Lynn, Helensburgh in Scotland, Street in Somerset and many more locations where projects were completed by the Sappers who were a fine bunch of men. The years rolled on and eventually the invasion took place which led to a victory for the Allies in 1945. Immediately the war was over all thoughts were on demobilisation and returning home. I enjoyed my Army service but like all others was glad it had finally ended.

During my Army years and after leaving Johnstone I kept regular contact with my beloved Roseleen, writing every week and speaking to her by telephone. Most of the leave I was given I spent at her home in Johnstone or at my home in Greenock. I bought a second hand Morris 10/4 from a local builder for Thirty Pounds. It was in great condition. I used it to drive to Johnstone from Greenock and even taught Roseleen to drive so that she could obtain a driving licence. We had become engaged to be married and were happy with the prospect of sharing our lives together after the war had ended and I was back home to begin a new life.

With the end of the war, demobilisation started and everyone in the Services was anxious to end their service with the military forces. Eventually it was my turn and I attended one of the Demobilisation Centres with other members of the Regiment. I received a 'demob suit' and all the other articles of clothing to start me out in civilian life. A travel warrant was given from

17. Our Wedding photograph, 1945

the base in Aldershot to take me to Greenock. What a joyous time. Full of memories, some happy, some sad. As I travelled home all my thoughts were on how quickly I could start to earn a living and how soon I could marry Roseleen.

On 12th June 1945 Roseleen and I were married in St Margaret's Church, Johnstone. It was a splendid wedding. There was a Guard of Honour from the Girls Training Corps (an off-shoot of the Air Training Corps) of which Roseleen was its Commandant. They lined up as we entered and left the Church. Little Alice McPhail, my sister's daughter, presented Roseleen with a silver horseshoe for luck when we left the Church. There were severe restrictions on travel so we took a train to Aberdeen and spent our honeymoon in the Douglas Hotel. It was while in Aberdeen that Roseleen bought her first pair ever of long trousers!!

After our honeymoon we set up home in Gourock. Roseleen by that time had moved on from the Bank and was working as Secretary to the Managing Director of Scottish Precision Castings at Hillington near Glasgow. I continued picking up the business of removing the black-out material from windows of factories, schools and business premises which is dealt with in the next Chapter of the book.

18. Alice McPhail hands a Good Luck Horse Shoe to Roseleen

19. Roseleen with parents, Dermot and 'Dirk' the favourite dog

On 21st November 1948 our son was born in the private wing of the Larkfield Hospital in Greenock. The Doctor who brought him into the world was Dr John Donald, a very dapper man, who always wore white gloves when seeing his patients. We called our son Dermot Hugh Hastings – Dermot from his uncle, Hugh from his maternal grandfather and Hastings from my maternal grandmother. My most vivid recollection of Dermot's early days is when he was just old enough to speak. He would get on his knees shaking the cot shouting 'I want my juice, I want my juice'!! He kept on shouting and shaking the cot until either Roseleen or I took the juice to his bedroom when there was silence immediately. A thirst quenched and a child silenced!

CHAPTER THREE

Return to Civilian Life

ON RETURNING TO GREENOCK I HAD TO turn my attention to the future and find the direction I could take to earn a living. I had no wish to return to my former work as a Plumbing and Heating Engineer – my aspirations had changed. While serving in the Royal Engineers I had been fortunate to have gained a vast amount of knowledge in building construction and was determined to set up my own business in the industry. On making enquiries I found there was a great difficulty in obtaining building materials as they were still under the control of the Ministry of Works. As I had no contracts from the Ministry or the Local Authority I was unable to secure the materials I required to set up the business.

It was then I had to give thought to what I could do until such time there was a relaxation on obtaining materials. It suddenly struck me that many houses had dirty windows as the men who had cleaned the windows prior to the outbreak of the war had joined the Armed Forces. I did a tour of the more affluent parts of Greenock – called the 'West End' – where there were many large detached houses and all manner of residential properties. I made up my mind there was an opportunity to take the 'bull by the horns' and create a Window Cleaning Company.

I registered the Gatehouse Window Cleaning Company, and purchased a wooden barrow and ladders. The name Gatehouse came from the village of Gatehouse of Fleet in Kirkcudbrightshire where my father was born. Pails and chamois leathers were obtained and I was ready to go. At first I set out on my own through the streets pushing the barrow which had a sign on each side indicating I was a Window Cleaner. At first I was somewhat embarrassed. Here was I, a former Officer in the Royal Engineers, pushing a barrow. However, all of that left me as I found the house owners very enthusiastic to make use of my service. My charge was One Shilling for one side and Two Shillings if cleaning the inside and outside. The charges were increased if there were larger windows and ladders were necessary. In no time I was inundated with customers who not only wanted the windows cleaned then, they wanted them cleaned every month. My father joined me although I did not allow him to climb the ladders. We soon employed two young men of sixteen who were seeking work. These two teenagers were the start of the labour force with the company when it appeared there was an opportunity to grow the business as there was no competition in the area from other Window Cleaners. As people saw the services the Gatehouse Window Cleaning Company could give, others started up in competition but we kept all our customers as they were satisfied with us. The town of Greenock was large enough to enable other firms to obtain work.

The first big break came when I secured a large contract from the Renfrewshire County Council. During the war it had been a requirement that all external windows in schools, business premises and offices had to be covered with a black-out material to prevent any lighting to be seen by German bombers who had attacked many areas in Greenock and Clydebank causing devastation and loss of life. Now the war had ended it was necessary to remove the black-out material from the windows to allow in the natural light. Renfrewshire County Council officials approached me to see if I would undertake the work of removing the black-out material and cleaning the windows at 131 schools, factories, offices and other public buildings in the County area. A survey was made of what would be required and I established that by using a razor of the type men had for shaving, the black-out could be scraped off and the windows made clean. I then discussed this with my father bearing in mind the possible problem of wages having to be paid to an additional labour force. We arranged an interview with the Bank Manager who agreed to fund the contract and provide cash for the wages. I also had meetings with County Council officials who gave an undertaking to make the payments immediately the work on any one property was completed. This took care of any potential financial problems.

At this stage the business was about to expand faster than I had anticipated and certainly was not, for the time being, going in the direction of the construction industry. I rented a property at No. 6 Brisbane Street in Greenock and bought two second-hand vehicles to transport the workers to the properties in the entire area covered by Renfrewshire County Council stretching from Wemyss Bay to Barrhead.

Word soon got round we were looking for workers, both male and female. Ladders, buckets, chamois and razors were provided. Within a month a labour force of thirty was employed and the company was on its way to success.

When other business firms saw what was being carried out at the various properties, many contacted me offering my company a contract to remove

RETURN TO CIVILIAN LIFE

the black-out materials. Firms like Scott's Shipbuilding, Kincaid Engineering and Gourock Ropeworks are only three of the many who had the material removed and the windows cleaned by the Gatehouse Window Cleaning Company. Not only was this a satisfactory solution for these businesses, there was an added bonus as many of the major companies arranged contracts for monthly window cleaning by my company. This arrangement ensured work for the labour force for some time. By employing my sister's husband Forbes McPhail and my brother Charles who had been demobilised from the Royal Air Force, I was able to hand over the supervision of these contracts to them who, along with my father, proved valuable assets in controlling the large amount of work which came my way so quickly.

The first break into the construction industry came by sheer chance although it was a demolition job rather than a construction one.

I happened to be in conversation with the senior Official in the Renfrew County Council Building Department when he told me it was the intention to demolish the many Anderson Shelters which had been built in a variety of places throughout the county – some even at the foot of back garden properties. These buildings had very thick walls and roofs to withstand possible bomb damage by the German enemy during the war. I told him I would be interested in carrying out the work if satisfactory terms could be agreed. Although there were a number of other construction and demolition firms around who could carry out this work, it was a case of first off the mark as far as I was concerned. As this work was different from the Window Cleaning Company, I registered a new company under the name of A. McQuarrie & Son, Building Contractors. It was a dream come true and the realisation of what I had my eye on before going to serve my country in the Second World War. The name of the company was to remain for many years and was de-registered in 1987 when it became Sir Albert McQuarrie & Son after Her Majesty The Queen conferred a Knighthood on me.

Having negotiated a rate which I thought would lead to a profit I signed the contract. From the start I thought I had bitten off more than I could chew. The concrete roofs had been reinforced with steel rods and thick layers of concrete. At that time it was not possible to use compressors as the Shelters were in places inaccessible for a compressor. I engaged a number of men who would hammer their way through the cement. A section was cut out in such a manner the roof would ultimately collapse. It was hard work, taking longer than I had planned. All I could hope for was to complete the work without too much of a financial loss knowing the profits from the Window Cleaning operations would continue.

During the time the two companies were operating I could see an opportunity to expand into construction. Due to the war many properties had no maintenance carried out for five years. This meant there was an abundance of work available not only in the private sector but the public one as well. At that stage I did not see my company entering into the construction of properties from foundation level. It was my view there were better opportunities for success in carrying out maintenance and renovation work. I made a careful study of the potential concentrating in the town of Greenock. I could see the route to success was to be independent of any other trade, to the extent all work undertaken would be under the control of the Director of the Company – that was me.

With the existing premises at No. 6 Brisbane Street in Greenock too small for the expanding business, a property at 32 Crawfurd Street and an additional warehouse in Robertson Street were rented. By finding these premises I was able to house the supplies needed to run the business on an independent basis. It was most fortunate work came flowing in. We had established a reputation in a short time for good and efficient workmanship.

To fulfil the desire for a strong workforce I had to 'poach' men of high calibre in the various trades to take over as foremen. I paid them better rates and offered a good bonus for productivity. Sign-writing caused me a difficulty until I heard of 'The Hawk'. His name was Thomson and he could do no sign-writing until the 'pubs' were open as he needed a 'dram' to get him started. He was one of the finest sign-writers I have ever come across. His work can still be seen in many Greenock premises.

All my efforts paid off and within six months the company was operating with employees in all trades within the building industry and totally independent.

Military Service resumed unexpectedly

A few months after I had been demobilised and returned to civilian life I received a telephone call from the Officer-in-Charge of the Army Welfare Service in Scotland enquiring if I would help by taking up an appointment with the Service. He explained the work would be of such a nature it would be of considerable help to servicemen and women who had been demobilised and were finding difficulties adjusting to civilian life, and also wives and families of military personnel still serving.

After giving this some thought to the request and as I could see the work taking up a lot of my time, I decided I wanted to help these people in their time of need. I accepted the invitation and was appointed Army Welfare Officer for the area of lower Renfrewshire which covered all the towns and villages from Kilmacolm to Wemyss Bay with the Headquarters situated in the Territorial Army Drill Hall in South Street, Greenock which was the Headquarters of the Royal Artillery Unit my brother Robert served with prior to the war.

It was fortunate I had not disposed of my Officer's Uniform as I was required to wear it when carrying out any duty with the Army Welfare Service.

My plan was to have the consultations in the Drill Hall several evenings a week, while I made myself available to urgent cases when they were notified to me. All the Scottish Area Headquarters of the Army, Navy and Air Force were notified of my appointment and would direct those seeking help to my office in the Drill Hall. I also had the services of the permanent staff at the Drill Hall who made the appointments for those wishing to see me.

On the evening of the first consultation session I arrived at the Drill Hall to find about twenty people waiting with a variety of problems. There were a few soldiers who had been given a permit of compassionate leave to look after the family business but were being recalled due to the expiry of the compassionate leave permit. The difficulties with some of the people were clear to see. My appointment gave me the right of access to any arm of the Forces right up to the War Office if I thought it possible to secure a satisfactory solution to the problems faced by the people. I did not hesitate to take the action necessary to secure the future of a business which would benefit the community in the aftermath of the war rather than see the people returned to their unit.

Other cases involved a wide variety of cases ranging from soldiers seeking extensions to leave, to others wanting out of the Service and return to civilian life – a view shared by many angry at the delay in the demobilisation programme. I helped as many as I could but told others, in no uncertain manner, the country's needs had to come first and their demobilisation would come in due course.

The most difficult cases I had to handle were matrimonial ones. These came in two forms. There were those couples who had married during the war but had been immediately separated due to the serviceman or woman being called back to their unit. The marriage had broken up and it was invariably the wife who was at a loss to know their position as all correspondence sent to the other party remained unanswered. In these instances I would write to the unit of the person concerned asking for an interview to be made with the serving person to determine whether there was any hope of saving the marriage. While I had a few successes, the majority of these marriages could not be saved and I had to inform the party who approached me in the first instance of the position. One very sad duty I had to undertake during my time as an Army Welfare Officer was to help the widows of servicemen killed in action. Some of these widows were in need of help for a variety of reasons. On several occasions I was able to contact the War Office in London securing recognition and justice for the widows. It was always at the back of my mind that many Greenock servicemen were killed in action, particularly at Dunkirk, and would never return to their loved ones. For this reason alone I always believed it my bounden duty to help the widows and families to the best of my ability.

Accommodation became a huge problem when servicemen returned home to join their wives, and, in many cases, children who had been born during the War. Very often the wives and children were living with parents in property which on the return of the husbands, became overcrowded creating all sorts of problems. As there was a shortage of housing throughout the area, I adopted a policy of contacting all agencies with property for rent advising them that these men had served their country and were justified to receive special consideration when properties became available for rent. The reaction I received from the Local Authorities and other agencies was splendid and through my efforts I was able to see a good number of families settled happily in their home.

Over the next year I continued with the Army Welfare Service whose needs became so much easier to such an extent that after a time I decided to give up my appointment and hand over to others to continue with the consultations as my own business activities required my full attention.

There is one story to record. It was the only time I had to deal with a bit of discord at the consultations due to the fact that I had been delayed by fifteen minutes and did not reach the Drill Hall until 6.45 p.m. There were a number of people waiting to put their case to me. As I walked towards the office, a man in the uniform of a Corporal stepped out and rudely started to berate me for not arriving in time. I learned he was seeking an extension to his leave. I looked him straight in the eye and said to him, pointing to my Epaulettes and Rank Badges 'What do you think these are, Christmas Trees? You address me as "Sir" and may I remind you I am doing this work without any payment'. He sharply retreated back into line to the amusement of others there. When it was his turn to put his case I duly listened but needless to say he did not get an extension to his leave as he could not produce sufficient evidence to justify me making an application to his Unit Commander.

I had enjoyed this unexpected return to military service and was pleased to have been responsible for bringing happiness to a large number of families in their time of need.

Serving the Community

The town of Gourock where we lived was originally a Burgh of Barony but after adoption of the General Police and Improvement (Scotland) Act of 1858 it assumed the status of a Police Burgh from then onwards. The Town Council comprised four Wards with three Councillors representing each Ward. The Council had a well designed Chamber where meetings were presided over by the Provost who was the senior member of the Council and who wore an ornate Robe of Office with Mink Collar and Facings. As customary in Scottish Town Councils the Provost had a beautifully inscribed Gold Chain decorated with the Burgh of Gourock's Coat of Arms. The Town Council was dissolved as a Burgh on Friday 9th May 1975 when it was incorporated into the new Inverclyde Council under the Government's reorganisation of Local Government. To many of the people of Gourock this was a retrograde step and, for some still residing in Gourock, continues to be a sore point.

It was a progressive town and many people who were employed in the adjacent larger Burgh of Greenock chose to live in Gourock as my wife Roseleen and I had done. After my return from the war I took an interest in the local Unionist Party which was quite active in the area. The Member of Parliament for West Renfrewshire, the constituency covering Gourock, was The Hon John S MacLay (later Viscount MacLay, now deceased). He also served as Secretary of State for Scotland and was a very popular gentleman.

In 1948 I was encouraged to contest the 2nd Ward of the Council as an Independent. Politics had not entered into the Town Councils at that time. All Councillors were elected as Independents. It worked very well as there was no political in-fighting during debates when the Council met. At the election I was successful and became one of the three Councillors for the 2nd Ward.

In these days no payments of any sort were made to Councillors. Meetings of the full Council took place once a month. Committee meetings took place in the evenings. I was able to carry out my duties as a Councillor without it interfering with the business.

In 1950 I was elected Dean of Guild in the Town Council. The Councillor holding this Office was Chairman of the Committee dealing with any matters to do with planning or other projects involving construction or rebuilding. When meetings of the Committee took place I wore a black Robe and the Town Clerk was present in his gown and wig as a lawyer. It was all very formal. When anyone addressed the Chairman it was preceded with the words 'Your Honour'.

Another Office I held within the Town Council was Vice Convener of

Parks and Gardens. Gourock was fortunate to have several large Parks and an abundance of areas which were planted with flowers according to the season. At Darroch Park, the main one in the town, there were several glasshouses where plants were brought on from seedlings and grown for planting out to give a wonderful show of flowers throughout the town. I had great pleasure serving in this Office and took a keen interest in the plants on show in the glasshouses. The Foreman, Alex Rollo, taught me how to grow orchids and for a good number of years I was successful at it!!

The Gourock Horticultural Society

At this time there was considerable enthusiasm by local people to form a Horticultural Society. I was requested by the other Councillors to call a meeting in the town with a view to creating one, provided local gardeners would support it.

The meeting was held in early 1950. It was attended by a large number of local residents who were extremely keen to form a Society. A vote was taken to do so and approved by all present. The Gourock Horticultural Society was inaugurated and held its first Annual Show in September 1950. I had been elected Chairman of the Society. One of the tasks I had to do was to find someone to 'Declare the Show Open'. I had read in the newspapers that Barbara Kelly – a noted actress, television and radio presenter was appearing in a Glasgow Theatre. Barbara and her husband, Bernard Braden who was Canadian, formed the famous television duo of *Kelly and Braden* appearing for many years on television and in radio. I sought Barbara out in Glasgow and explained to her my request to which without hesitation she agreed. Her presence at the Show was an outstanding success as large crowds came to see the great attraction for the first ever Show. The Gamble Institute was filled with blooms grown especially by the amateur gardeners. It was a magnificent display. After a few years the Show outgrew the Gamble Institute and found a new home in the Cragburn Pavilion, which could cope with the ever increasing number of entries. Cragburn Pavilion was owned by the Town Council which in later years was demolished to make way for housing. The Society returned to the Gamble Institute where the Shows continue to be staged with considerable success due to the magnificent work done by the committee.

I presented the first Trophy to the Society for the *12 Best Exhibits in the Show* naming it the R.S. McQuarrie Cup in memory of my brother Robert who was killed at Dunkirk in May 1940. Now there are over fifty Trophies presented at the Annual Show. The R.S. McQuarrie remains the principal trophy sixty-three years on from the Society being established in 1950.

I remained Chairman of the Horticultural Society although I had moved to other addresses away from Gourock. In 1979 when I was elected Member of Parliament for East Aberdeenshire I resigned as Chairman and was elected Honorary Vice President. At that time the Honorary President was The Hon John S MacLay MP and it was on his death some years later the Society invited me to be its Honorary President, a position I still hold. It is to the great credit of the members of the Society that every year two outstanding Shows are staged – a Spring Show and an Autumn Show. It is with pleasure that I have served as an Office Bearer of the Society for so many years. I was presented with the Royal Horticultural Society Medal for 'Long and Loyal Service' to the Society on reaching fifty years as an Office Bearer.

20. Presentation of the Royal Horticulture Society Medal for 50 years service

The Pensioners

There was another organisation I created during my time as Dean of Guild in the Town Council. It was the Old Age Pensioners Association. There were Associations in other adjoining burghs for the elderly and the Town Council saw the need for one in Gourock. I was delegated by the Council to call a meeting of Pensioners in the town to find what interest there was in setting up an Association. The decision was made easy as a packed meeting agreed to form the Gourock Old Age Pensioners Association on condition I would accept the role of Chairman. Whether it was a compliment to me at the age of 32, as I was then, or if they saw me as a pensioner I do not know but I accepted the Chairmanship and made sure the Association got off to a successful start.

In an effort to get the Association on to a good financial position I persuaded the Town Council to give permission for the Pensioners Association to take control and operate the car park behind the Continental Café on the seaside near the swimming pool in Kempoch Street. This was the only car park near the main street and even in those days was busy seven day a week.

At that time Town Councils were a bit more generous towards helping local Associations. It was not difficult to arrange for a By-Law to be approved by the Council imposing parking charges where formerly parking was free. I arranged for a hut to be provided for use as an Office for the Pensioners who were acting as Attendants at the car park.

The Pensioners Committee was delighted with this source of income and set up a group of male members who would turn up at arranged times to collect the charge from the car park users. The people using the facility who had not been paying previously did not object to the charge when they learned all the income went to the Pensioners Association. In the years that followed the income was used for outings and the Annual Christmas Party.

This system operated successfully for several years until the re-organisation of Local Government when the new Councillors decided to take over the car park as a Municipal one. To be fair the Council continued to pay for the Christmas Dinner for which the Association were most grateful.

It turned out to be a great Association. I held the office of Chairman for ten years and the Office of Honorary President for a further twenty years. My successors have kept the Association alive and it is pleasing to know of its existence sixty-three years after it was founded and still running smoothly.

Weekly meetings are planned with all sorts of entertainment. Outings are arranged and ever popular with the elderly. Recently a legacy of £20,000 was left to the Association by a member who wished the donation to be used for the outings and an Annual Christmas Party. I would suggest he must have been one of the members who was concerned at the loss of the car park income and wanted the Association to once more enjoy the free outings and Christmas Dinner – God bless him for his generosity.

A lasting memory I have of the weekly meetings is one occasion during my time as Chairman. The Association had a Chaplain, the Reverend Thomas Hamilton, from a local church. He was also Chaplain to the Greenock Prison. He asked me if it would be in order to bring to the weekly meeting a female prisoner who had a beautiful voice. I agreed and made the arrangements. There was plenty excitement among the members at the thought of a prisoner singing to them. When the young woman began to sing *I Know my Redeemer Liveth* from the Messiah there was a deadly silence in the hall. It was a perfect rendition of the beautiful solo. The applause was terrific. Then she sang *Panis Angelicus*. There was a standing ovation for her. It was one of the most wonderful voices it has been my privilege to hear. To this day the memory is still with me. I often wonder what happened to that young woman after completing her sentence. I have no way of knowing. I only hope she moved on to a better life, and perhaps able to use her lovely singing voice to her advantage.

During the time as a Councillor, I served these two organisations in the knowledge they were bringing together many people in the town of Gourock who may otherwise have been sitting at home with no real interest. No wonder there are so many people in Gourock receiving a 100th Birthday Card from Her Majesty The Queen. They have been kept active because of these organisations.

I retired from the Council at the end of my term in 1955 as it was necessary to devote all my time to the business. Yet another recession had fallen upon the Building Industry and all my energies were required to safeguard the employment of the workers in the two companies I had created. I had enjoyed my years as a Councillor and made many friends with whom I remained in contact for a number of years.

A Recession hits the Building Industry

In 1955 the building industry hit a recession which had a dramatic effect on my company. The Gatehouse Window Cleaning Company had no problems but the building company suffered a severe loss of business due to the financial crisis. For a number of years the industry continued to suffer from the recession which was not the fault of the operators of a building business. On this occasion we found ourselves right in the middle of it. Work was hard to secure and many contracts were only secured by extremely low price tenders which ultimately led to a loss in the company's earnings.

With the greatest regret I had to start a programme of reducing my workforce and paid off a number of the loyal workers. It was obvious the company would have to operate on a much lesser scale as there was always the danger of insolvency which I was determined to avoid.

During 1955 I was invited by a friend of mine in the sanitary pottery business to take up an appointment in the company as Commercial Director. The factory was based in Paisley. I thought long and hard as I had to ensure I had a good enough income to keep my wife and son. It would be possible

A LIFETIME OF MEMORIES

for me to keep the business going on its reduced scale and my father had good control of the Gatehouse Window Cleaning Company.

I found the temporary appointment of Director in the Pottery Company of great interest. It not only involved the Paisley factory known as Robert Brown & Co, other factories were located at Horwich near Bolton in Lancashire and in Liverpool. With demand being good in the north west of England I opened another two companies in that area. One sold all kinds of sanitary-ware for bathrooms and kitchens, the other, manufacturing goods for the pottery industry. My friend was delighted at the way I had helped develop these companies. Sadly he died very suddenly in 1960 and his death resulted in the entire firm being put on the market for new owners. This was not a body blow, as I still had my own companies operating on a smaller scale which were bringing in a satisfactory income.

With these changes I once more used my energies in another direction. The Paisley factory had been closed down due to the lack of a buyer. On a visit to the factory I saw there was a large stock of sanitary-ware in the warehouse. I approached the Liquidator and asked if I could purchase the stock. He told me there would be around 3,000 pieces of ware and asked what I could offer. Like a flash I just said 'two hundred and fifty pounds' expecting him to treat it as a joke. Immediately he said 'right it is a deal'. I could scarcely believe what I had heard and quickly got out my cheque book and paid over £250. As Johnstone was near to Paisley I rented a warehouse and transferred all the ware there. I did a deal with three brothers-in-law, Eddie, Vincent and Dermot McCaffery, to sell the goods at £1.00 per piece. I advertised the sale in the local and Glasgow newspapers. Within a month almost half the stock was sold which was not surprising at such a reasonable selling price.

I quickly realised there was a market for sanitary-ware in Scotland so I set up yet another company called Sanware (Johnstone) Ltd operating as Builders and Plumbers Merchants. I contacted a number of bath manufacturers and brass fitting manufacturers. Materials were purchased so that full bathroom suites and kitchens could be sold. I was pleased to have formed another company which was to operate successfully and give work to the building company of A McQuarrie & Son.

In light of this development I closed down the business in Greenock and transferred it to Johnstone. In 1963 we left Gourock and took up residence in Johnstone which was to be my work base for the next twelve years during which a number of life changing events took place.

Once we had settled into Johnstone, Roseleen purchased a grocer's business from her uncle. It was in the centre of a housing estate where business was particularly good in the evening when shops in the town had closed. After the death of her father, Roseleen bought one of his shops, which was ably managed by her brother Hugh, in another housing estate selling the same kind of goods. These two shops were run successfully and profitably by Roseleen who was an astute operator and quickly learned the tricks of the trade. I enjoyed helping out in the shops during the evenings and getting to know the customers who took advantage of 'late shopping'. In 1969 both shops were sold as by that time we were fully engaged in dealing with the Great Storm of 1968 which hit the west of Scotland on the 19th January and the subject of another Chapter. We purchased a house in Lady Margaret Drive, Troon and travelled daily to the Paisley Office.

Having successfully operated the two firms in Johnstone the next five years saw a considerable growth in the number of companies I was to create. I set up a company of manufacturers agents. This company undertook the sale of building and plumbing materials to a wide range of customers all over Scotland. I had appointed George McNaughton who had wide experience of organising a business of this nature to take over as Commercial Director. Sadly George died in 1970 at which stage the business was incorporated into Sanware (Johnstone) Ltd. By this time I had also taken over a pipe manufacturing company which provided pre-fabricated pipes and fittings for the plumbing industry. Although this firm only employed a small number of employees it was very profitable for some years. With a change in the manufacture of sanitary pottery designs the need for this type of product made by the company dropped considerably to the extent there was a very much reduced order book. The firm was later incorporated into Sanware (Johnstone) Ltd.

In 1964 I purchased Warewell Westcot Limited a building construction company which had been put up for sale on the retiral of the Director. This was a small business which had a solid core of customers. One advantage was the fact it had employed plumbers, electricians, tilers, painters and decorators. These were trades not previously been operated by any of the companies I owned. This was the company which was used as the main one when I was involved with the damage caused by the Great Storm. When the name of the parent company was changed from A McQuarrie & Son to A McQuarrie & Son (Great Britain) Limited in late 1969, Warewell Westcot was incorporated into the new company and all staff and employees were transferred.

Voluntary Activities

In 1967 I accepted an invitation to become Chairman of the Ardmillan

Housing Association Limited. This was a company formed with the support of HM Government to undertake the refurbishment on all classes of rented properties in the public and private sector which had been under the control of the Government Housing Corporation. Being Chairman of this Association did not preclude my company tendering for the work. The company had considerable success in being awarded contracts and an increase in the employees of A McQuarrie & Son (Great Britain) Limited was necessary. I remained Chairman of the Association until the end of 1972 when pressure of business prevented me from being able to fulfil the role of Chairman with satisfaction. The appointment was unpaid.

Coupled with the Ardmillan Housing Association, I was also invited to become Chairman of the Thistle Housing Society. This company was supported by the Government's Housing Corporation as an operating company engaged in new build houses to rent. I involved my company directly in the new build construction in Fenwick, Ayrshire and other areas in Renfrewshire. This brought the company to a state where work could be undertaken with all trades fully engaged on the contracts which had been successfully negotiated. There were many meetings to attend with Government and Local Government officials in connection with the ongoing work at sites where a great many houses were built by the Society which provided much needed places to rent and also houses for disabled people. The Society was one of the pioneers in providing special facilities for disabled people. Today such a facility is standard. It pleases me when I pass some of these developments to see them still being used for the purpose including entrance ramps and handgrips for the disabled. I was so glad it was possible for me to give time to these kinds of developments. I gave up the Chairmanship in 1973 due to the fact I was now living full-time in Gibraltar. It was with deep satisfaction I left knowing so many useful contracts for rented house had been completed during my time as Chairman of Thistle Housing Society. This appointment, like the other, was unpaid. I was more than willing to help others without seeking remuneration.

CHAPTER FOUR

The Great Storm of 1968

THIS CHAPTER IS ABOUT THE YEARS SPENT DEALING with the Great Storm which struck the west of Scotland on 14th January 1968. The strength of the gale reached a terrific 134 miles per hour causing devastating destruction to properties and the loss of twenty lives.

For me it all started that day just before midnight. My wife Roseleen, son Dermot and I were wakened from sleep with a thunderous roar of high winds and driving rain. We got out of bed, slipped into dressing gowns and came downstairs to the lounge which faced a main road in Johnstone where we were living at that time. On walking towards the window we could scarcely believe our eyes. Suddenly a thunderous roar took place. Garden huts, garage roofs and rubbish bins were trundling along the road battering everything. We heard a loud bang of masonry falling which turned out to be a chimney head from the tenement building some ten yards from our house which also had its roof torn off leaving the roof space exposed to all the rain. We stood speechless. I said to Roseleen, 'This will cost an awful lot of money to repair. I hope people have house insurance'.

At about 1.00 a.m. we were about to have a cup of tea when there was a loud noise in the house. Dermot and I rushed into the dining room to find the window and frame lying in the garden and rain pouring in through a large hole in the wall. Fortunately I had some plywood and straps in the garage and after being thoroughly soaked we managed to stop the rain from coming into the house.

In the morning as I drove to the office where I operated the building construction business there was destruction everywhere. Streets were strewn with debris and the street gullies were overflowing causing severe flooding. I had no idea the devastation had affected so many properties. The newspapers carried no news of the storm as they had been printed the night before. At the office there was much discussion of the situation. There was a difficulty in getting the men to work as the state of the roads strewn with debris of all sorts including damaged properties became impossible to access. That day at lunchtime, something happened which was to change my life for the next two and a half years.

As I drove home for lunch I saw the Burgh Surveyor, John Murdoch, leave his office. I wound down the car window and asked, almost jokingly, - 'Do you need any roofers, John?' He hurried over to me and said – 'Albert, I can do with all the roofers and labourers you can get me. Johnstone Castle and Cochrane Castle houses have been severely hit, roofs are badly damaged and rain is pouring in. The Council direct labour force is working on storm damage in the town and all other firms are working on damaged tenements'. I said to him – 'Give me an hour and I will endeavour to have men at these two locations to assess how the damage can be repaired'.

I rushed home, told my wife of the conversation with the Burgh Surveyor and that I had no time for lunch. I drove straight to the Labour Exchange and was given the names of all the roofers and labourers who were unemployed in the Johnstone area. I told the Manager of the Exchange the reason why I wanted these workers and the urgency. He co-operated well by telephoning those he could and by sending staff in their cars to collect the men and take them to my works. I returned to the office and organised my workforce with ladders and tools, and loaded them on to lorries. I had three at that time. I knew I had insufficient tools so I drove to the local ironmonger where I bought all the roofing tools he had in stock. On arriving at Cochrane Castle at 3.00 p.m. to see the destruction I was flabbergasted. Roofs were torn off; cars were buried in the rubble; streets and gardens covered with debris; scarcely a garage or garden hut left in place. I assessed at once re-slating was out of the question and hurried down to John Murdoch to ask for felt, tarpaulin and galvanised nails. He told me these items would be sent up immediately and I could purchase more wherever I could find them. I returned to the ironmongers and purchased all the stock he had. I then spent a short time at Johnstone Castle houses to find the devastation even worse.

It was obvious many more workers would be required. I returned to my office and phoned around all the nearby Labour Exchanges. Only Greenock could help and offered me ten roofers and fifteen builder's labourers. I told the Manager of the Exchange to arrange for these men to report to my office the next day. Within forty-eight hours the labour force had risen to sixty-six. In the meantime journalists were writing articles about the ferocious storm, photographs were taken which illustrated the extent of the damage not only to Johnstone and surrounding area but also to the City of Glasgow. Among the twenty people who died were three children. 100,000 houses in the City of Glasgow were damaged. A police report from one area in the city indicated seventy-seven people permanently homeless; 917 temporarily homeless; 5,373 roofs damaged; 1,997 chimney heads demolished; 226 gable ends of properties collapsed; 298 plate glass windows smashed; 950 ceilings down; 246 falls of masonry and 344 vehicles written off. The report states this was what had been identified so far. As it turned out the figures for all these categories rose dramatically when all reports were complete, with the total roof repairs reaching 254,000 and over 30,000 chimney heads down. The estimate of the cost of repairs was put at £35 million (at 1969 prices) much of which was paid by HM Government and Insurance Companies.

During these first few days I was not aware that a crisis in securing labour was developing. The Johnstone repairs were being carried out with considerable progress although life was difficult because the rain never ceased. I had assumed places like Glasgow, Paisley, Greenock and Clydebank would have sufficient workers within the direct labour departments augmented with employees from local firms to meet the need. That assumption was to be proved wrong very quickly.

On the Monday morning following the storm I was in my office when one of the staff told me a Mr Charles Coppleton wished to see me. He was shown in and introduced himself as Chief Clerk of Works for the Paisley Corporation and that he urgently required eighty roofers and 100 building labourers for the Ferguslie Park housing scheme and surrounding areas which had been devastated by the storm, as all available labour in Paisley was engaged on storm damage throughout the town. I did not hesitate because by that time I had the bit between my teeth. All the workers I was now employing were desperately anxious to get the roofs wind and water tight so people could return to their homes. I promised Charles Coppleton I would do my best. After he left the office I sat at my desk wondering what to do. Suddenly it hit me!!

There were many other areas in Scotland which had not been affected by the storm. I telephoned a great number of Labour Exchanges throughout the country advising of the vacancies and the wages which were on offer of between £100 and £150 per week – high remuneration at that time. The response was positive and men started arriving the following day. Additionally I contacted many small roofing and joinery firms offering sub-contract work in Paisley. These firms were delighted to accept as they did not have the people or the capacity to take on the work on their own. They were a marvellous help to me. Within the week Charles Coppleton had eighty roofers and 100 labourers operating in Ferguslie Park and many other areas in Paisley – a remarkable achievement.

People in the building industry were wondering how it was possible to organise a labour force of over 250 in a matter of seven days and be in a position to pay the wages. There were two reasons for this. One was the Local Authorities had undertaken to pay the invoices within twenty-four hours of submission. I engaged a surveyor whose job it was to assist the office staff, which had to be increased, in the preparation of the invoices to be submitted to the Local Authorities who did not always pay on time. A problem was looming. I called on Mr Roger Fleming, Manager of the Johnstone Clydesdale Bank, to explain the position. I asked for a facility in order to pay the wages bill while I undertook to pay into the Bank all receipts from the Local Authorities. He asked me to return within an hour which I did when he told me he had been authorised to let me have all the money I required on production of wages sheets and invoices. This was a load off my mind – an open facility with no security.

With the very much increased labour force I found it was not possible for me to monitor properly the work in the worst affected areas. I appointed three Foremen whose job it was to organise the labour and materials in specific areas. Scaffolding had to be erected before the workers could access the roofs to clear the damage and remove the fallen chimney heads. Masonry had become dislodged causing a risk to the workmen. The Foremen were instructed that a job had to be delayed if the safety of the workmen was in any way putting them into jeopardy.

Work in Johnstone and Paisley was progressing well. Greenock and Port Glasgow were appealing for aid. I made arrangements for the damage in these towns to be assessed and provided labour for temporary repairs to be carried out.

On the Saturday morning a week into the Storm I was in my office when I had a telephone call from Dr J. Dickson Mabon MP, Minister of State at the Scottish Office and Member of Parliament for Greenock. He was speaking from the office of the Lord Provost of Glasgow. He advised me there were 50,000 properties in Glasgow with no roofs and no tarpaulins. People were in desperate circumstances and he asked if I could help. I said I would be in Glasgow within the hour. This was my first visit to the city since the storm. Driving through the streets I was staggered at the damage. There was not one property in Paisley Road West which had not suffered roof damage. I was met at the City Chambers by Lord Provost Johnston and Dr Mabon. The situation was explained to me. The Town Clerk brought in maps on which the damaged properties were marked. He explained all available tradesmen in the city were engaged on storm damage and the Scottish Special Housing Association had drafted men in from Edinburgh and the

Lothians yet only a small percentage of properties had been attended to. Areas like Govan and the Gorbals and many others were desperately in need of help. The impact of the 134 mph gale had truly hit me.

21. Great Storm damage Glasgow City, 1968

Dr Mabon asked if I could carry out emergency repairs over half the city which would be followed by permanent repairs. I said 'Give me a large warehouse, loads of roofing felt and tarpaulins, timber straps and galvanised nails'. I told him these would be required by Monday while my workmen would make a start in the city the following day (Sunday) with materials borrowed from Paisley and Johnstone where the temporary repairs were being carried out without difficulty.

Over the weekend I set the wheels in motion in securing further labour. I instructed one of the Managers to search all Scotland and go into England if necessary and to advise all Labour Exchanges that workers were still being sought with high wages being paid.

On the Sunday I took fifty men to Glasgow to carry out repairs on some of the worst hit properties. I well remember the first property at No. 22 Cumberland Street where we had difficulty first of all in accessing the close and then to find debris from fallen chimney heads and roof timbers making access to the top of the building like an assault course. When I reached the top landing tears were brought to my eyes to find the flats with no heating of any kind and no water other than what was pouring in from the gaping holes in the roof. Despair was written on the faces of parents and children. The shock at seeing this terrible situation gave me the determination to forge ahead.

I then drove to Elmbank Street for a meeting with Mr Ian MacDonald, Deputy Town Clerk, who had overall authority for storm damage repairs and who was working seven days a week on the storm damage. He told me

22. Great Storm damage Glasgow City, 1968

23. Great Storm damage Glasgow City, 1968

THE GREAT STORM OF 1968

an old Bakery at Water Row had been allocated and the City building department had started to move materials into the building. On Monday morning we moved into Water Row with a new labour force which quickly rose to 400 tradesmen and labourers with a back-up office staff. By the week end the operation was going well. I had to purchase vans and lorries. Second hand buses were bought to bring men from Edinburgh, Lanarkshire, Greenock and Ayrshire. Lodgings were found for the men from the North of Scotland and England. In no time thirty-five lorries and vans plus twenty buses were used every day on the operations. More Foremen were assigned to specific areas with gangs of tradesmen and labourers. The entire project was run like a military operation.

Difficulties did arise mainly how to maintain contact with the Foremen and the workforce. On a visit to Water Row, Dr Mabon asked if there were any problems. I explained the one of contact. He told me there were a number of former Civil Defence Intelligence vehicles at the North Berwick depot. These vehicles had radio control fitted and they were available. I told him I would take six and asked the price. He telephoned the Scottish Office and was advised a price of £75 each. I was apprehensive of the condition at that price. Arrangements were made to travel to North Berwick next day when to my surprise on arriving at the depot, the drivers and I found these magnificent vehicles none of which had done more than forty-seven miles and had aluminium bodies which I learned later cost £3,000 each. They were fitted with desks and seats and wired up for radio. I could hardly believe my luck. I often wondered who made the error at the Scottish Office to sell them off at £75 each. The vehicles were driven to Glasgow where five were set up for control purposes in various locations which covered half the city. The sixth I retained as a headquarters and hired a driver to allow me to keep in contact with all the works taking place in the city and also in the other areas in the west of Scotland where the storm damage repairs were being carried out.

The former intelligence vehicles came in handy for another worthwhile purpose. Just at that time the Hon George Younger, Member of Parliament for Ayr and former Officer in the Argyll and Sutherland Highlanders led a campaign to 'Save The Argylls' as the Government had proposed to disband the Regiment. A Petition had been set up and George was asking for 100,000 signatures. I volunteered to have Petition Sheets in each of the mobile vehicles and as they were constantly on the move, many hundred of signatures were secured. When I looked at some of the completed sheets, I had never seen so many 'Jesus Christs' and Pop Stars as signatures to the Petition. The Petition must have had good results because the Government backed off and the Argylls were saved from disbandment.

Things were moving fast with new areas being tackled every day. With the large increase in the workforce it was necessary to find alternative office premises as the Johnstone office could not cope. I contacted the Estate Factor of the Elderslie Estates who advised me the offices which they had previously occupied in the Main Street, Elderslie were vacant and he could offer me the rental of the property. On seeing the large detached building I decided it would be most suitable for our use.

As more staff were being engaged to undertake the work connected to the storm it was possible to move in quickly. A large sign across the front of the building was erected with the name 'Thistle House'. I had purchased the Building firm of Warewell Westcot which became the principal name of the all operations of the storm damage repairs. At its peak the company engaged 1,000 operators covering all trades under my direction as Managing Director of Warewell Westcot. This firm was later incorporated into A McQuarrie & Son (Great Britain) Limited.

In addition to Thistle House I set up an office at the Water Row premises in Glasgow as the operations being carried out in the city and surrounding areas required greater supervision and monitoring.

It has never ceased to amaze me whenever I recall the days of the great storm just how easy it seemed to create and operate such a large workforce with little trouble. I think my Army Officer experience in the Royal Engineers of leadership and the need for quick decisions must have had something to do with it.

Over the next few months we worked steadily, with other towns and villages added to the list where repair works was required. With the rain persisting, properties which had temporary repairs required further attention. To consider permanent repairs was impossible when the workforce was still dealing with properties suffering from leaking roofs and fallen chimney heads. Emergency squads in buses dealt with severely affected properties until such time as permanent repairs could be made. It soon became quite obvious it was to be a lengthy operation. We worked an average of sixteen hours a day splitting the overtime in such a way that no worker became over tired to tackle the conditions of the roofs at a high height. In the first year we had very little scaffolding and much of the access to the roofs was made through the roof space. In what we called Phase Two, when bitumen felt and straps were fitted to roofs, scaffolding had been erected around the buildings and at the Chimney heads for the repair work. It was remarkable not one workman was injured during the entire operation due to our strict safety measures. As the months rolled on, the labour force reached 750

24. Great Storm damage Glasgow City, 1968

which later increased to 1,000 between direct company employees and workers from other firms under contract. Finance ceased to be a problem. The system was working.

The Local Authorities were able to pay bills as the Government provided millions of pounds for the storm damage to be repaired. The 30th December 1968 was a day of great satisfaction to us. After my weekly meeting with Mr McDonald at the Civil Defence Office when we were chatting he asked me if it was not time we were looking for payment from the city. I was taken aback as although I had interested myself in the financial side of the business the day to day running was left to the office manager. I was however aware there was no bank overdraft as all other Local Authorities were paying promptly as agreed. Mr McDonald said 'Do you know how much the city owe you for invoices submitted?' I confessed I did not. He told me it was over £350,000 and explained the task of dealing with invoices from so many firms on storm damage was such they were behind schedule. I told him to let me have a cheque for £250,000 on account. This was paid the following day. All of us enjoyed a very Happy New Year!! I learned from my building surveyor that he was aware of the situation and had submitted further invoices amounting to £200,000 for work carried out. Shortly afterwards the city fell into line and paid promptly which meant we were never short of funds pleasing the Bank Manager and justifying the confidence he had in me when I had approached him for facilities to pay the wages to the workers.

The beginning of 1969 saw the start of another phase to repair the properties on a more permanent basis. I had purchased millions of new and second hand roof slates and tiles from all over the UK. Thousands of properties throughout Glasgow had their roofs and chimney heads restored which gave me a great deal of satisfaction. It took a further eighteen months before the workforce could be reduced. During the time good friendships were made within the entire company and I was sorry when each squad of men were paid off. Ultimately we left Water Row and centred everything at Elderslie premises where a certain calm operated after a long period of intense activity and successful operations.

Here are a couple of stories I wish to share.
I always tried to visit as many jobs as possible each day and go on to the roofs. On one occasion I was in Scotland Street, Glasgow where the roof was being renewed. The lead was on the skews at the chimney heads and work was proceeding. The next day I returned only one man was on the roof – the others having been called to an emergency repair. I saw at once that the lead had been stripped from the chimney. I questioned the roofer who denied any knowledge of it. He had a smell of drink which was banned during working hours on account of the dangerous work. I said to him 'You are a liar. I tell you now, at this moment, there are three of us on this roof. You, me and him (pointing my hand upwards). If you do not tell me within one minute where the lead is there will only be two of us and you will not be one of them.' He saw I was angry and meant what I said. He blurted out 'It is in a pail in the roof space'. I shouted down to my driver to fetch the Police and ordered the man to get the pail and come off the roof with me. The Police came and collected him and the lead. Next day, he was in Court and sent to prison for fourteen days. The irony of it came six months later when the Police telephoned, asking me to collect the pail of lead. The last thing I needed was a pail of old lead. I had just received another handsome cheque from the City of Glasgow!!

Then there was the strike. I was sitting in the office at Water Row when the Govan Foreman came in to tell me about forty men in his area had gone on strike for more money. When I thought of the high wages these men were earning I was raging. I told the Foreman 'Go out there and tell these men I will give them five minutes to return to work otherwise they will be paid off at once'. The Foreman, Deveney, was a tough roofer from Gourock. I was told later he went out and in no uncertain manner, with a few colourful words, told the men what the Boss had said. His words were the strike was over immediately and the men returned to work. About an hour later a newspaper reporter arrived at the office and wanted to know about the strike. I said 'what strike?' He said we were telephoned and told there was a strike of workers here. I said 'did you see any strike?' to which he replied 'I saw nobody'. I told him someone must have been pulling his leg as there was no strike here. Off he went downcast at not having a scoop. It proved a journalist could be tricked but only if the problem was settled before his arrival. It also proved the necessity of using strong-arm tactics against tough tradesmen who would have disrupted these essential repairs. It was also a time when people could laugh at their own stupidities – like the woman in Hyndland who insisted her husband should wear his ARP helmet when going into the street during the storm winds. As soon as he left the tenement the hat blew off and smashed right through the windscreen of his car.

The permanent work carried on for another year. During that time I was making regular visits to Gibraltar where I had established another company called A. McQuarrie & Son (Overseas) Ltd. Our son Dermot along with Robert McClumpha, were directing the operations in Gibraltar (the subject of another Chapter). As the contracts in Scotland were completed the labour force was being reduced. I foresaw a time where it would be necessary for me to move to Gibraltar as the contracts being created there were substantial. This was discussed at length with my wife Roseleen and Dermot who agreed with me to move to Gibraltar.

I appointed David Mason one of the Managers in the storm damage operation to take control of the work in Scotland and advised him of my impending move to Gibraltar. I told him it was my intention to regularly return to Scotland so I could remain in contact with the operations and make such decisions as necessary. I must admit I was attracted to the idea of living in a warm climate and being able to swim in the sea in addition to aiding the people of Gibraltar at the time the border between Spain and Gibraltar was closed.

For the next year I regularly visited Scotland until all the contracts had been completed and the labour force paid off. At that stage I spent some time mothballing my companies in Scotland as working in Gibraltar was a full time occupation.

Many ditties were written about the Great Storm – some good, some not so good. MP Ian Davidson's ditty survived them all in the folk clubs for years after the damage had been repaired. I did not know the tune but this is what he wrote:

It battered Greenock's tenements and made the houses sway,
and trees and gates and garages were flattened on its way..........
to Glasgow's rotten tenements, and shook off their chimney heads
and some went down through the houses and they counted 19 dead.

The Rt Hon Brian Wilson, the former Energy Minister, in his article on the 25th anniversary of The Great Storm printed in the *Glasgow Herald* concluded with these words:

> It's an ill wind – but what would happen today
> Let's hope there is no anniversary repeat performance tonight
> For who would write the song
> Where would we get the roofers?
> And who would the Albert McQuarrie be of today?

(My thanks to Rt Hon Brian Wilson, Ian Davidson MP and *The Herald* for these extracts in the issue of 11th January 1993)

The media reported that I referred to The Great Storm as 'my storm'. This was quite true as I was totally focused on it almost every waking moment each day with the determination that those people affected would be taken out of their misery as early as possible.

The Great Storm of 1968 will never be forgotten. As I drive through Glasgow and the towns in the west of Scotland where we operated, my eyes always turn upward to the roofs and the chimney heads and my thoughts stray to those days in particular between 1968/1970. There the properties stand, proud and high – all signs of the great storm hidden from sight but not from mind.

So ended my involvement with the west of Scotland's Great Storm. It certainly was an amazing experience not only for me, but for all the labour force and also the thousands of people in the west of Scotland who had suffered from the 134 miles per hour gale.

CHAPTER FIVE

Answering the Call to help the People of Gibraltar

IN MID JULY 1969 while there was still a large number of employees with A. McQuarrie & Son Ltd completing the final phase of repairs to the buildings in the West of Scotland caused by The Great Storm of 1968, I received a telephone call from Mr Richard Buchanan, Member of Parliament for Glasgow Springburn. He advised me that General Franco, the Spanish Dictator had closed the border between Spain and Gibraltar as yet another attempt by the Spaniards to annex Gibraltar into Spain had been thwarted by the people of Gibraltar. 'Dick' as he was known told me all Spanish tradesmen who had been employed in Gibraltar had returned to Spain on the instructions of the Spanish Government, leaving many projects unfinished. The British Foreign and Commonwealth Office had received a plea for help from the Gibraltar Government as many of the unfinished projects were either of a military nature or of importance to the welfare of the people in Gibraltar such as hospitals, housing and health centres. From the military point of view the project was the refurbishment of the Gibraltar Regiment Barracks and the building of a new Regimental Headquarters.

Dick said he had been discussing the situation in Spain with Mr Michael Stewart, the Foreign and Commonwealth Secretary and the serious problems which had arisen as a result of the border closure. He commented to Mr Stewart of the huge storm in the west of Scotland where properties were severely damaged and how a labour force was recruited to deal with a serious situation. At this Mr Stewart asked Dick to find out if it would be possible for the company responsible for the storm repairs to gather together a force of tradesmen and labourers to travel to Gibraltar and to complete the unfinished contracts. Dick contacted me and arranged that I would meet Mr Stewart at his office in the House of Commons to discuss whether the proposal would be possible. Never did I think my company would be involved in considering operations in a place like Gibraltar which I had only visited with Roseleen while on holiday on a cruise ship.

I discussed the request with my wife Roseleen and son Dermot who had been responsible for a large part in the organisation of the storm damage repairs in the west of Scotland. They both agreed I should visit London to ascertain what would be required if a labour force of tradesmen and labourers from the company was sent to Gibraltar.

Prior to going to London, I sounded out Bob McClumpha, one of my Directors and a highly skilled tradesman, who had previously held managerial positions in a number of construction companies in Scotland. I also felt it necessary to sound out a number of employees in the various trades to find out if there would be any interest in going to Gibraltar. The general opinion was in favour.

The employees who were interested naturally wanted more information before making any commitment. They were given this after my return from the initial visits to London and Gibraltar and a good number volunteered to be on the list for selection.

I telephoned Dick at the House of Commons telling him I would be prepared to meet with the Foreign and Commonwealth Secretary for discussions. He was delighted and said a meeting would be arranged without delay. Within a few days I arrived at the Palace of Westminster and passed through security to reach the Central Lobby of the House of Commons. Little did I realise I would walk into the same Central Lobby ten years later as a Member of Parliament in my own right. At the Reception Desk I made a request for Mr Richard Buchanan and very shortly afterwards Dick met me in the Central Lobby and took me through the Voting Lobby to Mr Stewart's office behind the Speaker's Chair. Mr Stewart made me very welcome and thanked me for responding to his request for discussions.

The Foreign Secretary set out the position in Gibraltar highlighting the concern of the UK Government at the turn of events. Although there were a few Gibraltarian building tradesmen in a number of small firms none were in a position to undertake the kind of contracts which had been abandoned when General Franco closed the border. At the conclusion of the discussions I was deeply impressed at the concern of the Gibraltar situation shown by Mr Stewart. I returned to Scotland for discussions with Roseleen and Dermot, and the employees who would be involved if we decided to go to Gibraltar. The following day I had meetings with my managers and other employees explaining the situation. There was a good willingness to have a go. On that basis I decided it would be essential for me to visit Gibraltar, establish whether it would be feasible to take men out there, and under what conditions they would live while working in Gibraltar.

Within days I, along with two of my Surveyors, flew to Gibraltar and were greeted by no less a person than the Governor who had been informed of our impending arrival by the British Foreign and Commonwealth Office. We stayed at the Rock Hotel and on the first evening met Mr Joseph Gaggero, Chairman of the hotel directors. From that meeting a friendship developed which lasted until Joe's death, early in 2012, which caused me great sadness as over the years I lived in Gibraltar the friendship was very close.

Over the next few days we visited the main projects lying unfinished. I could see we would be faced with many challenges. Much of the equipment had been removed before the Spanish left. With the border closed the only way replacements could be secured was from Africa or the United Kingdom. I realised this would take time and the work may have to be carried out using normal traditional hand tools which would take much longer but the work would be done efficiently.

The question of where the men would live had to be dealt with. As hotel accommodation would be too expensive I approached the Military Commander who offered me a large building which had been Army Officers quarters. We carried out an inspection and accepted they would be suitable for our employees. The Army made a very generous offer to allow our workers into the dining room which was close by the former Officers' living quarters.

Having satisfied ourselves that we would accept the challenge I intimated the decision to the Governor and asked him to advise Mr Stewart immediately. I told the Governor we would return with the labour force within two weeks. I had been assured by the Military Commander that any equipment, or tools, we required to make a start on the projects would be provided willingly by the Army.

A list was made of the major projects and a plan drawn up on getting started. I accepted that on arrival in Gibraltar from Scotland the men would require a day or two to settle into the living quarters, eating canteen food rather than returning to wives and families each night. I established the majority of men who had volunteered to travel had never been overseas before.

We flew back to Johnstone wondering how easy it would be in finding volunteers from our workforce who would agree to work overseas. I need not have concerned myself. When the men learned that Bob McClumpha and Dermot would be in charge of the projects there were plenty volunteers prepared to go.

The first group of men flew to London and then on to Gibraltar in mid August 1969. Before departing from Glasgow Airport they were met by Provost Thomas Hannah of Johnstone who wished them well. Roseleen and

I were a bit apprehensive at seeing Dermot away but were comforted that Bob McClumpha in whom we had confidence would look after him. As Dermot was one of the team throughout the storm damage, he was well known to the men with whom he got on well. This, along with Bob McClumpha, gave us the assurance we needed in sending him thousands of miles from home. From then on it was Dermot's job to keep us informed of progress as I had to continue with the storm damage works in the west of Scotland in order to bring them to a successful conclusion.

In advance of the workmen leaving for Gibraltar I purchased a large van which was loaded with tools and other accessories which would be required. It was driven to Glasgow for embarkation on a ship to Cadiz in Spain. Because General Franco had closed the border between Spain and Gibraltar and shipping for Gibraltar was not allowed to enter Spanish waters, the nearest Port for freight to be landed was Cadiz before being transported by sea to Tangiers and then by ferry from Tangiers to Gibraltar. After a period of three weeks the van arrived in Gibraltar with the tools making the working life of the Scotsmen in Gibraltar easier and also more productive.

25. Group of workers off to Gibraltar, 1969

Completing the Unfinished Work

The first two projects which had to be completed as a priority were the Gibraltar Regimental Barracks and the new Regimental Headquarters at Europa Point. The barracks was a two storey long building of solid stone walls about three feet thick. The Headquarters was a new build adjacent to the Parade Ground which only had the foundations completed. This building was of concrete construction.

The other project was at No. 5 Secretary's Lane near the centre of Gibraltar and adjacent to the Headquarters of the Gibraltar Government. This was a straight-forward new build project to provide accommodation for Gibraltar Government staff as the official headquarters were in full use by Ministers and staff.

Work on both these projects was undertaken. Cutting through the walls at the barracks proved difficult as we had no compressors nor were there any available as they had been removed when the Spanish crossed the border back into Spain on the day of closure. In light of this problem we purchased compressors from Tangiers and had them shipped over to Gibraltar making life easier for the men who were cutting the openings in the walls to form new windows in the barracks.

It was obvious a larger work force would be required. To bring more men from Scotland would be difficult as the storm damage repairs had to be completed and the labour force there was fully occupied. I discussed this with the Minister for Labour in the Gibraltar Government who suggested I should try engaging building workers from Morocco. He put me in touch with the Senior Civil Servant in Tangiers who dealt with the employment of labour. After lengthy discussions with him we agreed that forty tradesmen and labourers would come to Gibraltar to work on the projects.

I had further discussions with the Minister in Gibraltar about accommodation. He managed to negotiate with the Army Headquarters to take over an unused barracks in Casemates Square which would accommodate all the men from Tangiers. Within a week the additional workers arrived and started work. At first the standard of workmanship of the Moroccans was poor, but with the patience of our foremen in training them the standard we required was achieved.

During these operations we encountered many difficulties, with two in particular. The first was obtaining material for the contracts. Some had been ordered from the UK and were stuck in Spanish Ports. Negotiations were necessary with a Spanish Shipping Surveyor in La Linea to have the containers re-routed to Tangiers for onward shipping to Gibraltar. To do this I had to fly to Tangiers, take the Hydrofoil to Algeciras, then by taxi to

La Linea for the discussions with the Surveyor as there was no telephone contact between Spain and Gibraltar. Several weeks passed before the containers arrived with progress of the contracts greatly hindered. In the interval we had to set up a purchasing agency in Tangiers to secure materials to keep the work going. We overcame the language problems and were able to establish a good working system between Tangiers and Gibraltar which allowed the work to move on much more smoothly.

The second problem was connected to the Moroccan labour force we had recruited from Tangiers. Every month, in the Holy Season of Ramadan all the Moroccan workers caught the Gibraltar to Tangiers ferry to be with their families during Ramadan. This lasted for two weeks three to four times each year, considerably delaying the progress of the work. We were helped by young people, including students, from many other nations travelling the world who would stop off in Gibraltar. We employed them as labourers initially and soon found out their skills were advantageous to us in restoring the productivity due to the absence of the Moroccans on Ramadan. When the Moroccans did return they always arrived carrying baskets of fresh fruit which was most welcome. I think the gift was intended as a softener for their absence!

In the early days of the work in Gibraltar, I was operating from the Company Headquarters in Elderslie supervising the operations on the second phase of the storm damage repairs. This phase was dealing with rebuilding chimney heads, removing the tarpaulin sheets, fitting felt and straps to the roof structures and finally fitting the slates which allowed families to live a normal life under a secure roof once again. Although the entire storm damage episode was challenging there was great satisfaction to see the roofs and chimney heads completed.

During this time I depended on Bob McClumpha and Dermot in Gibraltar to report on developments and progress in Gibraltar. After some weeks I decided to make a trip to Gibraltar. On arriving I proceeded right away to the former Gibraltar Regiments Officers Mess where the men from Scotland were dining. One of the joiners came up to me and said 'they have arrested Andy'. I asked why. He replied 'He was found stealing watches from a shop'. This was a serious incident. I consulted Dermot who confirmed a charge had been made against one of our joiners for theft. The case was to be heard on Monday. The joiner who told me of the case spoke to me again and said 'Can you not help as you are our Guardian!' I said it would be my intention to appear in Court. It turned out the man who told me about Andy was himself arrested on a similar charge. Both were to appear in Court on the Monday.

ANSWERING THE CALL TO HELP THE PEOPLE OF GIBRALTAR

On Monday morning I turned up at the Court and was allowed to speak on behalf of the two men. I explained to the Judge the men found drink at cheap prices and consumed more than they would have done normally, resulting in them committing an offence while under the influence of alcohol. I expressed the regret of the men and asked the Judge to deal lightly with them as they were in Gibraltar from Scotland carrying out the work to help the people of Gibraltar during the difficult times caused by the closure of the border. The Judge gave them a good telling-off and in the circumstances fined them a sum of Thirty Pounds each. I paid the fines into the Court at once. On leaving the Court the two men were loud in their praise in the way I had saved them from a prison sentence. When I returned to the Gibraltar Office my Surveyor, Charles Scarff, asked if he was to deduct the fines from the wages of the men (they were now earning £150 a week with food and lodgings free) at £10 per week. I said 'No way. Take the full sum off each of them on the next pay day'.

When the men found they were £30 light in their wages, far from being the Saviour when I saved them from a prison sentence, I was the biggest bandit on earth!! Needless to say that was the one and only incident of that nature all the time our men were in Gibraltar. I returned to Scotland knowing these men had at least learned a lesson.

In early 1970 Roseleen and I left Scotland for Gibraltar. We retained our home in Troon and purchased a flat in Gibraltar looking over to Algeciras in Spain only four miles away but unable to visit due to the closing of the border. I soon learned the only way into Spain from Gibraltar was the one I has used before by flying from Gibraltar to Tangiers then by Hydrofoil from Tangiers to Algeciras, which I did on a good number of occasions. We settled in very well and I took over the supervision of the contracts along with our son Dermot and Robert McClumpha.

Work on the two projects proceeded well and at the end of six months much of the work on both sites had been completed.

Motor Cruiser - a diversion from work

After living in Gibraltar for some months I became frustrated at not being able to enter Spain other than travelling through Tangiers to Algeciras. However an invitation I received from my friend Dr Toomey to accompany him on his boat to Algeciras changed my frustration into determination.

We sailed from the Marina in Gibraltar across the straits of Gibraltar. On the way we were intercepted by the Spanish Police Sea Patrol who came on board to check we were not carrying any illegal goods into Spain. They found nothing and we sailed into Algeciras Yacht Club where we tied up and had a thoroughly enjoyable day returning in the evening without a hitch.

I decided the best thing to do was to purchase a motor cruiser just like Dr Toomey. It was fortunate that one of my friends was returning to the UK on retiring from the Civil Service and had a cruiser for sale. I agreed a price with him and took possession. The cruiser had sleeping accommodation for six people although we never used it for any overnights.

The matter of who was to skipper the cruiser had to be resolved. Dermot was able to skipper the boat but he was not always available so I had to find someone else. I had no experience but was willing to learn. I mentioned this to the Group Captain of the Royal Air Force on a visit to the Officers Mess of which I was an Honorary Member. He said one of his Corporals was an enthusiastic sailor and would be well qualified to do the job for me at weekends when off duty. I jumped at the offer and met Corporal Walter who agreed to become the Skipper and Chief Engineer. On completion of the purchase Roseleen and I set sail to Algeciras. Just as happened on my trip with Dr Toomey, we were intercepted by the Spanish Police who came on board to examine our passports and look around the boat for any illegal goods. Communication between us was difficult as they spoke little English and we only had a smattering of Spanish. We were not unduly hassled and the police were soon on their way. On reaching Algeciras Yacht Club a ferryman, provided by the Club, took us ashore after we dropped anchor. We spent a great weekend at the Reina Cristina Hotel only a short distance from the Yacht Club returning to Gibraltar on Monday. After a time and once I had the ability to take control of the boat we decided to sail through the Straits of Gibraltar to Estepona Harbour. This was a great thrill and was done without any difficulty. On several occasions we even sailed to the Jose Banus near Marbella which was only then being constructed as a Marina.

Using the boat in good weather was easy but there were times when it was too tricky to put to sea in rough waters. In these cases we flew to Tangiers and caught the Hydrofoil to Algeciras. I would telephone one of my business friends in Tangiers who would meet us from the Gibraltar plane and see us on to the Hydrofoil, with this plan being reversed after our weekend in Spain. It made these weekends so much more enjoyable with such a good friend willing to make our journeys more comfortable.

During these trips into Spain we were intrigued to see so many residents of Gibraltar sailing or flying into Spain by the same methods as we did. Rather than staying in hotels they lived in their own flats which were located in and around La Linea, the nearest town to Gibraltar. Since we were now spending many weekends in Spain we decided to purchase an apartment.

The Spanish economy was not good at the time and properties were not selling. An apartment was bought fully furnished which allowed us to take immediate occupation. For the rest of our time in Gibraltar we enjoyed many times at the apartment as the complex was complete with a swimming pool which I used a lot. One benefit of the apartment was we could entertain our Managers at the apartment by taking them over in the boat and giving them a break from the work in Gibraltar.

The one thing lacking when we visited Spain was our own transport. We had been using taxis to drive us to Marbella but this was not really satisfactory. I considered buying a car in Spain. When discussing my proposal with Mr Capurro, a garage proprietor in Gibraltar, he suggested I buy one from him with it being brought into Spain by the manufacturer. I ordered a Mercedes from him and rather than the delivery of it to Spain, Roseleen and I flew to Stuttgart in Germany, collected the car from the works and drove it to Spain. It was a great experience for us. The car was kept in a lock-up garage at the Reina Cristina Hotel which was so convenient for us when we planned to spend time in Spain. Having the car made such a difference to our travels in the Costa del Sol and we were able to see so much more than was possible before we bought the car.

When we left Gibraltar in 1975 we sold the car but retained the apartment for future use in the hope the border would be re-opened. In later years we sold the apartment to a Naval Officer who was retiring from serving in Gibraltar and wished to reside in Spain.

26. Our family at Dermot & Libby's Wedding

The years spent making these regular visits into Spain were all part of the allure I had about being in a warm climate but able to work at the same time.

A Wedding in the Rock of Gibraltar
In September 1972 our son Dermot was married to Elizabeth Gareze daughter of Colonel Pepe – of the Gibraltar Regiment – and Mrs Gareze. A good number of our relatives came over from Scotland for the wedding including my sister Margaret and her husband Forbes who played his bagpipes at the entrance to the church and again during the reception followed by a Luncheon in the Officers Mess at the Gibraltar Regiment.

Dermot and Libby (as she is known) spent their honeymoon in London and returned to Gibraltar two weeks later with a Labrador dog they had named Sammy who became a firm family favourite. They took up residence in a dwelling house in Engineers Lane.

In October 1972 Roseleen, Dermot and I with Libby flew to Scotland for a celebration to mark their wedding at a Dinner in the Rockfield Hotel, Paisley hosted by us for our friends who had been unable to travel to Gibraltar for the wedding. We reserved accommodation at the Royal Scottish Automobile Club in Glasgow where I was a committee member. On the evening of the Dinner the four of us met in the foyer to await the car to drive us to the event. As Libby emerged in her entire wedding outfit some of the staff, who were unaware of the reason for the event, were taken aback as Dermot and Libby had been occupying a double room at the Club – and now appeared to be just getting married!! After hearing the explanation the staff broke into laughter and wished them well. We returned to Gibraltar the following day. As we left the RSAC the staff gave Dermot and Libby a good send off as a married couple!

27. McQuarrie and McCaffery families in Paisley

On 31st January 1974 Dermot and Libby had their first child – a daughter who they called Catherine Mary and our first grandchild. Our second grandchild was born to Dermot and Libby on 17th February 1975 and named Jonathan. This gave us a lasting attachment to Gibraltar as Catherine and Jonathan were born in the Territory. In the years that followed Dermot and Libby had six more children – Louise, Roseleen, Robert, Stephanie, Elizabeth and Dermot Junior. All six were born in Scotland. Now they are grown up – some married with family of their own giving me eleven great grandchildren – with perhaps more to follow!!

Next major works in Gibraltar

The next major project was the extension to St Bernard's Hospital. This was a project to add new buildings and install a lift into the existing building. The existing hospital was built on a hill and approached through a number of narrow streets which made access to the site difficult. One of the major difficulties was to keep the hospital in operation while building the extension.

After several months of very demanding work the project was completed, and we handed over a fine modernised hospital to the Government of Gibraltar. As there was an acute shortage of medical facilities prior to our project the extra facilities came as a huge relief to the Government and the people. In 2003, the existing hospital was replaced by a wonderful new St Bernard's Hospital built on reclaimed land within easy reach of the centre of Gibraltar making it much more convenient for all using it. The Government of Gibraltar has ensured that the equipment is of the most up-to-date and staffed by highly trained medical personnel.

On Wednesday 4th April 2004 at the celebrations for 300 years of Gibraltar being attached to the British Crown, I presented a Bronze Bust of Her Majesty The Queen to the people of Gibraltar which had been sculptured and donated to Gibraltar by Professor Nadey Hakim, an eminent Transplant Surgeon based in London. The Bust is positioned at the entrance to the new hospital.

Professor Hakim handed over the Bronze Bust to me in London before I boarded a flight to Gibraltar. It was very heavy and was packed into a suitcase which I was able to pull on to the aircraft. The crew took possession of it during the flight to Gibraltar and on arrival assisted me in negotiating the stairs from the aircraft to the tarmac. It was then I spotted a wheelbarrow which I was given permission to use. I wheeled the Bronze Bust to the Custom Hall where I was questioned as to what was in the suitcase. I told the Customs Officer it was a Bronze Bust of Her Majesty The Queen.

His reply was 'this will be the only time when Her Majesty will arrive in Gibraltar and carted along in a wheelbarrow!!' The next day I had the honour of presenting the Bust to the Chief Minister at a Ceremony in the House of Assembly before it was taken to its home in the new hospital.

28. Bronze Head and Shoulders of Her Majesty The Queen
The work of Professor Nadey S Hakim MD, PhD, FRCS, FRCSI, FACS presented by him to The People of Gibraltar to celebrate 300 years of Gibraltar's connection with the British Crown

Conversion of King George V Hospital

While a number of projects were underway the next major one was the conversion of the King George V Hospital into one for the mentally disturbed. Once more we had to tackle difficult situations because of the security work involved. There was a problem in the supply of padded cells for people who sadly were of a violent nature. Nothing suitable was available in Gibraltar. I flew to Tangiers where I had hoped to source something suitable in the hospital. There was little in the way of padded cells which frustrated me as there was an urgent need for them at KGV Hospital. It was impossible to acquire these from Spain as the manufacturers were not allowed to trade with Gibraltar firms due to the closure of the border.

After careful consideration I decided the best course of action was to return to Scotland and visit the secure unit at Carstairs Hospital in Lanarkshire. The doctor and staff were most helpful. I took careful measurements of a padded cell and the general construction. I knew some of the materials required would not be available in Gibraltar, so I made enquiries for suppliers in Scotland and arrange for the materials to be taken by air to Gibraltar via London. Fortunately the goods arrived quickly and the King George V Hospital project was completed to the entire satisfaction of the Gibraltar Government.

Varyl Begg Estate Development

The next major project we undertook was one of the largest yet tackled. The Government of Gibraltar had a severe shortage of homes for the people and decided to embark on the creation of a new housing estate on reclaimed land near the harbour. The Chief Planning Officer asked if I would undertake the work of such a project. At first I was a bit reluctant as my labour force was engaged in a number of construction projects in the Territory. After a little thought I agreed and work started. It was then that there was a little bit of good luck. Taylor Woodrow, one of Great Britain's largest builders, sent a labour force to Gibraltar under a fine Manager, Charles Walters. This firm were able to take on the major role at the estate with my company continuing to work well along with Taylor Woodrow employees.

This contract continued over many months. All sorts of problems arose particularly with the shortage of materials due to the closure of the border between Gibraltar and Spain.

The estate was named Varyl Begg after a former Governor of Gibraltar. When it was completed there was great rejoicing by the people who had been lucky enough to secure a home with a fitted kitchen and bathroom. I was delighted my company along with Taylor Woodrow had been able to bring pleasure to these families.

Meantime my labour force completed many projects including several for the military whose numbers at that time, inclusive of all the Services, was 30,000.

The New Health Centre Project

The completion of the Varyl Begg project came at a very good time. My company had been invited to tender for a new Health Centre in Casemates Square in Gibraltar. In late 1972 I was advised by the Government Planning Officer that my tender for the work had been accepted. I knew this was going to be a challenge as we would run into the same problems as happened in the construction of the Gibraltar Regiment Barracks at Europa Point and all other works. The existing building was of stone with walls three feet thick. It had been occupied for many years as the Command Pay Office for the British Forces stationed in Gibraltar and Naval vessels calling at Gibraltar. The two story building was a long one with the windows constructed in arch form. It was a very imposing building but its structure was not suitable for conversion and would have to be demolished. The Government Architect, Michael Azzopardi, in drawing up plans retained the arched windows in the new design. Our joiners and concreters proved their ability in first of all forming the arches in timber followed by pouring the concrete into the timber shell for each window. There were sixty-four arches in the front facing Casements Square with forty on Line Wall Road at the rear of the building.

29. Gibraltar Health Centre under Construction

The external cladding was built with special bricks imported from England.

The work of demolition began with, as I thought, great difficulty created because of the three feet thick walls. Very soon it became apparent a crane with a large ball was necessary. I flew to Tangiers to hire the crane which was taken by the ferry operating between Tangiers and Gibraltar. Because of the Border being closed it was impossible for me to obtain one from Spain It took two weeks to demolish the property and remove the debris to Europa Point where it was tipped into the sea.

30. The Health Centre completed and in action

31. Gibraltar £10 note showing Health Centre

The construction of the new Health Centre then commenced. The tradesmen in the company took great pride in their work and the skill of their workmanship was to produce to the last brick a fine example of their skills. During the weeks and months which followed the building slowly became an outstanding feature in Casemates Square. It was finally completed in 1974 when the people of Gibraltar had a Medical Centre better than anything they had before. I was immensely proud when the Chief Minister, the late Sir Joshua Hassan formerly opened the building with me standing by his side. It was a great achievement by all the operatives of the company who were engaged in its construction. A photograph of the Health Centre is depicted on the Gibraltar Ten Pound Bank Notes. Some of these Bank Notes I have collected as souvenirs of the finest project my company undertook in Gibraltar. I was absolutely thrilled when the local firm of monumental sculptors called Anis and Company produced a huge engraved granite slab with the words:

Constructed by
A. McQuarrie & Son (Overseas) Limited
1974

32. Standing beside the stone tablet, 1974

33. The Tablet at the Health Centre entrance

This building stands today as a fitting reminder of the Scottish workers who volunteered to help the people of Gibraltar in their time of need.

The Final Project in Gibraltar

The final major project in which my company was involved concerned the building of a new hotel in Gibraltar. We were responsible for all the joinery work including the making of the balustrades for the staircases which were designed to resemble the Victorian era. To make these I purchased a joinery company from a local firm who had all the wood turning equipment. This firm had employed skilled workers from Morocco who were given the job of making the special items for the hotel. This was done in a splendid manner. When the work was completed it was much admired by all who visited the hotel and to this day is in mint condition having been so well maintained by the hotel staff.

By this time our Scottish tradesmen had been operating in Gibraltar for five years returning to Scotland for a three week annual leave in groups to their homes. In that time we had been able to train the Moroccan labour we employed to a high standard. During the years we had also been able to engage a number of builders from Portugal who arrived through Tangiers and then by ferry to Gibraltar. Soon it was decided to return all the Scottish workers to their homeland over a period of a month which allowed for as little disruption to the contracts still being undertaken. Many of the men were sad to leave Gibraltar as the people had been kind to them and appreciated how much they had helped them with the problem of the border closure between their City of Gibraltar and Spain.

A change of Direction

At this stage another incident happened to me which was to mark the end of my time living and working in Gibraltar. I had been adopted as prospective Parliamentary Candidate for the Constituency of East Aberdeenshire to contest the next Westminster General Election – more about this in later Chapters. Dermot was in agreement that Roseleen and I should return to Scotland and take up residence in East Aberdeenshire. I gave Dermot the opportunity to take over the company in Gibraltar but he advised me his real interest was a career change into television which he had been doing in his spare time for some months with Gibraltar Broadcasting Corporation. He had been producing a programme called *The Thistle of Scotland* which was broadcast in the Costa del Sol and Gibraltar. I was aware of his keenness to further his interest in television and to in due course return to the United Kingdom and seek work in BBC or ITV.

Our decision was the correct one as it turned out. When Dermot returned to Scotland he secured employment as a Presenter with BBC Scotland at the Aberdeen studios. After a time he moved to Grampian Television where he was the first TV Presenter in the world to broadcast from a helicopter on the blow-out at the Bravo Oil field in the North Sea. The famous Red Adair, an American who was renowned for extinguishing fires in oil fields, came from America and was successful in putting out the fire. In 1978 Dermot joined Scottish Television. After many years with STV he took up opportunities with television companies in London, Rome and Sweden before he received an invitation from Fox Sports International to take up an appointment as Senior Vice President and Executive Producer in Los Angeles where he remains at the time of my writings.

After long and careful consideration we all agreed that the Gibraltar operations should be wound down over a year as the crisis which existed in Gibraltar when we first arrived had by this time been dealt with. There were sufficient local building companies operating to handle the contracts and general maintenance work.

Before moving on from Gibraltar I recall an interesting story. It happened in 1973 in conversation with a friend who owned and operated a hotel. He told me he was having difficulty in securing supplies of whisky to the 'Rock'. The following day I telephoned an acquaintance in Glasgow. I explained the position to this Executive of a Distilling Company who immediately offered me an agency to sell supplies of 'White Heather' whisky in Gibraltar. Within two weeks supplies of the whisky were being sold at great pace. The wholesale price of a 70ml bottle was **one pound sterling**!!

The demand for the whisky by many businesses in Gibraltar meant I had to set up an office with staff to handle the orders. I formed a new company naming it Europa Agencies Limited. Very soon further agencies were secured for French and Italian Wines and other goods which were in short supply in Gibraltar shops. This business operated until I had completed all our contracts in Gibraltar. I sold it to the local casino owner who had been one of the major customers for White Heather whisky to keep his customers happy!!

So ended six years of operating in Gibraltar. What started out as a sort of errand of mercy due to the closure of the border ended with a considerable number of buildings constructed by Scottish tradesmen helped by the Moroccans and others, who sought employment in Gibraltar from many countries, which stand today as a tribute to the workmanship of all the workers in the company helped by the organisational skills of my son Dermot and Robert McClumpha, the two Directors who organised the business in Gibraltar from the start in 1969.

Although I left Gibraltar to pursue a political life, I never lost contact with many of the people I met there. We still visit often and I take great pleasure in seeing the buildings each time I return. My interest in Gibraltar returned in 1981 when as a Member of the British Parliament I took a leading part in the British Nationality Bill affecting Gibraltar which is the subject of another Chapter in the book.

CHAPTER SIX

A Lighter Side of Life

THE 12TH OF JUNE 1970 was the date of our Silver Wedding. To celebrate it, Roseleen, Dermot and I set sail on the Cruise Liner *Orsova* from Southampton on a trip which was to take us to the Bahamas. The *Orsova* was one of the P & O ships, giving accommodation to 690 first class passengers, 809 passengers in the tourist class and 641 of a crew. Roseleen and I reserved one of the staterooms with a private balcony where we could enjoy the relaxation and the sunshine. Dermot had his own cabin and a steward to look after his needs during the trip.

34. With Roseleen & Dermot on the Orsova, *1970*

As we sailed the seas, friendships were established with other passengers and in particular two families from Fiji. They were Mr & Mrs Watti Tagilala and Lieutenant Colonel G. Mati and Mrs Mati. Watti was a senior Civil Servant. Every evening we met up and had great fun which made the cruise so enjoyable.

On 12th June 1970, the date of our Silver Wedding Anniversary we held a Cocktail party for twenty-five friends on board the *Orsova* including the Captain and other Chief Officers. There was plenty of champagne, a wonderful buffet provided by the Chefs and Liqueurs to end off a very special Anniversary.

35. The Party on the Orsova *with Fijian friends*

I came to an agreement with the Captain to pay for all the drinks and he would supply the food. When I received the account for the drinks amounting to £65 I was staggered at the low figure for twenty-five guests and paid up rapidly in case an error had been made!! We said goodbye to our Fijian friends when they left the *Orsova* for the journey by air to their home in Fiji. Before doing so they invited us to visit them in October for the celebration of Fiji's Independence from Great Britain which was to be attended by H.R.H. Prince Charles. We promised to make every effort to be in Fiji for the Independence celebrations. The *Orsova* sailed on to the Caribbean. It was a wonderful trip and when we eventually returned to Gibraltar we decided if circumstances permitted we would keep our word to our friends and return to Fiji in October.

Fiji Independence - Monday 10th October 1970

Having been reminded in a letter about the Independence celebrations from Watti Tagilala we decided to make the trip to Fiji. In preparation for the visit and as Dermot and I would be wearing our McQuarrie tartan kilts, Roseleen had a skirt made up in the McQuarrie tartan. When we boarded the aircraft at Heathrow one of the crew members asked Roseleen if we were an entertainment group as we were dressed in tartan outfits! We explained the reason for the tartan outfits was because we were to be attending the Independence celebrations in Fiji and wanted to show our national dress as Scots. We kept up the joke about being an entertainment group for some time afterwards.

We arrived in Fiji on 4th October 1970 and were met by Watti at the airport where we were presented with a garland representing a warm welcome. We checked into the Grand Pacific Hotel where we were treated as VIP guests during the entire time of our visit to Fiji.

On the first evening Watti and his wife held a Reception for us in their home where we met their twin daughters who were eight years old. Whenever we met them again they knelt and addressed me as Ratu Mac - Ratu meaning Chief!! The principal guest at the Reception was the Prime Minister, Ratu Sir Kamisese Mara and his wife. The Prime Minister was late in arriving. When he did appear and walked round the room, all the ladies knelt including Watti's elderly mother, and kissed his feet! There was an abundance of food and refreshments, and in accordance with etiquette no one could start eating until he and I, as the other VIP, had selected our food. It was a most impressive evening.

Later in the week a Party was held at the home of the Commanding Officer of the Fijian Regiment. This was in interesting evening. The guests were seated around the dining table in the grounds of the house. There were several courses but it was the main course of chicken which was a surprise to us. The chickens were taken from the ground where they had been placed in parcels of foil in the morning and cooked by the heat of the soil. They were delicious. Despite promises to do so Roseleen never tackled it in our garden!!

Saturday 10th October 1970. It was to be one of great rejoicing as Fiji gained its Independence as a Dominion. The event was held at Albert Park

A LIGHTER SIDE OF LIFE

in Suva which was packed by Fijians young and old who wanted to be part of this historic occasion. From what I could see there must have been well over 20,000 people in the Albert Park.

36. At a House Party in Fiji with friends, 1970

*37. Prince Charles handing over
Independence Documents in Fiji, October, 1970*

One of the major parts of the official proceedings was the handing over of the Constitutional Documents, confirming the Order in Court and the Independence Act, by H.R.H. Prince Charles to the Prime Minister Ratu Sir Kamisese Mara who was seen to be pleased to accept on behalf of the people of Fiji. The Prime Minister knelt on a cushion to make his ceremonial speech of acceptance to H.R.H. Prince Charles. I noted he spoke in Fijian and a large number of Fijians joined the Prime Minister in the final words of his address.

There followed the raising of the new Dominion's National Flag of Fiji. A platoon of Fijian soldiers in red uniform led by a Captain raised the flag to the new flagpole which had been erected in front of the dais. The Colonel of the Fijian Regiment called out 'present arms' to all the troops on parade. It was a splendid sight. There was a roll of the six drums situated at the base of the dais. As the drums were 'rolling' the flag was slowly raised to the top of the flagpole at the same time as three aircraft of the Royal New Zealand Air Force came into view and flying over Albert Park in a triangular formation leaving trails of white smoke This was the moment the people of Fiji had been waiting for – their Independence – and finally it had come. There was tumultuous cheering and flag waving from all the people in Albert Park. Those of us in the Grand Stand joined in the cheering waving the flags we were presented with on arriving at the Park.

38. Albert Park Fiji Independence Celebrations

The final part of the Ceremony was a brilliant exhibition of marching by all the troops to the music provided by the Fijian Military Force Bandsmen. There followed a 21 Gun Salute in honour of the great occasion.

At the conclusion of the marching the Parade Commander called for three cheers for Her Majesty The Queen and the Dominion of Fiji. H.R.H. Prince Charles, the official party and guests joined in the loud cheers of the people in the Park. The Fijians added their own symbolic chant of Kaila, Kaila, Kaila – the Fijian shout of joy.

As we left Albert Park at the end of the Ceremony we were thrilled to have attended this most wonderful occasion and one of the never-to-be-forgotten times in our lives.

The Government of Fiji held a Gala Dinner in the evening at the invitation of the Prime Minister Ratu Sir Kamisese Mara and attended by HRH the Prince of Wales who brought a message of congratulations on Fiji's Independence from Prime Minister Edward Heath MP on behalf of the people in the United Kingdom. It was a glittering affair to end a special day. It was an honour for Roseleen, Dermot and I to be invited to the Dinner.

The celebrations continued with a Thanksgiving and Dedication Service on the occasion of the Attainment of National Independence in Albert Park on Sunday 11th October 1970. Many thousands attended this most moving Service led by the National Leaders of all the Church denominations in Fiji. It was a wonderful time of great rejoicing and expectation for the people of Fiji which we had shared with them. The Fijians carried on rejoicing for several days with many parties being held.

On Tuesday 13th October 1970, during his visit to Fiji, Prince Charles found himself in a little difficulty. He was in one of fourteen punts on a fishing drive. The fast reef tides proved difficult for the Fijian fishermen who were steering the punt which Prince Charles was in along with his Equerry, Nicholas Soames – nephew of Winston Churchill, now the Rt Hon Nicholas Soames MP with whom I served in my years as a Member of Parliament. Late in the afternoon the Prince's punt became trapped in the reef tide. The craft quickly filled with water. Prince Charles who by this time was soaking wet kept bailing it out with a small enamel bucket. He was determined to continue in order to see the fishermen spearing the fish. However the rough water prevented the fishermen from continuing and they were frustrated at not being able to show Prince Charles their method of catching fish by spearing. Reluctantly he agreed to return to Suva for an engagement at Government House. The officials in the party were relieved.

Having enjoyed a most marvellous and memorable occasion we travelled back to Gibraltar feeling proud we had been invited to the historical event in Fiji.

A trip to the Far East

In November 1974 Roseleen and I decided to have another break from work. Although we enjoyed Gibraltar we were constantly under pressure from the contracts we were undertaking in Gibraltar and in particular the many problems we encountered in the construction of the new Health Centre at Casemates Square.

This time we flew east to Singapore. We stayed at the magnificent Raffles Hotel which had been occupied by the Japanese forces during the Second World War, since when it had been completely refurbished and returned to its former glory. Raffles Hotel is one of the famous hotels in the world situated in the heart of Singapore, a bustling city. The ambience within the hotel made it easy to relax and to enjoy cuisine and delicacies either local or international. Our accommodation was a suite and comprised of sitting room, bedroom, dressing room and bathroom. This was opulence which we had not known before. Air conditioning, telephone, fridge, television and other facilities which are now taken for granted, were provided, making the stay most comfortable.

39. Raffles Hotel Singapore

While sightseeing we came across The Tanglin Club which was restricted to English speaking members. As a member of the Royal Automobile Club in London I introduced myself. We were welcomed as visitors into the Club where there was a swimming pool and tennis courts, and well appointed restaurants and bars. We enjoyed our few days using the facilities of the Club.

The Chinese market is a must for all visitors to Singapore. We joined the throngs of people in the evening milling around the stalls packed with all sorts of goods and locally produced food which was bought by the Chinese people. Before leaving Singapore I got measured for a suit by the Hotel Tailor, a man called Henry. It took forty-eight hours to complete and was a good fit and a very reasonable price. Roseleen also made use of the Tailor who made up several dresses for her with which she was delighted.

From Singapore we flew to Hong Kong where we checked in at the Peninsula Hotel on the ocean front. It was a magnificent hotel with beautiful rooms. The day after arriving we learned about the horse racing which was due to take place that evening at the Hong Kong Racecourse. I called the Racecourse office to find out times and charges for entry. I was put through to the Secretary and explained to him I was a member of the Ayr Racecourse in Scotland. He welcomed me and told me to take a taxi to the Racecourse where he would meet us at 7.00 p.m. at the Executive Entrance which was well signposted.

At the appointed time and place we made ourselves known to a Steward who had been instructed by the Secretary to take us to one of the VIP Suites overlooking the winning post and with a wonderful view of the course where the Secretary awaited us. The VIP complex had its own dining room where race-goers could enjoy a splendid assortment of delicious food during the evening's entertainment. These suites had their own betting area which was very convenient! We could hardly believe our good fortune and thanked the Secretary for his invitation to us before the races began.

Before the first of the six races we placed our bets. I failed but Roseleen bet on the winner of each of the six races. Added to that there was a bonus prize of 500 dollars in the last race which, needless to say, Roseleen won – what a night!! We returned to our hotel to celebrate Roseleen's winnings even although there had been no shortage of champagne at the races. The following morning we arranged for a bottle of the 'best bubbly' and floral arrangement to be delivered to the Secretary and his wife for all the kindnesses we received at the races.

During the next day we were having coffee in the hotel lounge when a gentleman sitting near us came over and asked if we were from Scotland as he had overheard us talking. We told him we were and on holiday from Gibraltar, where my company was carrying out a number of contracts. He explained his home was in Bearsden near Glasgow and he was a Bank Manager representing one of the Scottish Banks. In the course of our conversation he told us he was on the Committee of the Hong Kong St Andrew's Society and said it had a flourishing membership of ex-patriots from Scotland to Hong Kong. Mr Dempster then invited us to attend the St Andrew's Ball which we were pleased to accept. Pushed under the door of our room that evening was a beautiful invitation, showing the Coat of Arms of the Hong Kong St Andrew's Society, from 'The Chieftain and Committee of the Hong Kong St Andrew's Society' inviting Mr & Mrs Albert McQuarrie to attend the St Andrew's Ball on 29th November 1974. Dress was Evening or Highland. Fortunately I had my Highland Dress with me and Roseleen had a Ball Gown so we had no problem with dress. It was a wonderful evening when we met many people with whom we kept contact for years.

40. At Burns Society Dinner in Hong Kong

On to Tokyo

In Tokyo we reserved a room in the New Otani, a very modern hotel set in gardens with lakes stretching a considerable distance down a hill from the hotel. Dressing gowns with New Otani printed into the fabric were provided. Among the information in the room there was a note which read that guests could take the dressing gowns with them on departure, if they so wished. I did and it hangs in my wardrobe at home in as good condition as it was thirty-nine years ago.

Having been told that we must take a trip in the Bullet Train to Kyoto we arranged with hotel reception to secure tickets for us. On the arranged day we taxied to the Tokyo Station where we found hundreds of people rushing around to catch trains but we were completely lost as to what to do or where to go. We could see no signboard indicating from which platform the Bullet Train would leave. I kept asking for help but when I started to speak the person seemed to laugh – it appeared nobody spoke English. We were becoming concerned as it was nearing the time for the train to depart when we were fortunate on approaching a young man for help, to find he responded in English and he was making his way to catch the Bullet Train to Kyoto. We followed him gladly! With a sigh of relief we found the train forty-five minutes after arriving at the Station. The journey to Kyoto was a very pleasant one with the young man sitting beside us as we hurtled through the countryside on the fast speed train. It transpired he was studying law in London and was home on holiday. On arriving at Kyoto we thanked him most sincerely for coming to our aid.

Kyoto was the capital of Japan for more than two centuries from the year 794 to 1868 AD. At that time it had a population of one and a half million people and was the fifth largest city in Japan. During our visit we saw some fine examples of silk fabric, embroidery work, porcelain and lacquered goods. We visited Temples, Museums and Shrines and were amazed at their beauty. As we did not want to venture too far from the station, we were pleased to have had the opportunity to see these before the journey back to Tokyo on the Bullet Train travelling at such high speeds without any discomfort or noise.

After a few more sightseeing days in and around Tokyo we returned to Gibraltar having had the pleasure of tasting a little of life in these places which we had only dreamed about but were now a memorable reality.

CHAPTER SEVEN

Entering into National Politics

IN 1963 I WAS INVITED BY Major Alan Anderson (now deceased) who was President of the Scottish Conservative and Unionist Association to put my name forward as a Prospective Candidate for the Westminster Parliament. I did so and was placed on the Candidate's List. I made a number of efforts to be selected including Maryhill, West Dunbartonshire and Paisley. I was finally successful with the selection for the Kilmarnock Constituency against Rt Hon William Ross, the Labour Secretary of State for Scotland, later Lord Ross of Marnock. I knew there was no hope of winning but I was determined to put up a good fight for the sake of the Party.

The Kilmarnock Association was fortunate to have a fine Headquarters near the town centre. There was a full-time Agent by the name of Vincent Calder. He was an enthusiastic young man who stuck rigidly to the rules. He would not even allow me to buy him a cup of coffee in case it broke election law! After a few years Vincent moved on to set up a company supplying refrigerators to stores throughout Scotland. This turned out to be such a success that he was known to call on his customers driving his Rolls Royce with the personalised number plate of VC 1. I was delighted to have such a vibrant person as my Agent.

The election was called in 1966. I had spent many months nursing the constituency with a great band of workers. The result was as expected. Willie Ross was returned. The difference in this election was that I had managed to reduce his majority. I was the only Conservative and Unionist Candidate in Scotland at that election to reduce a Labour majority and increase the Conservative vote. Mr Ross was not at all pleased, but I was!

Having achieved this little bit of success in my first effort, Associations took a more considered approach to my applications as a Prospective Candidate. One classic example of this was in 1967 when a by-election was called in the Pollock Constituency. At that time Pollock did not have many public sector houses owned by the Local Authority as is the case today. On a Saturday evening John Mitchell, the Chief Executive of the Scottish

Conservative and Unionist Association telephoned me to ask if I was interested in contesting the seat for our party. In response I had to tell him I had been nominated as the Prospective Parliamentary Candidate for the Rutherglen Constituency and I did not want to let them down. The party selected Professor Esmond Wright who, with the determined efforts of many supporters, including The Hon George Younger MP for Ayr, his wife Diane and myself who spent many hours working in the constituency ending each day with an evening meal of fish and chips from a local shop. We had no time for dinner elsewhere and enjoyed the experience of eating fish suppers out of a paper bag! I sometimes wonder what my future political life would have been had I accepted the offer from John Mitchell to contest Pollock as Professor Wright won the seat. As it happened I was living in Gibraltar in 1970 and had resigned as the Candidate in Rutherglen since I was unable to 'nurse' the seat. Even with the election of a Conservative Government in 1970, Rutherglen remained a Labour Seat.

During the time I was living in Gibraltar I retained my name on the Candidates' List for Westminster. When the Constituency of Caithness and Sutherland in the north of Scotland were seeking a candidate for the 1974 election I put my name forward. I received a letter from the Constituency Chairman indicating the Executive would be interested in interviewing me for the vacancy, but I would have to pay my own expenses which I agreed to do. I flew from Gibraltar to London and on to Wick via Glasgow. I arrived early in the day, hired a car and made a quick survey of the area. I knew this was only a small part of the constituency but at least it would give me a little knowledge about the kind of activities which took place in Caithness.

When I arrived at the Association Rooms that evening I heard there were three candidates on the short list. I knew both the candidates from meeting them at Candidates Conferences. The Committee had planned the interviews in such a manner that none of us would meet during the course of the evening. I was last of the three to be interviewed. Amongst the extensive questioning I was asked how I would nurse the seat from Gibraltar. I told them if I was selected as the Prospective Candidate I would come back from Gibraltar and take up residence in the constituency until after the election. As the interview took place in August with the election forecast for October 1974, I knew it would be possible for me to stay in Scotland for a period and be able to nurse the seat which covered a vast area in the north of Scotland.

Later that evening I was called back to the rooms when the Chairman advised me they would like me to be the candidate to contest the seat for the party at the forthcoming General Election for the Westminster Parliament. I accepted the invitation which was greeted with applause.

I had read the constituency record of voting and was aware the sitting Member of Parliament, Robert Maclennan (now Lord Maclennan of Rogart) had a good reputation as a Constituency MP. In the 1970 General Election my great friend Patrick Maitland (later Earl of Lauderdale, now deceased) contested the seat in difficult circumstances as the candidate for our party. A prominent local farmer in the area had intimated his interest and his wish to be the candidate for the party. However, he was not acceptable to the members in Sutherland – a part of the constituency – as they had made it known they wanted Patrick Maitland. The result was that at the election, many Conservative electors in Caithness withheld their votes for the party so much so that Patrick Maitland failed to win the seat. The resultant bitterness lasted for many months and to some degree was still there when I was adopted as the candidate. Fortunately as I was to take up residence in the constituency I was able to make my presence felt and approach many of the disillusioned seeking their support. I even made contact with the dissident member who had opposed Patrick Maitland and while he would not publicly support me, he indicated he would not make any adverse comment about my Candidature, which was comforting.

In due course Roseleen, Dermot and I arrived in Wick. We rented a Lodge which had been newly refurbished on the outskirts. It was a splendid property and ideal for the duration of the election campaign. Situated nearby was the large home occupied by an enthusiastic supporter. The Lodge had not been occupied since its refurbishment – even the cutlery in the drawer was still in its wrappings. The open fireplace was enjoyed every evening after returning from the day's campaigning. Looking back on the few weeks spent at the Lodge - although we were fighting a campaign we did have a wonderful time when many a fine liqueur was tasted!

During the few interesting weeks we spent in the constituency many incidents come to mind but there were two in particular relating to the Lodge which I wish to share. At the end of the first week of our stay we had a visit from the local Sheriff. He was a great character who enjoyed a drink. The trouble was his visits became nightly. He would arrive about 10.30 p.m. and seldom left before 1.00 a.m. As our sleep was necessary to continue the campaign we devised a plan. On hearing the Sheriff's car in the driveway we switched off all the lights in the house, kept quiet and ignored the ring of the doorbell. Eventually the Sheriff got the message and his visits ceased.

The other situation was to do with the local grocer. In Gibraltar our cocktail cabinet was well stocked with liqueurs. After settling in at the Lodge we located the local licensed grocer's shop. Dermot and I visited the shop and requested a bottle of Drambuie, one of Cointreau and one of Tia Maria. The Grocer told us he did not stock any liqueurs but he would make sure our request would be fulfilled by the afternoon of the following day. From then on he carried a stock of these liqueurs. I often wondered what demand there was for these drinks after we had returned to Gibraltar!

The campaign was intensive. To begin with we found such a difference in the personalities of the people we met in Caithness compared to those in Sutherland. We found travelling from place to place tiring but despite the distance involved we were determined to return to the Lodge each evening, despite many kind offers of accommodation by generous party supporters. All the meetings arranged by the campaign Secretary were very well attended. Each Saturday we arranged a Motor Cavalcade when thirty or more decorated vehicles travelled from Wick to various towns. On one occasion we drove to Dornoch where an election meeting was to take place.

The supporting speaker was Rt Hon Gordon Campbell, the former Secretary of State for Scotland. As he began his speech one of the audience, who had a little too much to drink shouted at him 'would you shut up; it's McQuarrie we have come to hear'. I reassured the person he would have the opportunity to hear me after the former Secretary of State for Scotland had addressed the company. This placated the person and Gordon delivered a rousing speech. I then followed which seemed to satisfy the interrupter!

The election was held in October 1974. Several weeks of hard campaigning by me and other candidates resulted in a good percentage of electors casting their vote. Covering the entire constituency there were a number of cars fitted with loud speaker equipment. The convoy toured many of the areas of Caithness and Sutherland playing a recording of a song entitled *McQuarrie for me* to the tune of *A Gordon for me*. Here are the words:

> McQuarrie for me, McQuarrie for me;
> I'll vote for McQuarrie as our new MP.
> The Labour, the Liberal and the SNP
> Don't worry us at all as they'll very soon see.
>
> It's Albert McQuarrie who'll win at the Poll
> He'll knock down your Rates and keep you off the dole;
> The other three parties will run in despair
> When they learn that Albert McQuarrie is there.
> *(The Chorus was then repeated)*

Victory, however, despite the most valiant effort, did not come. The sitting Member of Parliament was elected but I was able to secure a creditable vote for our party. Although naturally disappointed the Association Committee were pleased at the result which raised their hopes for success in the future.

Following on from the election the Association Chairman asked me if I would continue as their candidate. At that time I honestly did not see the Conservative and Unionist Party making sufficient inroads to unseat the sitting MP. I declined the offer. I appreciated the disappointment of the members of the Association and particularly those who had worked so hard in the campaign but I really wanted to contest a winnable seat. Roseleen, Dermot and I returned to Gibraltar where I once more took charge of the current contracts while new projects were undertaken.

I had intended to take a rest from politics at this stage but early in 1975 I received word my name had been submitted to the East Aberdeenshire Association for consideration as the prospective Parliamentary Candidate for the next Westminster election. I researched the constituency to find it had been represented for thirty-six years by the renowned 'Bob' Boothby (Lord Boothby of Buchan and Rattray Head) now deceased and for twelve years by Mr Patrick Wolrige-Gordon, now deceased. The Conservative hold on the constituency had been lost in February 1974 when it was captured by the SNP who also held it at the October 1974 General Election. At once I was enthusiastic. This is the kind of challenge I was looking for – a winnable seat. I advised the Party Headquarters in Edinburgh I would be pleased to have my name considered and would wait to learn of any decision.

From Gibraltar to East Aberdeenshire

In May 1975 I received a communication from Party Headquarters. I had been placed on the Short List and was to be interviewed by the Executive Committee of the East Aberdeenshire Conservative and Unionist Association at the home of its Honorary Treasurer, Mr J. Alexander Dingwall-Fordyce who was also a member of the Grampian Regional Council. The letter arrived with the date and time of the meeting. At this point, so soon after the October election, my wife Roseleen was none too keen on another venture into national politics. With a little persuasion I got her to agree I would have one more 'shot' for what I saw as a very possible winnable seat, given a fair wind for our party at the time of the next General Election. As Labour had won the October 1974 election with a wafer thin majority, dependent on the votes of the SNP members, there was every possibility that Labour would be forced to call a General Election at anytime.

Some days before the selection meeting, I travelled from Gibraltar to a hotel in the town of Ellon in the East Aberdeenshire Constituency. With a map to guide me and having established the constituency boundaries I drove to the two main towns of Peterhead and Fraserburgh, both important fishing ports in the north east of Scotland. The rich agricultural land stretching from the coast to the Grampian Hills supported many farming enterprises both large and small. I felt as each day passed that this was the area I wished to represent. I rehearsed my speech for the selection meeting until I was word perfect in my mind. The meeting was held on a Sunday afternoon. I was met by Mrs Mary Dingwall-Fordyce, wife of the Honorary Treasurer who put me at ease. After the meeting was over she told me she had put a name in an envelope of the candidate whom she thought would be selected and it was mine! I think Mrs Dingwall-Fordyce was pleased with her prediction.

I was delighted with the interview. My speech was greeted with genuine applause. Several questions were asked of me. My answers appeared to satisfy the committee although I nearly made an enemy when I criticised the Regional Council only to find that Mr Harry Sim, the Vice Chairman of the Association, was also Vice Convener of the Grampian Regional Council. My response to his comments must have satisfied him as he remained a firm and sincere friend until his death years later. I was elated when, after the selection committee deliberated on the performance of all three candidates, I was told the members had agreed unanimously to nominate me as the Prospective Parliamentary Candidate for East Aberdeenshire a seat which I felt was one I could win.

I telephoned Gibraltar as soon as I could to tell Roseleen and Dermot I had been selected as the candidate. Neither was totally pleased as they foresaw another upheaval in our lives. I was therefore a little apprehensive and returned to Gibraltar right away to appease them and to instil enthusiasm at the prospect of my becoming a Member of Parliament.

On returning to Gibraltar a series of discussions began. I had passed my 57th birthday and felt it was time to start winding down my companies in Gibraltar and Scotland. My initial thoughts were to become a full-time candidate. The Government was so vulnerable there was a view it could fall at any time.

After many hours of discussion Roseleen and I decided to leave Gibraltar to take up residence in East Aberdeenshire. On arrival in Aberdeen I bought a Jaguar car, booked in at a hotel and began the search for a suitable home. The guarantee I gave to Roseleen was that the home had to be acceptable to her. A very interesting meeting then happened which helped me keep my promise to Roseleen. When in Gibraltar we struck up a friendship with the RAF Chaplain and his wife, Gerald and Margaret Mungavin. We knew they had moved on from Gibraltar but did not know where. It was on a visit to the town of Turriff while house-hunting that we heard a voice calling 'Roseleen'. It was Margaret Mungavin. We were both surprised and delighted to see her in Scotland and in Turriff. Gerald who was a Scottish Episcopalian Minister was now the Rector of St Congan's Church in Turriff. When Margaret heard the reason why we were in Aberdeenshire she immediately told us of the ideal home. At that time it belonged to the Treasurer of the Church who was due to be transferred to London and was about to put his house on the market. Margaret contacted the gentleman and made arrangements for us to visit Teuchar Lodge some five miles from Turriff and reasonably central to the constituency.

41. Teuchar Lodge my Constituency Home

We visited the property the following morning. After viewing the house and the grounds Roseleen agreed it would be very acceptable to her. I fully agreed with her sentiments and within a short time Teuchar Lodge became our home from where I would set out every morning in my pursuit to become the Member of Parliament for East Aberdeenshire.

Shortly after I took up residence at Teuchar Lodge I was approached by a number of fishing skippers who were demanding a fifty mile fishing limit for Scotland. In the knowledge of the importance of the fishing industry in the constituency, I readily agreed to join the campaign. I supported the fishermen in their determination to achieve their goal by attending meetings with them Members of Parliament and local Councillors.

42. At No. 10 Downing Street with Fishing Petition

In June 1976 the fishermen of the north east of Scotland set up a petition to create a fifty mile fishing zone to be exclusive to Scottish fishermen. Petition forms were circulated in towns and villages in the north east – in particular the many fishing villages dotted around the coastline of the area. I was requested by a number of skippers to take an active part in the campaign and show that the Conservative Party was behind the fishermen. Following many meetings, a rally of several hundred paraded through the streets of Aberdeen calling for a fifty mile zone to protect the livelihood of hundreds of people connected directly and indirectly with the industry. I was in the forefront of the parade at the request of the fishermen.

43. With Party Supporters at Downing Street

By this time I had secured the support of Scottish Conservative Members of Parliament and Candidates in the North East. Thousands of signed petition forms were collected, handed to the Prime Minister at 10 Downing Street for information before being presented to the European Parliament in Brussels. The campaign also had the support of Lord (Bob) Boothby who had become a firm friend of fishermen during this time representing East Aberdeenshire. He was still trusted by the fishermen who appreciated his continued support and interest.

On 20th June 1976 a delegation comprising of Mr Joe Mitchell Association Vice-Chairman, Mrs Christine Sutherland Association Secretary and myself, travelled by train with the Petition. At the House of Commons we were met by Alick Buchanan-Smith MP, Russell Fairgrieve MP, Lord Boothby and Jimmy Lovie from the Scottish Fishermen Producers Organisation along with Roddy McColl, the Secretary. We were also joined by Candidates and Agents from the north east constituencies.

Afterwards the group travelled to Brussels to hand over further bundles. Although some concessions were made for a fifty mile exclusive zone, the Labour Government never accepted these concessions. The fight continued and the fishermen knew we were backing them to the full. In return the fishermen supported me by giving me their vote when the Election took place on 4th May 1979. It was heartening for me to witness at the count of the votes the following morning that the fishermen and the farmers supported me ensuring that I would sit on the green benches in the House of Commons representing them and all the people of East Aberdeenshire.

After the loss at the February 1974 General Election when Mr Patrick Wolrige-Gordon who had been the Conservative and Unionist Member of Parliament for twelve years (having followed Lord Boothby) was defeated by the SNP Candidate Douglas Henderson, the local Association suffered a further blow in October 1974 when Douglas Henderson held on to the seat at the General Election.

44. With Edward Heath in the Constituency

The double blow devastated the activities of the Association to such an extent that morale was low and branches were folding due to the lack of membership. There was however a hard core of solid Conservative and Unionist activists led by Sandy Dingwall-Fordyce, Joe Mitchell and Alexander Pittendrigh, all successful businessmen in their own field. At what I can only describe as a powerful meeting held in the Headquarters in

Mintlaw, a plan was drawn up to visit every town and village within the constituency over the next few months with a concerted effort to revitalise the branches again. In this respect the late Joe Mitchell gave up time every week to drive me around the area, to meet people and to arrange meetings which I would address. This proved very successful and over the ensuing four years the membership of the Association had increased, twenty-five branches were created revitalising every part of the constituency. We were ready for the battle to regain the seat and had high hopes of succeeding. In November 1976 Mr Edward Heath MP the former Prime Minister visited the constituency in support of my campaign, met the Association Office-Bearers before delivering a rousing address to a capacity company at a dinner held in a local Hotel.

Bredero Limited

45. With Alan Chisholm and Sandy Cook of Bredero

Following on from my selection as the Candidate for East Aberdeenshire Conservative and Unionist Association much of my time was spent getting to know the constituency and its people, I then found I had spare time which I wished to put to good use. I learned of a company called Bredero which was about to begin work on a new housing estate in Ellon – part of East Aberdeenshire Constituency. This firm which was based in Edinburgh were searching for a Site Manager to oversee the construction. I telephoned the Edinburgh office advising that I would be interested and was immediately connected to the Managing Director Mr Alan Chisholm, to whom I explained who I was and my business background both in Scotland and in Gibraltar. He confirmed the vacancy in Ellon advising me that interviews for the appointment would take place the following week. Mr Chisholm invited me to attend the interview session which was to take place in an Ellon Hotel. On the day of the interview Mr Chisholm was joined by a Company Director Mr Sandy Cook who was a Chartered Surveyor. At first they suggested I was too highly qualified for the work intended but I was not willing to allow this from preventing me securing the appointment and explained more fully my wish to continue my involvement in the building industry but not to operate the business as I had done for many years. The job was awarded to me so I can only assume I must have said what they wanted to hear.

A few days were spent in the Edinburgh office acquainting myself with the plans for the project. Amongst other items it was necessary for a hut to be sited within the development area where I would work from and where all drawings and specifications for the project would be kept. I arranged a meeting with the contractor, Stewart Milne. This meeting took place in my new site hut. This was the first major building contract for Stewart Milne as previously he had been engaged in fitting bathrooms and kitchens in tenement properties in Aberdeen. (In the years that followed Mr Milne successfully built up his company to become a multi-millionaire and Chairman of Aberdeen Football Club). I wonder if that first meeting was an omen for the success he has achieved!

Between 1975 and 1979 I undertook work for Bredero in Banchory, Peterculter, Aberdeen, Peterhead as well as Ellon where an extension to the original development of new homes received the go-ahead. As the Ellon development project was developing without delay the question of marketing the houses arose. By this time I could see some potential activity for me and despite what I had said at the interview about not wanting to set up a building company again I saw no problem in setting up as an Estate Agent. My proposal was put to Mr Chisholm and Mr Cook who agreed to let me handle the sales.

As my hut was too small for anyone else to work daily I purchased a caravan with the sole purpose of using it as a Sales Office situating it at the entrance to the development and near to the Showhouse. I employed local ladies with experience of an Estate Office and opened up for business.

With the discovery of oil in the North Sea and Aberdeen, a hub for exploration, only a short distance from Ellon I soon discovered that oil related companies were purchasing properties for managers and staff who were arriving into the north east of Scotland and for the most part were working off-shore. It was essential that these workers had houses in the area where they would relocate and maintain a family unit. The system was that the Oil Company leased the fully furnished property for a period of years. I saw yet another opportunity and made myself known to the Shell Headquarters in Aberdeen to find out if Shell would be interested in taking over houses in Ellon. The response was good and after a visit to Ellon by the Property Director of Shell, ten homes were taken on lease. This was a great start to my selling efforts as I was able to secure a good annual payment for the leases. The sales staff at Ellon, were well satisfied with their work as all the other houses were sold on completion.

46. The Capsule at Paisley Shopping Mall

The success of this project led to the further developments I mentioned earlier. In each case I hired staff who either located in a hut on site or in a caravan – luxury in heated show houses was not a 'perk' in these days. As the number of houses being built was ever increasing it was necessary to appoint a Sales Manager. I was aware that I could not afford to allow the business side of my life to interfere with my campaign to win the election whenever it took place. I appointed Barry Anderson who had experience of organising a Sales Office and this appointment worked to advantage for all.

I continued my involvement with Bredero working closely with Mr Sandy Cook who was responsible for all the Scottish projects after Alan Chisholm moved to England to take over the Bredero's project at Hammersmith in West London and a shopping centre in Epsom. I acted as a Consultant on various projects undertaken by the company including the Bon-Accord Centre in Aberdeen – a major operation which the company so successfully completed. On the completion of the house building projects by Bredero in the north east of Scotland, I closed the Estate Agency business to concentrate on the work of a Member of Parliament.

On losing my seat in the House of Commons in the 1987 General Election, Alan Chisholm, the Managing Director of Bredero, invited me to take up an appointment as a Consultant for the Paisley Town Centre project which the company was embarking upon at a cost of £60 million including a town centre shopping complex. At the time I had not intended to move from the north east of Scotland but after much consideration I accepted his offer as Consultant with the Bredero Offices near to the development. After a considerable amount of ground preparation work, a time capsule containing information on the project including bank notes and copies of local newspapers was buried into the foundations in 1988.

As happens with all developments and in particular those in restricted areas as Paisley, was the project took four years to complete. The complex was opened by Deputy Provost William Orr in the absence of Provost George Murray who had taken ill just hours before the Opening. Within a few months HRH The Princess of Wales accepted an invitation to visit the shopping centre when she unveiled a plaque to mark the occasion.

Arising from my involvement with Bredero and after the completion of the Paisley Shopping Centre Alan Chisholm invited me to take up a Directorship of Hunterston Development Company. This company was based at Fairlie in North Ayrshire. I was to represent the Bredero Company which had a substantial shareholding in Hunterston. I accepted the invitation and acted as the Bredero Director on the Hunterston Company Board of Directors until 2010 when Clydeport bought the company at which time all Hunterston Directors resigned.

This ended a long connection with Bredero which began in 1975. I enjoyed working with Alan Chisholm and Sandy Cook over many years and still retain contact with them.

Back to National Politics

The result of the October 1974 General Election was that Labour emerged with a wafer thin majority and were dependent on the members of the Parliamentary SNP to keep it in power. It was thought this situation could not last a full term but it survived until March of 1979 when the SNP withdrew its support on a Confidence Motion forcing Prime Minister James Callaghan to call a General Election. How well I remember that night. The Association was hosting a fund-raising event which I was to address in the Pitfour Arms Hotel in the village of Mintlaw. Around 10.30 p.m. that evening I received a call from my friend George Younger MP for Ayr who told me the Government had fallen. There was tremendous applause when I made the announcement to the gathering and a feeling of elation that at last we were to have the opportunity to regain the seat for our party. Several thoughts went through my mind. Would the enthusiasm everyone displayed in support of my candidacy be maintained and would I find in any one part of the constituency a lack of support? Roseleen and I returned to Teuchar Lodge in the knowledge the real campaign had begun – sleep did not come easy!

47. George Younger MP receives a lobster from Jimmy Lovie on a visit to the Constituency

There followed an intensive campaign when I spent every day visiting businesses and factories and often ending the day by addressing Branch meetings. I did have to work hard as I realised that SNP had mustered effective groups in some areas and Douglas Henderson had been a good and popular Member of Parliament. Right from the start I knew it would be a hard fight but I was also fully aware that over the four years I had conscientiously worked in the constituency and Mrs Margaret Thatcher had gained popularity. Her visits to the constituency were an outstanding success and nationally the Polls were predicting a Conservative and Unionist victory which I felt was helping me. The campaign workers many of whom spent their entire day working either with me or in the various sub-offices throughout the constituency had a feeling that success was within reach and therefore enthusiasm was high. It was all worth it. On 3rd May 1979 I was declared to have been elected as the Member of Parliament for East Aberdeenshire with a majority of 538 – not as large as I had hoped but good enough for the Presiding Officer who refused a demand of the SNP for a recount. Even more wonderful was the news that the Conservative and Unionist Party had secured 339 Seats against 268 for the Labour Party with the SNP reduced from eleven Seats to two. Our Party formed the next Government with Margaret Thatcher as Prime Minister. The success of our party was felt widely in East Aberdeenshire Conservative and Unionist

48. Margaret Thatcher visits Peterhead, 1978

Association and amongst thousands of voters there and throughout the country. East Aberdeenshire was one of the seats the pollsters did not reckon would be taken from the SNP. My victory was headlines with Scottish Television reporting 'McQuarrie sensationally snatches East Aberdeenshire'. One of the proudest people watching was my son Dermot who by that time was a Presenter at Scottish Television in Glasgow.

49. Celebrating election as a Member of Parliament at Aberdeen Beach Ballroom with Roseleen

Several weeks before the election was called, the King Edward Branch made plans for a function on Friday 4th May in the local hall. When Roseleen and I arrived we received a huge welcome. It was a great feeling and a humbling one at the same time. I addressed the company after which I was presented with a box of King Edward cigars in a fine wooden box which I have in my possession to this day. It was known that I enjoyed a King Edward cigar from time to time but have not smoked for many years.

The week after the General Election which saw Margaret Thatcher elected as Prime Minster, she kept her word to visit Scotland. On the Saturday afternoon the Perth City Hall was packed to capacity with Conservative and Unionist supporters who enthusiastically welcomed the

ENTERING INTO NATIONAL POLITICS

Prime Minster to Scotland. The newly elected Conservative and Unionist Members of Parliament were given a standing ovation when they and their wives took their seats on the platform behind the Prime Minister. Margaret Thatcher delivered a rousing speech promising to implement the promises which the party had made in its Manifesto. One was the promise to increase the pay of all ranks in the Police Force throughout the country and she announced it would be implemented from that day. This brought another of the six standing ovations during the speech, the last of which lasted for four minutes. The Prime Minister was overwhelmed at the great display of loyalty from her Scottish members.

On my way home to Teuchar Lodge from Perth on the Dundee Aberdeen road I was pulled into the side by a Police speed car at a junction to Fettercairn. My pleasure and delight for the Prime Minister's Rally in Perth was such that I let my mind drift not realising I was exceeding the 70 mph limit. I wound down the car window. The Police Officer looked in and said 'Oh, it's you Mr McQuarrie'. As my photograph had appeared in all the north east of Scotland newspapers on my election I was easily recognised. The Police Officer added 'Please give my thanks to the Prime Minister for the substantial pay rise which is much appreciated. Now be on your way and take care.' I was glad the Prime Minister's announcement that afternoon in Perth had saved me from a 'booking' so early in my time as a Member of Parliament. On driving home I made sure I did not exceed the speed limit as other Police Officers may not have recognised me so readily and may not have heard the good news from the Prime Minister.

I was eagerly looking forward to my first visit as a Member of the United Kingdom Parliament the topic of another Chapter of the book.

CHAPTER EIGHT

Entering the House of Commons as a Member of Parliament

AFTER MY ELECTION AS A Member of the Westminster Parliament for the Constituency of East Aberdeenshire I soon found out that no official information on what action to take or when to be present in the House of Commons was forthcoming. On reflecting when I was elected to the Gourock Town Council many years earlier, I recall receiving a package from the Town Clerk confirming my election as a Councillor of the Burgh of Gourock and advising me of the date when the Statutory Meeting of the Council would take place at which I should be present.

I was therefore surprised that nothing of this nature was provided following my election as a new Member to Parliament. After a few days I learned from one of the Scottish Members that the Swearing-in of Members would take place the following week. We made our plans to be at the House of Commons for this Ceremony so Roseleen and I travelled to London and checked in at the Victoria Hotel. I was filled with anticipation at the prospect of entering the Palace of Westminster as a Member of Parliament in the United Kingdom.

The history of the Palace of Westminster is a long and fascinating one dating back to the 11th century. Within the Palace which covers eight acres there are 100 staircases and 1,100 rooms. Over the centuries there were a number of fires but it was in October 1834 that the Palace of Westminster was burned down by a fire which started in furnaces below the Lords Chambers. It was fortunate that the famous and historic Westminster Hall which was completed in 1099 was saved from the devastation and which hundreds of visitors pass through daily. Following the fire it is understood that Members of the Parliament were offered alternative meeting rooms for their sessions but refused. Temporary accommodation was found which allowed Parliament to operate as it had done since the 13th century. Over the next thirty years the structure as we know it today was rebuilt. During the

the Palace of Westminster suffered severe damage from German Bombers on a number of occasions. In May 1941 an attack by the Germans destroyed the Chamber of the House of Commons. It was restored on the instruction of Prime Minister Winston Churchill who arranged for it to be reduced in size as a debating Chamber. The result of this can be seen when on certain days of important speeches in the House of Commons, Members are seen sitting in the aisles because there are insufficient seats for the 652 Members. The present Government proposal, if successful, to reduce the number of Members of Parliament to 600 should help considerably in assuring seating for all Members.

Although I had made several visits to the Palace of Westminster during my career leading up to politics, it was only when I walked into Parliament Square from Victoria Street and seeing the Police Officer on duty at the door that I fully realised that this particular day in my life was to be a memorable one.

On arriving at St Stephen's entrance I was greeted by a large notice informing the public that the House of Commons was closed. Not only that, I found my way barred by a policeman who wanted to know what I was doing there! Having been made aware that this may happen I handed him one of my Election leaflets as proof of my identity. He referred to a list of MPs then smiled and said 'Right up to the Central Lobby, Sir. You'll find your way from there'. I walked up the long corridor from the entrance adjacent to Westminster Hall, admiring the beautiful paintings and many statues of earlier Prime Ministers. I was later to learn that the long corridor was the original House of Commons. I entered the magnificent Central Lobby with its enormous stained glass windows symbolising the Patron Saints of Scotland, England, Ireland and Wales. On this occasion there was nobody around the Central Lobby.

Like the new boy on his first day at school, I was lost and wondered what to do. Then I thought 'When in trouble, ask a policeman'. I walked towards the policeman, handed him another of my leaflets and asked for guidance on what to do. He decided the best course of action was for me to visit the office of the Sergeant-at-Arms which I did and was greeted by a lady whose name I learned was Miss Frampton. She took me under her wing.

First of all the Official Pass which would allow me access to the House of Commons had to be obtained. This was done and I was the proud owner of the card complete with my name and photograph signifying that I was a Member of Parliament. Miss Frampton directed me to the Members' Corridor – an area which on my previous visits I had wished to enter but could not. It was a thrill to walk along the corridor and not have the duty policeman tap me on the shoulder and say 'Excuse me, sir. Are you a Member?' This time as I passed he saluted me and said 'Good Morning sir'. The Members' Post Office was my next stop where I found a large bundle of mail waiting for me. I found my way to the Members' library which was packed with other Members dealing with mail. There was no space available. Eventually I found a quiet corner in a corridor which had a desk and it was there that I began my work as a Member of Parliament. Later that day many Members complained about the lack of office accommodation. The Whips Offices of both major parties were virtually under siege from Members requesting space. The trouble was that the incoming Government was not the same political colour as the outgoing Government and the former users of the offices were determined to hang on to their accommodation as long as possible. In the meantime I was given a locker along the corridor to the Members dining room to store my papers until an office was allocated to me. It took me four weeks to obtain an office and then learned that the previous occupants of the office had been Shadow Ministers under Mrs Margaret Thatcher and were Ministers in the Government. I thought – there may be hope for me!

Soon I became acquainted with the vastness of the House of Commons – the corridors, the many staircases, the meeting rooms, the dining rooms and tea rooms. At the end of each day many Members leave by way of the Palace yard door where there is a bell, when pushed, flashes in Parliament Square at the entrance to the Palace yard indicating a Member is calling for a taxi. This arrangement works well for both Members and taxi drivers who can pick up good fares each night. During the first few days the important procedure of the swearing-in of Members took place. Each member approached the Despatch Box on which is the Holy Bible. The Member then takes the Oath of Allegiance to Her Majesty The Queen, signs the Members Book and is introduced to the Speaker of the House who, at this time, was the Rt Hon George Thomas, a kindly gentleman. He gave me a friendly welcome wishing me well serving in the House of Commons.

The House of Commons is full of tradition and ceremony which has been copied by other Parliaments all over the world. One of these traditions takes place each day at 2.30 p.m. before the House business commences. If a Member wishes to guarantee a seat in the Chamber, he obtains a small green card from within the Chamber, signs it and places it into the brass holder in the seat of his choice. In doing so no other Member of the House may occupy that seat for the remainder of the day. I endeavoured to attend prayers on most days. Members stood when the Speaker and his Chaplain approached the Chair. The Chaplain opened with a few words before saying 'Let us Pray' at which point the Members present turned to face the wall. After doing this for a few days I decided to find out the reason for this practice.

I approached the Speaker's Chair and addressing him in the customary manner said 'Mr Speaker, sir. Why do we turn and face the walls when your Chaplain says "let us pray"?' Mr Speaker replied by saying 'Albert, I have been in the House of Commons for thirty years and still don't know the real reason'. Nevertheless he gave several explanations which had been related to him. The first was that in the days of the Tories and the Whigs members were instructed to turn their backs on each other during the time of prayer so that they would not hurl abuse at each other. The second reason, he said, was that as there are no kneelers for Members in the Chamber and by turning round Members could use their seats as kneelers.

Where to stay?

When I arrived in London after the election to take my seat, the situation of a home was most uppermost in our minds. Roseleen and I, at the first opportunity, began the search to find suitable accommodation within a reasonable distance of the House of Commons. We hired a car, visited Estate Agents and viewed properties only to find other Members had been quicker off their mark than we were due in many cases to their easier access to London. After a few days we rented a basement flat at Tedworth Square, just off Kings Road and near the Tube for Westminster. This flat was not what we had hoped for but we were glad to take it as the only one available after our search. We returned to our home in the constituency glad to have somewhere to stay in London once the House returned from summer recess.

Roseleen was not happy but accepted the situation until such time we could find a more suitable property. We lived for several months in a basement flat which required lights on at all times of the day and that situation made me determined to waste no time in the search for a house. Then I had a stroke of luck. One of my House of Commons friends told me he lived in the district of Kennington in a house rented from the Duchy of Cornwall Estate Office and that he believed a house had become vacant. Without wasting any time I drove to the Duchy Office in Kennington, explained to the Office Manager what I wanted and that I wished a property near to the House of Commons. I was told there was a house on two floors at 21 Sancroft Street, Kennington which the Duchy would be prepared to let me have on a rental. There was a garage attached, a garden at the rear and this was exactly what we were looking for. The Office Manager agreed to 'hold' the offer until Roseleen had seen the house. She was delighted with it. (I learned later the house had been occupied by Mr John Stonehouse, a former Member of Parliament and Government Minister of some note).

The Lease, drawn up for the tenancy of the house, starts off with the words *'This Lease made the fifth day of August One Thousand nine hundred and eighty between His Royal Highness Charles Philip Arthur George, Prince of Wales, Duke of Cornwall and Rothesay, Earl of Chester and Carrick, Baron of Renfrew. Lord of the Isles and Grand Steward of Scotland, and Albert McQuarrie Esq, MP'*. It then goes on setting out the conditions attached to the occupancy of the property. The Lease hangs in my home as a reminder of the happy times spent at 21 Sancroft Street. It was important to me that Roseleen was content in our London home as she saw little of me when there were late night sittings very often continuing into the early hours. She made many friends in the area with whom she played bridge and golf at Dulwich Golf Club – two of her favourite hobbies.

Having signed the Lease I was anxious to take occupancy and set about furnishing the house – as it was entirely void of anything. Furniture, beds, linen, crockery, cutlery along with all the other domestic requirements were purchased. In these days all expenses were borne by the Member from his own resources - there were no claims from Government coffers. There was a maintenance grant which was insignificant to the cost of fitting out a house for occupation.

After I occupied No. 21 Sancroft Street I discovered the adjoining houses were lived in by other Members of Parliament. In 1985 the Duchy adopted a policy of selling off the houses. I was offered the opportunity to purchase No. 21 for £29,000 as a sitting tenant. At that time I turned the offer down as we already had our house in the constituency and had retained our house in Gibraltar. In this instance I made an error despite Roseleen advocating we should accept the offer to buy. In 1987, after I lost my seat in the general Election the house was sold by the Duchy for £85,000!

Back at the Commons!

On my first day, amongst other things, I was directed to the Members' Cloakroom on the ground floor adjacent to the Palace yard. In this room there were sufficient hangers for every Member. On every hanger there is a canvas loop which was used in days gone by for members to hang their swords as for obvious reasons they were not allowed in the Chamber. I saw no swords hanging in the Members' Cloakroom!

ENTERING THE HOUSE OF COMMONS AS A MEMBER OF PARLIAMENT

In the Chamber itself and on each side of it there are two distinct lines which are two and a half swords length and were placed there many years ago to prevent Members attacking each other across the floor of the House. Today, the attacks are verbal – much safer than swords!

50. House of Commons Chamber showing the Red Lines and White Line Bar at the House

Amongst other fascinating traditions I would comment upon is the 'Bar of the House'. This is a coloured bar on the carpet extending a few yards beyond the entrance to the Chamber from the Members Lobby almost in line with the seat which is occupied by the Sergeant-at-Arms when the House is sitting. As Members enter and leave the Chamber it is expected of them to bow to the Speaker's Chair whether it is occupied or not. When watching proceedings from the House on television, I am disappointed to see that many Honourable Members no longer carry out this tradition. As the Mother of Parliaments is renowned the world over I think Mr Speaker ought to draw the attention of Members to this tradition so that it is not lost in what is now referred to as the modern world. Once traditions are forgotten it is unlikely they will ever be resurrected again.

There is one other matter which I would make comment upon and it is that many speeches made by Members, and sometimes even Ministers, are read. I well recall when George Thomas was Speaker of the House how he 'ticked' off Members for reading their speeches! Members were expected to 'prepare' their speech referring to notes rather than straight reading.

Membership of All Party Groups

Joining one of the many All Party Groups which operate within the House of Commons creates an added dimension to the work of an MP. At the top of the list, I believe, are the Commonwealth Parliamentary Association and the Inter Parliamentary Union which are affiliated to many other Parliaments in the Commonwealth and which I joined early on. Amongst other Groups I became involved in was the British Gibraltar All Party Group. My interest in Gibraltar had been maintained since returning to the United Kingdom in 1975 and because of my recent and direct involvement with Gibraltar I was elected Chairman of the British Gibraltar All Party Group, a position I held from 1979 to 1987 when I lost my seat. Due to legislation which was proposed for territories like Gibraltar there was a period in 1981 when a big battle was fought with the UK Government. I devote a further Chapter in the book to this subject.

51. On the Terrace for Members only section

I joined the Scotch Whisky All Party Group and was elected Secretary, an Office I held from 1979 to 1987. This was a high powered pressure group as the whisky industry is of such importance to the economy and labour of Scotland. I attended a number of receptions every year where representatives of the Whisky industry were able to catch the ear of Members as a means of reinforcing the importance of the industry in Scotland. As anyone who attended these receptions would tell the representatives from the various companies were more than generous with their 'drams' and often a tasty range of 'nibbles'. It has been known for some Members having 'one too many' and requiring help back to the House of Commons to sleep it off! I hastily add I was never one of them!

52. The Terrace with Bill Walker MP and friends

Representing a constituency where the fishing industry was important I joined the Conservative Fisheries Sub-Committee becoming their Vice-Chairman from 1979 to 1987. I also sat on the Scottish Conservative Back Bench Committee, the Select Committee on Scottish Affairs, the Select Committee on Agriculture and the Private Bill Procedure.

Being a member of these Committees allowed me to gain a wide knowledge of how Government works and how effective Members can be in presenting cases to Ministers. In a number of cases, Government ultimately takes action to the benefit of the people of the Member's constituency.

I was actively interested in the Groups and Committees while there was an added advantage in that there was always the possibility of representing the United Kingdom Parliament on visits to countries affiliated to the Commonwealth Parliamentary Association. It was my good fortune in 1981 to be selected for a visit to Australia. Included in the trip was New South Wales where a forebear of my Clan was the first Governor General. He was Major General Lachlan McQuarrie who was much loved by the people. I believe he changed the spelling of his name when in Australia. More can be read about my visit to Australia with a Parliamentary delegation in a later Chapter.

One of the privileges given to Members of Parliament is access to the famous Terrace in the Palace of Westminster which looks on to the River Thames. No member of the public may enter the Terrace unless accompanied by a Member. Within the Terrace there is a section specifically restricted to Members only. In my time Members were able to access this area of the Terrace from the Members Restaurant and it was where they could relax on pleasant warm sunny days watching the small cruise boats sail closely by the Terrace.

The intriguing and colourful history of the Palace of Westminster will always be of interest to the general public and so I was always delighted when friends and constituents came to visit which ended with tea and biscuits on the Terrace. Today there is a Terrace Restaurant both for Members of the Commons and for the Lords and their guests but not for the public. I have fond memories of times spent on the Terrace when politics was always the main subject for discussion. I hope this long standing tradition continues and the Terrace will forever be a 'hallowed place' within the Palace of Westminster.

Very quickly I grew into Parliamentary life, acquainting myself with the customs and as each day dawned I felt I was serving my country again but this time in the comfort of a place where history was being made.

CHAPTER NINE

Down to Work as an MP

HAVING SETTLED INTO MY office and engaged Barbara Sartin as my Secretary in the House of Commons the first major event was the Queen's Speech to the Members of the Lords and the Commons in the Lords Chamber. I was lucky enough to secure a seat in the Lords Gallery which gave me a splendid view of Her Majesty delivering the Speech.

Prior to the Members of Parliament proceeding to the Lords for the Speech, they wait in their 'place' for the call to be made by Black Rod to attend the House of Lords. Black Rod is an Officer of the House of Lords who carries out this ancient tradition and who on this particular occasion walks from the House of Lords across the Central Lobby towards the House of Commons Members Lobby. On approaching the Commons Chamber, the door is closed preventing Black Rod from entering. He reaches for his baton, knocks at the door three times at the place easily seen by the markings where this ancient tradition has been performed over the centuries, before the door is opened. Black Rod then enters the Commons Chamber and walks forward until he reaches the Mace which rests on the table in front of the Speaker's chair. He commands the Members of Parliament to attend upon Her Majesty in the Chamber of the House of Lords. Black Rod turns and leads a procession from the House of Commons with the Prime Minister and Leader of the Opposition immediately behind him followed by Government Ministers and Shadow Ministers and Members from all parties. At the conclusion of the Queen's Speech, Her Majesty leaves the Chamber of the House of Lords and is escorted to her carriage. Members of the House of Commons return to their Chamber to debate the contents of the Queen's Speech which culminates with the voting procedure a few days later.

The Maiden Speech and Questions to Ministers

One of the great moments a new Member of Parliament experiences is delivering his/her Maiden Speech in the House of Commons. This is the first occasion when the new Member rises in the Chamber to address the House. Members are advised by the Whips that the speech should be non-controversial, and should commence with a tribute to the former Member of Parliament for the constituency.

I was fortunate to be given an early date. On 13th June 1979 I took my seat in the Chamber at 2.30 p.m. for prayers. Mr Speaker called me at 8.06 p.m. I rose to deliver my Speech. It was a thrill to be addressing the House, knowing that by tradition there would be no interruption from other Members at any time. As a Maiden Speech allows the Member to make an appeal for help to Ministers on a particular issue, I chose to speak on Widow's Pensions. The speech was not long and I am including it as it is printed in Hansard.

> I begin by paying tribute to my predecessor, Mr Henderson, who during his period of service in this House worked most assiduously for his constituents. In that connection he was carrying on the highest tradition of Members elected to serve the constituency of Aberdeenshire East, and I hope I shall be able to carry on that tradition and dedication during my time in the House.
>
> I am delighted to have this opportunity of addressing the House for the first time. I represent the fine constituency of Aberdeenshire East, which is a long way from this Chamber. Thanks to modern travel, I am able to commute to this lovely City of London - and the Palace of Westminster – take part in the proceedings of the House, and then return to the green fields of the beautiful agricultural areas in my constituency and the rolling waves of the North Sea, where the oil and gas come ashore to aid this country's economy.
>
> Aberdeenshire East is one of the largest fishing communities in Europe. From the harbours of Fraserburgh and Peterhead, the fishing fleet sails out to catch fish not only for direct consumption but also for the fish processing industry which has many factories in my constituency. This industry plays a large part in the export drive. The fishermen have a hazardous job, often in rough seas, and sadly, a few of the boats never return to harbour. This leaves the community to face another disaster, with the wives and children mourning the loss of the breadwinner.
>
> In this context I wish to draw attention to a matter which affects every industry, because when calamities like this take place they leave behind the widows. There are three million widows in Britain today and I wish to remind the Chancellor of their plight. I am aware that in the past many Rt Hon and Hon Members have fought for the rights and pensions of widows, but with very little success. Therefore, I make no apology for bringing the matter before the House once more.

I am very pleased the Chancellor of the Exchequer proposes to complete the exemption from tax of war widows' pensions. The Royal British Legion, of which I am proud to be a member, has fought very hard for this, and I am sure the organisation will be delighted to learn of the Chancellor's decision. However, I remind the Chancellor many of the widows today are in this category because their husbands died after the war as a result of wounds sustained during the war. Those widows do not enjoy the rights of classification as war widows.

I want all tax to be removed from widows' pensions. I also want to see the existing anomalies removed. I urge the Chancellor to give us an indication he will consider these matters. When a woman is widowed, she falls into one of several categories. Up to the age of 39 she receives £27.30 for twenty-six weeks, after which she receives nothing at all. Surely it is quite wrong to assume she can go out to work or remarry. She may neither have the health nor the capacity to take on a job, and she is more than likely to have children of school age. She may not wish to remarry. Yet the State forces her after the twenty-six week period to take to take one of these alternatives or to throw herself onto the social security system. Widows aged between 40 and 49 receive a pension ranging from £5.85 a week to £18.14 a week. From 50 to 60 years of age the rate is £19.50. I have purposely omitted mentioning children's or earnings-related allowances to widows, as many are out with these categories. For those who are, the difference is not significant enough to improve the desperate situation in which those widows find themselves. The widows receive no unemployment or sickness benefit. They cannot apply for industrial injury benefit, education grants, maternity or invalidity allowances. Even the child benefit is deducted from the widow's benefit pound for pound. They are in a constant poverty trap – and it is a trap from which this House must remove them. Why should widow's pensions not be paid in full on the same scale to all widows rather than have the variations which now exist? Why should all these other anomalies exist when the husbands had paid national insurance contributions all their working lives so that in the event of their death the widows would receive a proper pension?

Then there is the worst feature of all – the taxing of the widow's pension if she chooses, by need or desire, to take up employment. It is wrong the pension should be taxed when the purpose of providing the allowance was to support the widow in the event of the husband's death. By all means tax the earned income, but leave the widow's pension alone and give the widows the full benefit of that allowance.

I ask my Rt Hon and Learned Friend the Chancellor of the Exchequer to give serious consideration to improving the lot of these three million widows – a figure which increases daily. Will he endeavour to remove the anomalies by providing a standard widow's pension for all age groups, and grant the various benefits which are not now available to widows? Will he also indicate whether it is possible to bring in the complete tax exemption for widow's pension, as is proposed for the existing war widows?

We have a moral obligation to look after these widows. Other needy groups may criticise, but if we make a start with a group which is the largest and which is suffering most, we shall at least have made some headway for others in the future.

Greater recognition should be given to the changed circumstances of married women after the death of their husbands. I further ask my Rt Hon and Learned Friend the Chancellor seriously to consider amending legislation on the income tax liability, pension rights and social security rights of all widows, irrespective of age, on the death of the husband. If we can do something for the three million widows who have lost their loved ones, we shall have the satisfaction of knowing we have achieved something which is badly needed. We shall also be seen to be a caring House and we shall earn the gratitude not only of the widows but of the Nation itself.

As I sat down at the end of my speech, I was pleased to have delivered it with satisfaction. I decided to remain in the Chamber listening to other Members making their Maiden Speeches, a number of these Members in later years becoming Ministers.

Within the procedures of Parliament there is an alternative method of securing information from Ministers on issues other than when the House is sitting, and it is Parliamentary Questions. When a Member has a matter of concern in the constituency, a Question can be submitted to the appropriate Minister to look into the matter and lodged at the Table Office. In due course the question and the response is published in Hansard for the record. There were many issues from my constituency which I raised and I had no hesitation in making use of this system to get a satisfactory answer. Here is just one example of a question from the member and the reply from the Minister:

'Fish Processing (East Aberdeenshire) (11th June 1979)
Mr. McQuarrie
To ask the Secretary of State for Scotland if he will visit the fish processing factories in East Aberdeenshire, in view of the continued threat to employment and the very existence of these factories due to the shortage of supplies and the high price paid for such stocks as are available.

Mr Younger: I have at present no plans to do so but, as I indicated to my Hon. Friend on 23 May-[Vol. 967, c*149*] - the position of the industry is being kept under review. In response to a request from the Herring Buyers'

Association, my Noble Friend the Minister of State, Scottish Office, and my Hon. Friend the Minister of State, Ministry of Agriculture, Fisheries and Food will meet the Association's representatives on 26 June, when these matters will no doubt be discussed.'

This response gave me the opportunity to assure the members of the fish processing factories in my constituency something was being done about the problem.

All during my time as a Member of Parliament I made use of the Parliamentary Questions to Ministers including the Prime Minister. My question to the Prime Minster on the 19th June 1979 is most interesting as it related to the matter of devolution in Scotland. At the time the ultimate decision was to take no action. Now thirty-three years later we are engaged in a debate where the Nationalists want to separate Scotland from the United Kingdom. I sincerely hope the result will be **No** once more. There is no doubt in my mind we are better under the United Kingdom than a separate and isolated Scotland. This is my question to the Prime Minster and her answer.

> Mr. McQuarrie asked the Prime Minister if she has fixed a date for setting up the all-party talks on the proposed constitutional changes in governmental working in Great Britain.

> The Prime Minister: My right hon. Friend the Chancellor of the Duchy of Lancaster will be approaching parties with Seats in Scotland about the possible framework of inter-party discussions.

Making use of the written Questions was a most useful tool to highlight issues within the Constituency worthy of attention while keeping the name of the Constituency of East Aberdeenshire to the fore.

My first Summer Recess

In July of 1979 the House rose for the recess. It would not sit again until October after the Party Conferences were over. As Roseleen and I did not take a break after my election we planned to cruise around the Greek Islands and on to Egypt and Israel. Our cruise liner was the *Daphne*, a splendid vessel with a fine swimming pool which I enjoyed immensely. From the liner we visited many interesting places in the Islands before travelling on to Egypt and Israel.

On a short stop-over in Cairo we took a trip to see the Pyramids on the western side of the Nile River. This turned out to be a fascinating excursion for me. To see many of these tombs built of blocks was wonderful but it

53. At the Pyramids in Cairo

was the moment when I climbed up about 10 feet on one of the Pyramids to find to my amazement on a ledge a loose stone of about 6" long by 3" deep and 2" wide. I carefully carried it under my arm as I cautiously returned to the ground. This piece of a pyramid sits proudly at my home to this day as a personal reminder of a very fine holiday to a place with such history.

We sailed on to Israel enjoying the pleasures and relaxation of the liner before taking a full day trip to Jerusalem which was yet another exciting day. One of the outstanding features we saw when arriving in the city was the bronze 'sculpture' like a huge candelabrum surrounded by iron railings, known as the Menorah. Our guide explained to us it represents one of the oldest symbols of the Jewish faith. Later we were fortunate to meet a Rabbi who explained the Menorah is a seven-branched candelabrum which is lit in the Sanctuary of the Temples every evening. It is cleaned in the morning, the wicks replaced and fresh olive oil is poured into the cup-shaped containers of the Menorah. Later we learned that today many of the Menorah are electrified.

54. In Jerusalem at the Menorah

Moving on to the Seat of Israel Parliament called the Knesset, we saw how it was built on a hill in a district known as Givat Ram. Much of the finance to pay for the building was left to the State in the Will of James A. de Rothschild, a very wealthy member of the Jewish Community. This new building was dedicated on the 31st August 1966. It is a splendid building with, at the time of our visit, many up-to-date facilities lacking at the Palace of Westminster although I much prefer what we have and the history of the Palace of Westminster.

Included in the visit to the Old Town of Jerusalem was a tour of a number of buildings connected with the rich history of the town. Many have been retained in their original construction, reminding people of the profound history it holds which the people of Israel can be justly proud.

The final visit of this fascinating day took us to the Wailing Wall in the eastern part of Jerusalem. I had often heard of the Wailing Wall which is a sacred place and visited by so many people every day looking towards the wall often with their hands placed on the wall while praying. We saw people pressing Prayer Petitions into the seams of the wall with a plea for a cure of an illness or a plea for a remedy to a problem. Roseleen and I made our way to the Wall and with our hands pressed on the Wall said our prayers followed by placing a written petition into the Wall as others were doing.

55. Back on board the Daphne

DOWN TO WORK AS AN MP

We departed Jerusalem glad to have the opportunity of seeing the wonderful city and the custom of the Jewish people. It took us back to the days of our childhood when Jerusalem was an important part of the religious lessons at school. Like other places we have visited the memories of this visit will never leave us, but I do have to say there was something very special about this one.

Later in the evening we met up with friends in the Cocktail Bar of the *Daphne*. With high spirits we told them of our most wonderful day to one of the most historic places in the world. The following day we relaxed while sailing back to Athens for our flight to London and onward to Aberdeen and our home at Teuchar Lodge.

Back to work as an MP

During the House of Commons Recess a Member's mail is re-addressed and delivered by Special Delivery each day to the Member's home address. It is clearly marked 'MP's mail for urgent delivery'. During the time we were cruising a number of these packages had been despatched from the House of Commons Mail Office to my home awaiting my attention on my return. Having cleared all mail prior to our holiday, I was surprised to find the bundles of mail which had to be dealt with – the holiday was well and truly over! I tackled the constituent's queries the very next day seeking the help of the staff at the Constituency Office in Mintlaw to type up letters to the constituents and also to the person or firm who could help with the case raised by the constituent. Within a short time I saw it was necessary for me to make arrangements for my mail to be dealt with on certain days which would allow me to get out into the constituency to meet the people in their own area.

My plan was to visit every town and village in the constituency in addition to calling on businesses where I would be able to meet people at work. I purchased a Camper Van - not to sleep in – which I would use to get around and which was suitable for me to meet constituents to discuss their problems. The local newspapers printed the notice of the date, time and location of the places I would visit from Monday to Friday. Constituents took advantage of my visits to their community to seek the help of their Member of Parliament. This proved to be an outstanding success which I continued each summer. Saturday mornings were left for engagements like coffee mornings while Sunday was a day of rest and a day spent with family other than attending church where the elderly Minister on walking up the aisle before the Service would exclaim, without fail, 'Oh, here's our Member of Parliament; good day Mr McQuarrie'. His remark every Sunday embarrassed me a little until I remembered the saying 'I don't mind what you say about me, so long as you mention my name!'

The summer recess was a busy time with continual constituency work undertaken for individuals and firms related largely to the main industries of the area of agricultural and fishing and the indigenous businesses related to them. Before returning to London for the start of a new Parliamentary session, I attended my first Party Conference as a Member of Parliament. It was paramount solidarity was shown towards Margaret Thatcher at her first Conference as Prime Minister in her tremendous efforts of turning around the fortunes of the United Kingdom which she did with the support of her backbenchers like me.

The House of Commons then became busy with Members returning to their offices after the long summer recess, to their respective committee work, dealing with mail - which took priority - collected daily from the Member's Post Office and taking part in the debates in the Chamber. On many occasions it was not unusual to be approached by a journalist from the 'Lobby' – the term used for press reporters who had access to MPs in the members' Lobby – for comment on some topical issue in Government or an incident in the constituency which the Member would be keeping his eye on. I learned fast one should never be backward in making comment to the journalists as it was their job to feed the comment or information to the national or local newspapers which in turn gave publicity to the Member and also was a means of informing constituents of the work of their MP.

In an earlier Chapter I mentioned the majority of Members are appointed to Select Committees which generally met in the morning and additionally there is the All Party Group Committees who meet regularly each month. The British Gibraltar Group was of particular interest to me as early in 1981 the Home Secretary had issued proposals to force the people of Gibraltar to be Dependent Territory Citizens ceasing their right to be British Citizens which they had been since 1704. The proposal and the outcome is the subject of another Chapter in the book.

I made a decision to attend the Chamber as regularly as possible as debates very often affected my constituency. By taking my seat on the 'green benches' it also gave me the opportunity to catch the Speaker's eye if I wished to raise a matter on the subject being debated and which would result in some positive action by the particular Minister answering questions from the Despatch Box. Such occasions always drew comment from the Journalists of the local newspapers, who reported the story, giving publicity to the Member which was no bad thing!

With the election of a Conservative Government voted in to turn the fortunes of the country around, and although the House of Commons was a busy place there was much to be attended to in the constituency. It can be well and truly said, like a housewife, an MP's work is never ending as issues are raised by constituents and all sorts of situations develop within Local Government and in Communities where the Member is invited to take an interest for the benefit of the people. In representing a fishing and farming area whose hard working leaders were seeking assurances restrictions in work practice would not be imposed by the European Economic Community, it was necessary for me to attend meetings with the industries' representatives and to give assurances I would take their suggestions and their grievances to the Minister.

In October 1979 I made a last gasp effort to save the Buchan freight line from closure. Over the previous months I had been in negotiation with British Rail pleading for the line to be retained. As the response was negative I set up a meeting with Mr Kenneth Clark, Minister of State at the Department of Transport. I arranged for a representative from Grampian Regional Council and Banff & Buchan District Council to be present at the meeting. We met Mr Clark at his London Office. He was told that it would be catastrophic if the line was to close and the track lifted. For two hours we tried to explain to the Minister the serious situation which would arise. Mr Clark indicated he would investigate the situation as soon as possible hoping the closure could be avoided. After two weeks I met Mr Clark who advised me after careful consideration the closure would have to take place. Sadly the line closed, the track was lifted and the line became the Buchan and Formartine Walkway the responsibility of the Local Government who bought the track for £1.00.

The current ongoing talk of cutting public expenditure brings back to memory a speech I made in October 1979 to members of the Peterhead Branch of my Conservative and Unionist Association. There was much discussion at that time about the decision taken by the labour force at Lawsons of Dyce to turn down a consortium takeover package which would have secured 600 jobs. The package with a value of £2½ million included a 12 per cent increase in pay for the workers which the workers felt could be improved. In addressing the Branch I made it clear the Government would not tolerate such actions and I made the suggestion the country was turning into one of greed by the actions of some workforces. I added this Government would stick to its principles of the three C's – consideration, conciliation and co-operation and made it clear there was no intention on the part of the Government to place unnecessary restrictions upon the public, but the Unions would be required to 'toe the line'.

It is ironic that the words used in the situation at Lawsons of Dyce in 1979 are virtually repeated by the present Conservative and Liberal Coalition Government in these years of austerity some thirty-four years on.

The successful and activity packed year of 1979 was concluded over the Christmas and New Year at Teuchar Lodge with our son Dermot, his wife and children who were watched over by the ever faithful Sybil Wallace our Housekeeper. It was a joy for us to be together and to be joined by two friends of many years, Peggy and Chris Paterson who were regular visitors to Teuchar Lodge from Greenock and in later years from Largs in Ayrshire.

CHAPTER TEN

Mr Fish and the Buchan Bulldog

THERE ARE VERY FEW Members of Parliament who receive a 'nickname' from the media which sticks to them. When I became a Member of Parliament, never in my wildest dreams did it occur to me I would be the recipient of a nickname. It is a journalist's delight for anyone to have a nickname and in my case it was not just one but two which were given to me by journalists in the Scottish media. They were Mr Fish and the Buchan Bulldog. The former was given for raising matters about the fishing industry in the Commons but it did not last long. It was overtaken by 'The Buchan Bulldog'. This chapter sets out how it arose and how it has remained in use by the media even up to the present time.

In 1979 the fishing industry, both offshore and onshore, was suffering badly because of other European fishermen plundering our waters. I fought hard in the Commons Chamber by way of questioning Ministers at length to obtain justice for my constituents bearing in mind that the combined fishing ports of East Aberdeenshire were the largest in Europe. As a result of my speaking on this matter so often, the Labour Opposition Members called me 'Mr Fish'. The media became aware of this, referring to 'Mr Fish' when reporting my activities on behalf of the fishing industry at Westminster, especially my efforts to gain a fifty mile fishing limit for all Scottish fishermen which included a visit to Brussels when the case was put to Members of the European Parliament. I did not object to 'Mr Fish' so long as it attracted the attention of the Ministers. I even pressed the Prime Minister to step in and persuade her Ministers to take action which she certainly did. During discussions she promised to visit my constituency to see the position for herself, a promise which was honoured.

While I was fighting for the fishing industry I was on a similar course for the farmers in my constituency who were being adversely treated by the European Union regarding farm subsidies. There was an urgent need for a proper Common Agricultural Policy covering the European countries within the Union which would not discriminate against our farmers. I had a number of meetings with the Secretary of State for Agriculture, Fisheries and Food (Mr Peter Walker) and the Minister of State (Mr Alick Buchanan-Smith) pressing them for a fairer Common Agriculture Policy from Europe which would safeguard the farming industry. Both had a positive outlook on the need for a reformed CAP and were well aware of the concerns expressed to them by the National Farmers Union and other farming organisations. The farmers acknowledged how the Ministers were striving to secure a reformed CAP while I was watchful the farming industry did not suffer further difficulties on subsidies.

56. The Buchan Bulldog canvassing

Luckily the farmers did not label me with a nickname. It was fortunate because on 20th June 1980 in an article by William Raynor a journalist writing in the *Aberdeen Evening Express* profiled me with the heading 'The Buchan Bulldog' which was accompanied by a large photograph of me. At once the name 'Mr Fish' ceased and I found myself with a new nickname which was adopted by the media.

William Raynor headed his article with the words 'Within the last 24 hours East Aberdeenshire's battling Tory MP has been nuzzling Employment Minister James Prior into action over a dispute at St Fergus Gas terminal; and, much more important for the region as a whole dug his teeth deep into Scottish Home and Minister Health Minister Russell Fairgrieve and the Grampian Health Board'. William Raynor completed the heading of his article with the words, printed boldly, **The Buchan Bulldog**.

This was the introduction to the name 'Buchan Bulldog'. Readers may be interested in the article written by William Raynor. I thank *Aberdeen Evening*

MR FISH AND THE BUCHAN BULLDOG

Express for permission to print extracts.

Bulldogs have one quality above all. Once they get their teeth into something, they stand firm and square and won't let go.

So if the MP for West Aberdeenshire has any illusions that a pat on the back or a few soothing words will be enough to persuade the MP for East Aberdeenshire to drop his latest bone of contention, he's likely to be disappointed.

The former, of course, is Russell Fairgrieve, whose job as Scottish Minister for Home and Health comes embarrassingly close to the bone, which in this instance is the competence of the Grampian Health Board to serve the best interests of the people within its bailiwick.

The latter is his Tory colleague Albert McQuarrie – a man whose stocky frame, heavy jowls and determined glint give him more than a passing resemblance to this most canine breed.

Not only that. Even where bones have been much less juicy than the Health Board's refusal to allow advanced heart surgery in Aberdeen, or its threat of closure against outlying maternity units, Albert McQuarrie has shown in the past that he can play bulldog with the best of them, and play to win.

Early in the life of this Parliament, he was the leader of the Scottish Tories who took their protest against Government plans to axe promised defence jobs in Glasgow. The group took the matter right to Prime Minister Margaret Thatcher in Number 10, and extracted a satisfactory compromise.

He may have the makings of a cartoonist's dream, and some of his opinions may seem, naïve and easy to ridicule, but he has proved that he is not to be underestimated.

This is just the mistake said to have been made by members of the dispirited Tory Association in East Aberdeenshire who thought he'd be no more than a stopgap, giving them time to find someone more suitable after the next sure-fire defeat.

And just the mistake made by the man they thought would again defeat them - the conscientious usurper from the SNP, Douglas Henderson.

But had he and they looked more closely at Albert McQuarrie's background, they might have learned otherwise – or been better prepared.

Perhaps what helped to make Albert McQuarrie such an ungaugeable quantity was his fierce pride, not just in being British but, most unusually for an aspiring

Tory, in being a battling Clydesider, working class to boot.

He is a man without synthetic airs and graces. His father, an ex Scots Guardsman, worked in the shipyard at Greenock, was six foot four, and wore a belt which was swiftly removed if any of the young McQuarries needed to be chastised.

It was in no sense cruelty,' says the MP 'It was discipline, and it had a great effect on my life.

He has the fondest memories of his childhood, and although he says he's been very lucky with his own son. Dermot, a one-time reporter for STV, (now with Fox International in the USA as Senior Vice President and Executive Producer) he's sad that the sort of respect he felt for his parents is not as widespread among teenagers today.

He was a Junior Imperialist when the war claimed him to the Corps of Royal Engineers in a bomb disposal unit, and when the war ended he rejoined what had become the Junior Unionists. From there, his interest in the lot of the elderly took him on to Gourock Town Council – where he says "my political life really started". He became Dean of Guild.

Meanwhile, he had gone into the building business with his father, and married a Renfrewshire girl named Roseleen. At the expense of his political ambitions, his business prospered, although his wife recalls hearing him say, early on in their marriage, one day he was going to sit in the House of Commons.

His first try was in 1966, a bad year for the Tories, against Willie Ross the Secretary of State for Scotland (late Lord Ross of Marnock) whose majority in Kilmarnock was 14,000.

But Westminster's loss was Glasgow's – and later Gibraltar's – gain. When the great storm of January 1968 stripped tenement roofs in their hundreds, McQuarrie became the biggest private contractor, employing between 750 and 1,000 men on repairs.

And after General Franco closed the Rock's border a year later, McQuarrie had a telephone call from Michael Stewart, the Foreign Secretary. The colony had lost all its Spanish building workers, and one of McQuarrie's friends, an MP who was also a director of his company, had suggested he could help. He exported his workforce, topped it up with Moroccan building trade workers from Tangiers, and spent over six years in Gibraltar building barracks, housing, hospitals, health centres and schools.

He returned to Scotland and, as a face-saver for the Tories, whose candidate had fallen pregnant, was given five weeks to fight Robert MacLennan in Caithness and Sutherland for the October 1974 election. He failed to win but would have stayed on to fight again had East Aberdeenshire not come out of the blue.

Until the SNP captured it in February that year, it had been over fifty years in Tory hands, first under Robert Boothby, then under Patrick Wolrige-Gordon. McQuarrie thought it was winnable and started nursing it in earnest when he moved to Teuchar Lodge at Cuminestown. His business, which had almost abandoned building to become the selling agency for Bredero Homes, was moved to Ellon. It's an arrangement which some in the light of Bredero's involvement with Aberdeen District Council, may regard as a little too close for comfort, but which he fiercely and openly defends. It is right and proper, he insists, for his business to be in his constituency and subject to the same vicissitudes.

It certainly did him no harm. He restored Tory morale, built up the party organisation made himself known "I don't care what you say about me," he told one friend, "but just keep mentioning my name".

His enthusiasm and his confidence paid off, as did the efforts of the ladies recruited by his wife to canvass in marginal wards, and he slid into Parliament last May with a majority of 558.

In a party still, if unfairly, saddled with the grouse-moor image, he cuts an incongruous figure, and among more progressive Tories, his views on emotive issues like capital punishment for terrorists, and for the killers of women, children and police officers – "it's the old story." he says, "an eye for an eye, a tooth for a tooth" – no doubt set tongues a-tutting.

Extracts from William Raynor's article.

From that date on it became quite common for Members and Ministers to use the expression 'The Buchan Bulldog' when referring to me in the Palace of Westminster. An illustration of this occurred on 22nd June 1981 when an article by James Naughtie, a journalist at the *Scotsman* (now a Presenter on Radio 4) with the heading 'The Buchan Bulldog makes his mark'. He made a number of comments in the article which are worthy of inclusion in my memoirs. I set out a few of the paragraphs and express my thanks to Scotsman Publications for permission to publish them.

Albert McQuarrie; "Mr Fish" "The Buchan Bulldog". Names to conjure with indeed. It can safely be said that the Honourable Member for East Aberdeenshire is now firmly established as one of the Commons favourite characters.

That is not to say that Mr McQuarrie is seen as a figure of fun. The Prime Minister would be the first to admit after his spectacular revolts over petrol prices and the effect on Gibraltar on the Nationality Bill that Albert can be troublesome when he is firing on all cylinders - as he always seems to do.

Over the past month or two as Westminster hearties have assessed the fortunes of the 1979 intake of MPs the name McQuarrie has been popping up with remarkable – some would say, alarming – regularity. He has made an impression. The Opposition tend to give a good natured moan as he rises in his place, and it is said that the Tory Chief Whip has now given up calling him in for a dressing down for rebelling – or threatening to rebel – against the Government.

Mr McQuarrie has the makings of a Commons character. First of all he looks the part. He is a substantial figure and he sits just two benches behind Mrs Thatcher where he has the advantage of catching the Speaker's eye quite easily and standing more or less in centre stage.

Mr McQuarrie's record as it is remembered by his colleagues, consists of a series of well-timed banana skins slung in the path of the Government. On petrol prices he was the most voluble opponent of the 20p rise introduced in the Budget. He helped to reduce the Government's majority to their lowest level since the General Election.

On Gibraltar he spoke passionately for the rights of the inhabitants of the Rock (speaking from his own experience) and helped build up the head of steam which might yet burst out on the Government in the Lords. On sundry other issues he has been well forthright.

The strength of the McQuarrie approach is that he clearly revels in the attention it brings. But that, of course, irritates his colleagues. There were some awkward moments during the petrol revolt when five rural Tory MPs decided to conduct a detailed investigation into the oil companies' pricing policy and the disparities between city and rural costs. Albert, who was leading the public rebellion, was not particularly amused and made his feelings known. Where, he asked, were they in the Opposition lobbies when the vital vote was called?

So facts. Mr McQuarrie became known at one stage as "Mr Fish" because of his dedicated defence of the interests of the North-East fishermen, a role which he has filled with enthusiasm and commitment. In this context he is apt to make reference to Lord Boothby, an illustrious predecessor in East Aberdeenshire with whom, not unnaturally, Mr McQuarrie finds some affinity.

He {Mr McQuarrie} speaks in the House, most would admit, with great force. But probably just as important he has developed the art of the audible intervention. As Mr Michael Foot springs to the despatch box, a loud cry of "rubbish" may occasionally be heard. It is always worth betting 5p that it is Mr McQuarrie.

In committee he intervenes regularly, more often from a sedentary position. But what is notable is he is just as ready to heckle a Minister as an Opposition spokesman if he thinks he should. He doesn't care.

Naturally this leads to slight contretemps with the party from time to time. After the Gibraltar episode, one MP suggested unkindly that there should be designed after the manner of the Anti-Nazi League badges, a lapel badge saying "Rock against Thatcher".

Yes Mr McQuarrie is a strong supporter of the Government. After the petrol revolt he was heard to say to the objectors who argued the Government needed the income that his action would help to teach the Cabinet "wets" to make more cuts. So it is not always a simple rebellion. Sometimes it is confusing.

But it is safe to state that there will be more of them. Albert McQuarrie had decided that the Commons is the place to make a noise, and indeed that it is hardly worth being there if you do not. So we can expect some more fireworks from that direction. **Extracts from article by James Naughtie.**

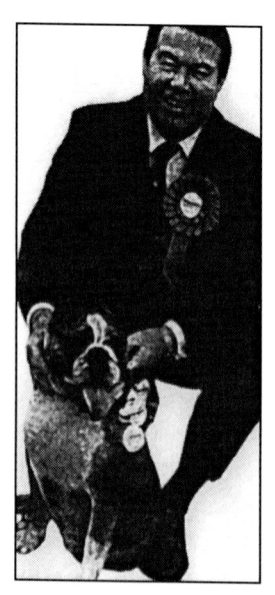

57. The Buchan Bulldog and Dog

As the name stuck to me during my service as a Member from then on I made good use of it during the 1983 General Election when I was selected to contest the new seat of Banff and Buchan, arising out of Parliamentary Boundary Revision. I found a good Tory supporter who had a bulldog. My photograph was taken with the dog and that photograph was used in part of

137

my Election Address to the electors of Banff and Buchan. It most certainly worked as I almost doubled my majority against the same candidate I had defeated in 1979!

I became quite accustomed to being called the 'Buchan Bulldog' in a variety of headings in the local and national media. When I addressed the Peterhead Probus Club, the *Buchan Observer* came out with the heading 'Buchan Bulldog wows Probus' and gave a detailed report in my speech which covered the time when Her Majesty The Queen conferred the Knighthood on me. The speech was well received as was evident by the newspaper heading.

On another occasion when I was addressing the Gordon Constituency Conservative and Unionist Association the *Aberdeen Press & Journal* reported with the heading 'Buchan Bulldog loses none of his bark or bite'. Reporting on the same meeting, another local paper issued an article with the heading 'Buchan Bulldog's Rallying call to Gordon Tories'. Another headline by a Scottish newspaper reporting on political speech I had made headed the article with the words 'The Buchan Bulldog Barks Again'. I could go on and on with many more examples.

I recall one heading which stated 'Buchan Bulldog roars out his defiance at Sir Keith'. This referred to the time when Sir Keith Joseph was Secretary of State for Education. He had brought out proposals to cut student grants which brought fierce opposition from many back-bench Conservative MPs. Around 200 Members attended a meeting to which I had requested Sir Keith to attend. He was visibly shaken at the reception given to him by the MPs.

In my speech I made it clear that many Members were not prepared to accept his proposals, stressing that I had not seen such strength of feeling on a single issue since becoming an MP. I challenged Sir Keith to revise the proposals and return with a set which would be acceptable to the Conservative Members. After listening to a number of Members speeches on the matter Sir Keith agreed to take the proposals back for amendment. This pleased me and my colleagues. We saw it as a good step forward.

Here are a few more quotes referring to the Buchan Bulldog – the first from a Member's speech in June 1981:

> The Government has been forced to capitulate because of pressure from its back-benchers, notably the Hon Member for Aberdeenshire East (Mr McQuarrie). Having had their backsides bitten by the Buchan Bulldog, the Government is determined to muzzle the Bulldog and put him back in his kennel by introducing measures such as this Motion.
>
> I am glad to see the Hon Member for Aberdeenshire East (Mr McQuarrie) in the Chamber. I nearly called the Buchan Bulldog my Hon Friend. He listens

with respect to what I have to say, whether or not he agrees with me. People speak about the Hon Gentleman in glowing terms all over Scotland because of his courageous stance in backing my Private Member's Bill and his courageous stance in favour of the good people of Gibraltar.

I hope that other Government Back-benchers will follow the Buchan Bulldog's courageous example. I am sure that his constituents hold him in a higher regard than ever. Now is the time for people, whatever their party allegiance, to stand up against the Government and their ludicrous, unjustifiable proposal, because it is one of the worst acts of vandalism in the history of Scottish education.

In conclusion it is most interesting how the name 'Buchan Bulldog' still attracts the media twenty-six years after losing my seat in the British Parliament. I am grateful to have been given a nickname which runs on whenever I am mentioned in the media. I wish to express my sincere thanks to all the journalists and media who continue to call me 'The Buchan Bulldog' and assure them I am still barking at 95 years plus!

CHAPTER ELEVEN

The British Nationality Bill, 1981

A MEMBER OF PARLIAMENT IS often asked to support something which is at odds with the Government. I was asked by other Members to lead a protest against a Government proposal. The issue was the British Nationality Bill 1981 introduced by the Secretary of State for the Home Department, Rt Hon William Whitelaw. Meetings were arranged with Ministers and ferocious battles took place in the House of Commons.

Mr Whitelaw stressed the existing nationality law was out of date and needed to be replaced. The section which raised the ire was the intention to create two classes of citizenship for those living in the Dependent Territories and others in the British Colonies. Under the new Bill they were to be classified as Dependent Territory Citizens and British Overseas Citizens.

I was contacted by Members of the Government of Gibraltar who had already passed a Motion in the House of Assembly condemning the proposals which they saw as the removal of a right which the people of Gibraltar had enjoyed since 1704.

58. Aerial view of Gibraltar

THE BRITISH NATIONALITY BILL, 1981

They were outraged, Mr Whitelaw would not budge on the terms of the proposed Bill. Protests were held throughout Gibraltar and Members of Parliament who supported Gibraltar deluged Ministers demanding changes to the Bill. The Secretary of State for the Home Department refused to make any alteration at all.

At the Second Reading in the House of Commons on 28th January 1981, Members on all sides of the House attacked the proposals. They made powerful speeches leaving the Secretary of State in no doubt about the strength of feeling against the proposal.

The depth of concern in Gibraltar was such, Sir Joshua Hassan, the Chief Minister, and other Gibraltar Ministers flew to London to meet with Members from all sides of the House to gather support for an Amendment to be made to remove the proposal designating the people of Gibraltar as Dependent Territory Citizens. At 6.24 p.m. on 28th January 1981 I was called to speak - reported in Hansard at Column 968/969/970 of 29th January 1981 - for which I am grateful.

This huge problem concerning Gibraltar had been taken up by me as leader of the Commons Protest Group and also as Chairman of the All Party Gibraltar Group. I am sure readers of this book will find it interesting to learn of the tremendous effort made in support of the people of Gibraltar. I have inserted extracts from my Speech into the book for the record.

Mr Albert McQuarrie (Aberdeenshire East):

I speak as Chairman of the British Gibraltar Group, and in that capacity wish to refer specifically to Part II of the Bill, which seeks to create a new definition of British Dependent Territory Citizens, and to Schedule 6, which includes the Dependent Territory of Gibraltar which will be required to accept Dependent Territory Citizenship status if the Bill is passed.

The Minister is well aware of the considerable concern which has been expressed in Gibraltar about the Bill. It is seen as downgrading its citizens from their present position, which they consider to be Gibraltar British. They feel this sense of belonging to Britain will be removed if the Bill is passed with Schedule 6 in its present form.

In his written reply to my Parliamentary question my Right Hon Friend the Home Secretary said although the proposals in the Bill laid down that birth in, or other close connection with, Gibraltar would qualify the holders for Citizenship of the British Dependent Territories *"this decision in no way alters the Constitutional position of Gibraltar in relation to the United Kingdom"*. My Right Hon Friend also indicated the people of Gibraltar have the right as "United Kingdom nationals for European Community purposes" – [*Official Report,* 15

January 1981; Vol. 96, c.612] to enter the United Kingdom to seek and take up employment.

There is a strong case to consider the special factors which relate to Gibraltar. At present, no restriction is placed on the number of Gibraltarians allowed to enter the United Kingdom for employment, and to settle. They are subject to no form of control after entry, nor are they required to register with the police. They are eligible for any type of employment in Britain and their employment is not conditional upon there being no local labour available.

These agreements were made in 1968 by the then Labour Government, and although assurances have been given by successive Governments there would be no change in the future, the passing of the Bill will give this Government, or any future Government, the right to withdraw these concessions and to place upon Gibraltar restrictions which do not exist at present. Therefore, what assurance can my Hon Friend the Minister give, if Gibraltar is not removed from Schedule 6 and its people will not lose the rights they enjoy now? I hope the assurance will be forthcoming when my Hon Friend winds up the debate.

59. Changing the Guard at Governor's House.
I am next to him on the balcony. He is in uniform

THE BRITISH NATIONALITY BILL, 1981

There is also the question, in support of the Gibraltarians' wish to become British citizens, of the proposals by the Commission to the Council of the European Communities, dated 31 July 1979. It concerns a Council directive on a right of residence for nationals of member States independent of the pursuit of an occupational activity in the territory of another member State. If this proposal were to be approved by the Council of Ministers, Gibraltarians, as United Kingdom Community nationals would have the right of abode in Britain. If they have the right of abode by the 1968 assurances, and the 1979 proposals, surely the Minister should accept this strengthens the case for the Gibraltarians to be excluded from Schedule 6 and retain their position, or at least have the right of dual nationality.

Over a period of many years the national status of the people of Gibraltar as British subject citizens of the United Kingdom and the Colonies has been shared with the people of the United Kingdom, and has been a source of great pride to the Gibraltarians. Their ties with the people of the United Kingdom have been stronger than anywhere else in the world. Gibraltar has been a British fortress and naval base for nearly three centuries, which has resulted in a deep sense of patriotism and identification with Great Britain. The measures in this Bill will, therefore, create a most unfortunate divide, which would be a sad reflection on Great Britain, when the Gibraltarians' loyalty to Britain is so deeply felt by all who live there in difficult circumstances.

If the Minister cannot see his way to make this gesture now and undertake to remove Gibraltar from Schedule 6, when the Bill goes to Committee Hon Members who are selected to serve there will table amendments which should be acceptable to the Minister and result in the Government agreeing to the request of the Gibraltarians in respect of their citizenship position. It will maintain the depth of trust which the people of Gibraltar have for the United Kingdom. As dual nationality is being retained in the Bill, it should be given to Gibraltar. We honoured Malta during the last war for its gallant effort against the enemy; Let us now honour Gibraltar by acceding to this simple request – one which is paramount to the future of all who live and work in Gibraltar, and who trust this Government to give them a fair deal.

I can only conclude by referring to a very simple, but impassioned, appeal that I have received from a group of ordinary people in Gibraltar. It is one of many that I have received. It states: "I am a Gibraltarian married with three sons. We are very proud to be British and to live in British Gibraltar, like the majority of Gibraltarians. I would like you to do all in your power for us please so that we can get the nationality citizenship of the United Kingdom when the White Paper comes out and keep Gibraltar British for ever. God bless our Queen.

Your faithful servant."

That letter, with others like it, has been sent to me because of the proposals in the Bill. Those who have written are like the 400 ex-Servicemen who stood by Britain in two world wars and the members of the Honourable Order of the British Empire who live in Gibraltar. They are all begging the Government not to alter the existing status of the people of Gibraltar.

Need I say more? The letter says it all. I hope that my Hon Friend the Minister of State will indicate that he will take the matter back for consideration and make amended proposals in respect of Gibraltar before the Bill comes back to the House on Third Reading.

Despite the most strenuous efforts on the part of every Member who was supporting Gibraltar we failed to persuade the Government to change course. The Bill was sent to a Committee of the House for examination to be returned later to the Chamber with a report on any Amendments. Although we were disappointed, the fight to gain justice for the people of Gibraltar continued.

On 2nd June 1981 the Bill returned to the Chamber for the Report Stage. Before the discussions commenced Mr Deputy Speaker made a statement from the Chair with the permission of Mr Speaker. A new Clause 7 would be entered into the Bill, the terms of which had been agreed in Cross-Party discussions and also Lord (Nicholas) Bethell who was our campaign leader in the Lords.

On that evening I was called at 10.45 p.m. having sat in the Chamber from 2.30 p.m. In these days Members spent many more hours in the House of Commons than it appears happens now. By courtesy of Hansard I am including here for the reader's interest the record of the New Clause and extracts from my speech.

> '**Mr Deputy Speaker:** I understand that the Hon Member for Aberdeenshire East (Mr McQuarrie) wishes to move new Clause 7 and it will be convenient for the House to take with it new Clause 6 – *Provisions of section 227(4) of the Treaty of Rome* – and the following amendments:
> No. 86, in clause 46, page 34, line 32, at end insert 'and Gibraltar'.
> No. 84, in Schedule 6, page 51, line 41, leave out 'Gibraltar'.
> I should inform the House that Mr Speaker has agreed to this procedure.
>
> **New Clause 7**
> RIGHT TO REGISTRATION BY VIRTUE OF UNITED KINGDOM NATIONALITY FOR EUROPEAN COMMUNITY PURPOSES
>
> 8A. Notwithstanding the provisions of Part II of this Act a person who has a right of abode in a British Dependent Territory to which the provisions of Article 227(4) of the Treaty of Rome apply or who is a United Kingdom

THE BRITISH NATIONALITY BILL, 1981

national for European Community purposes by virtue of the operation of Article 227(4) of the Treaty of Rome shall be entitled, on application, to be registered as a British Citizen. – [Mr McQuarrie]

10.45 p.m.

Mr Albert McQuarrie (Aberdeenshire East): 'I beg to move. That the clause be read a Second time.

I have to declare a special interest in the new clauses. Two of my grandchildren were born in Gibraltar. I also spent six and a half years in Gibraltar in a business capacity, erecting hospitals, schools, public buildings and Ministry of Defence and local authority housing. In that time I developed a deep affection for the people of Gibraltar.

New clause 6 and amendment are embodied in new clause 7, and I therefore propose to speak to the new clause and not to move new clause 6, a proposal which has met with the approval of Mr Speaker.

New clause 7 seeks to grant to the people of Gibraltar the right to registration by virtue of the status they now enjoy as United Kingdom citizens for European purposes. The acceptance of the new clause is essential if the House is to be seen to be safeguarding the interests of the Gibraltarians. It is accepted they have the right of abode as Community nationals by virtue of the operation of article 227 (4) of the Treaty of Rome.

It fully justifies the claim Gibraltar should be classed with the Isle of Man and the Channel Islands, people who enjoy full British citizenship under the Bill. None of the other dependent territories will be affected as the present status of the Gibraltarians was granted when we entered the EEC.

It is acknowledged that successive Governments have permitted Gibraltarians to enter and live in Britain and to be considered as equals when applying for employment in Britain. This is only at the discretion of the Government of the day and can be removed at any time if circumstances in the United Kingdom are such that the continuation of the discretion is difficult or impossible to maintain.

The people of Gibraltar live in constant fear these existing rights will be removed. The fear is genuine when one considers there is always the possibility of a future British Government withdrawing from the EEC, which would at once remove the Gibraltarians the right to be United Kingdom citizens for Community purposes under article 227.

The fear has been expressed in Gibraltar by the Chief Minister, Sir Joshua Hassan, Mr Peter Isola, the leader of the official Opposition, Mr Joe Bossano, an independent Member of the House of Assembly, and all Members of the House of Assembly.

It was summed up conclusively by the late Mr Samuel M Benady CBE, QC, Leader of the Bar in Gibraltar, who said in his address at the opening of the legal year in Gibraltar last year:

We have had many verbal assurances that the Gibraltarians would be afforded special treatment if they wish to enter, or reside, in the United Kingdom. These are mere assurances, but in law they have no right. Great Britain has said time and time again that it will sustain and support us, but I as a loyal British subject say to Britain – from these ancient benches of our Supreme Court – it is no use sustaining the body if you do not sustain the spirit.

Mr Benady said that in 1970, repeated it in 1977 and said it again in 1980, but the cry has gone unheeded by successive Governments. It is for the Government to answer the call. To approve new clause 7 would cause no upset for any other dependent territory or to any independent State. Mr Benady and his wife, Pat, were dear friends when I lived in Gibraltar.

My Right Hon Friend the Prime Minister has been made well aware of the deep feelings held by the vast majority in Gibraltar that they should not be classified as citizens of British Dependent Territories. My Right Hon Friend the Lord Privy Seal has been inundated with representations opposed to the Government's proposals. All have gone unheeded.

My Hon Friend the Minister of State, in a circular sent to those who wrote to my Right Hon Friend the Home Secretary protesting about the proposals, stated that the Government was aware of the strength of feeling in Gibraltar but felt bound to adhere to the view that "connections with Gibraltar should qualify people for citizenship of the British Dependent Territories and not for British citizenship".

Why should it be contrary to the purposes of the Bill to say for historical or some other reasons people from one territory should be treated differently from the rest? It was a closing of the door completely when the Minister of State, in a letter of 19 February to the Hon Member for West Stirlingshire (Mr Canavan), stated Gibraltar was not the only dependent territory for which people could make a claim for special treatment and to make an exception would go a long was towards nullifying the whole idea of citizenship for dependent territories.

Even in the letter, the element of fear for the future held by the Gibraltarians was shown up when the Minister of State wrote that under the Government's proposals they would become citizens of the dependent territories would not 'materially' affect their existing position in relation to the United Kingdom. Yet

THE BRITISH NATIONALITY BILL, 1981

he has stated consistently the Gibraltarians would not be affected by the Bill. How does he, therefore, justify his remark they will not be 'materially' affected?

My Hon Friend the Minister of State concluded his letter by stating he was convinced the Government's proposals were on the right track. The proposals have been rejected totally by the people of Gibraltar as a sell-out and a reduction to second-class citizenship with no legal guarantees for the status the Gibraltarians now enjoy.

60. Gibraltar's New Marina

[New clause 7, if accepted by the House, will give the Gibraltarians a right on application to be registered as British citizens. These two words 'on application' mean that any person from Gibraltar can opt for British citizenship or retain his Gibraltarian status. It must not be forgotten that for more than 300 years the Gibraltarians have been under British rule.

There is no need to dwell on the hardships, abuses and difficulties inflicted on Gibraltar since 1954. They are well known in the House and the country. It is sufficient to say that the patriotism for their own city and for Britain was aroused to a degree never known before. In the 1967 referendum, 12,138 Gibraltarians voted in a poll of 95.8 per cent for British sovereignty. Forty-four people voted to be linked with Spain. This situation remains as strong today. While the majority of Gibraltarians work in harmony with Spanish people, they do not want Spanish citizenship.

The new clause will give them the right to choose. It will also remove the stigma which was placed on the people of Gibraltar after the Bill was published, when Spanish newspapers reported Gibraltar, on the passing of this legislation, would be nothing more than a colony of monkeys (a disgraceful assertion).

Shall we allow this Bill to be the final chapter in the long history which has existed between the Gibraltarians and the British people? 'Solid as the rock' means more than just a piece of hard stone to the Gibraltarians. It means a steadfast determination never to give in.

If new clause 7 is not accepted, it will be to our undying shame we have let down the people who are more British than the British, who served this country in its time of need through two world wars and who now look to this House to grant them the legal right to become British citizens if they so choose. This is what new clause 7 will do.

All in Gibraltar and many hundreds of thousands of supporters of Gibraltar in Britain and overseas look to the Minister to accept this new clause. If he fails to do so, we shall divide the House in an effort to secure success for the desire of the Gibraltarians to remain first-class British citizens with legal rights.

The Home Secretary presented the case for the Government in a speech which endeavoured to justify the reason why the Government could not accept the New Clause. It is worthwhile recording extracts from the speech which appeared to satisfy a majority of Members. We were not convinced at his comments and tried to make the point that the New Clause gave the people of Gibraltar security of the position they had enjoyed since 1704.

Extract from Mr William Whitelaw's speech – 02/06/1981

The clause was moved with great passion and feeling, which I fully appreciate, by my Hon Friend the Member for Aberdeenshire East (Mr McQuarrie). As he said, it would not remove Gibraltar from the ambit of British overseas citizenship. Rather, it would entitle a citizen of the British Dependent Territories from Gibraltar to have British citizenship if he asked for it. The clause does this by enabling those who have the right of abode in a Dependent Territory to which article 227(4) of the Treaty of Rome applies, and those who are United Kingdom nationals for European Community purposes through their links with such a territory, to be entitled to acquire British citizenship on application.

'In seeking to make a more coherent and logical system of citizenship, we were influenced by the argument the status of the remaining dependencies should be positively recognised in citizenship terms. This is why we created a separate citizenship of the British Dependent Territories to be held by those who have

THE BRITISH NATIONALITY BILL, 1981

ties with the dependencies. It is not a second-hand citizenship. We regard it as a parallel status to British citizenship, held on like terms.

Having created this citizenship, I believe it would be wholly unacceptable to exempt one dependency from it. This is precisely the sort of anomaly we sought to erase in the Bill. The clause would make an exception for one dependency, which would lead to demands for others, which could scarcely be resisted.

If we gave way to other dependencies, we would be back to where we are now, with an unsatisfactory position. Alternatively, we would have a new British citizenship with immigration commitments for the future which I am sure, nearly every Hon Member would regard as unacceptable. It is important I say this to the House. It is why I do not believe we should give way on the amendments.

I have explained the simple and straightforward reasons why I cannot advise the House to accept any of the amendments to give Gibraltar a special position. I fully understand the views put on behalf of the people of Gibraltar. However, I am convinced that I should be wrong and irresponsible in the long run to take any other position.

The Government have given specific assurances to Gibraltar. There is no question of the administrative concession which enables Gibraltarians to enter the United Kingdom freely being withdrawn as a result of the Bill. This concession is not affected. We have made it clear we intend to ensure the rights now enjoyed by the people of Gibraltar as part of the European Community should continue. Even if the circumstances were to alter, we have made it clear we do not foresee the Gibraltarians would normally face any difficulty in entering the United Kingdom as they wish.

I understand the arguments put by my Right Hon Friend and other Hon Members for making Gibraltar a special case. I do not believe, however, in the context of the Bill, that a special case can be conceded without consequences for Hong Kong. I cannot recommend the House to accept. On that basis, I must ask the House to reject the clause.'

End of Extracts

All our efforts seemed to have meant nothing to the Government in its determination to introduce the two new clauses of citizenship. It was not helped by the statement from Mr Timothy Raison saying 'the Government had carefully considered the representations and while the strength of feeling was accepted he did not think the House should accept New Clause 7 put forward by the Hon Member for Aberdeenshire East (Mr McQuarrie)'.

In the winding up speech, (extracts having been printed), by the

Secretary of State for the Home Office Mr Whitelaw, it was made quite clear the Government had no intention of letting New Clause 7 be incorporated into the Bill.

All we could do was to force a Division in the hope sufficient Members would support the people of Gibraltar by inserting new Clause 7 into the Bill.

Sadly when the Vote was taken the Ayes (us) had 248 vote and the Noes 273 – a majority against us of 25 which was a considerable achievement for our efforts and did not please either the Prime Minister or the Chief Whip. We were determined to fight on.

The Bill was sent to the House of Lords for consideration. This would be an important time as we would have to persuade the Lords to overturn the decision not to accept New Clause 7 and send it back to the Commons as part of the Bill.

I had an immediate meeting with Lord Bethell when we planned to introduce an amended New Clause. This was done at a Sitting of the Lords which I attended and watched with much interest on 22nd July 1981. The amended New Clause was carefully worded which we hoped would find favour with the Lords. Lord Bethell made a robust opening speech in support of the New Clause, ably supported by Lord Hughes, a former Scottish Minister in a previous Government. They were strongly supported by Lord Boyd-Carpenter, Lord Merrivale, Viscount Boyd and a number of Peers from both sides of the House.

The Government put up a fight to oppose the Amendment led by the Lord President of the Council (Lord Soames) who made a powerful speech to reject it. He was supported by many Peers including the Lord Chancellor (Lord Hailsham) who defended the Government's proposal to remove from the people of Gibraltar the rights they had since 1704. After six hours of debate a Vote was taken which resulted in a majority of 38 by the Lords to accept the new Clause as an Amendment to the Bill and return it to the House of Commons for approval. There was much rejoicing in Gibraltar at the news but I knew the battle was not over. I had a meeting with William Whitelaw, the Home Secretary, to discuss the Lord's Decision. After a period of discussion, and arguments, Mr Whitelaw told me he would not be changing his mind. This made me even more determined to defeat the Government, if necessary, when the Bill returned to the Commons after the Recess.

When the House of Commons resumed early in October 1981 I set about seeking support from Members on all sides to vote for the Lords Amendment when it was called in the Chamber. The response was most

THE BRITISH NATIONALITY BILL, 1981

encouraging to the degree I was certain we could overturn the 25 deficit we had on the Report Stage and win the vote in the Chamber.

On ascertaining the matter would be debated on 26th and 27th October I sought a meeting with the Home Secretary. We met on the Monday morning when I asked him whether the Government would be accepting the Amendment from the House of Lords. He said nothing had changed. The Government would be rejecting the New Clause. I made him aware that we had enough support in the House of Commons to defeat the Government and we were determined to do so if necessary. I reminded him that we had lost by only 25 votes last time and would find little difficulty in securing extra votes to win at the votes. He told me he would consider what I had said and would contact me the following day. I left him in the knowledge he was well aware of the new situation.

The next morning I had a call from the Home Secretary's office advising me that Mr Whitelaw was still rejecting the Lords New Clause but was bringing in another Government Amendment which should meet the requests we were seeking. A copy of the new Amendment was sent to my office in the House of Commons later that morning. When I read it I had a feeling of great joy as it was just what we had been working towards. I was asked to keep the information confidential until the Home Secretary made his speech at the Despatch Box.

I was in my place in the Chamber early. I did not want to miss one word of what the Home Secretary said. Additionally I wanted to try and ensure I could catch the Speaker's eye after the Home Secretary had spoken. I had prepared a speech after I had been given the good news by the Home Secretary's office.

The debate continued immediately after Questions. A good number of Members made speeches in support of the new Amendment. Others who were interested in some Dependent Territories were not in favour as they saw a situation of Gibraltar citizens receiving more favourable treatment than other territories.

On 27th October 1981 the Home Secretary wound up for the Government. I am setting out some of his comments which are pertinent to the case for Gibraltar. I hope readers will find them interesting.

The Amendment proposed by the House of Lords:

> A person who is a United Kingdom national for European Community Purposes by virtue of the operation of any of the pre-Accession Treaties listed in Part 1 of Schedule 1 to the European Communities Act 1872 shall be entitled, notwithstanding the provisions of Part 11 of this Act, on application, to be registered as a British citizen.

Mr William Whitelaw: I beg to move, that this House doth disagree with the Lords in the said **amendment**.

Mr Deputy Speaker: With this we may take the Government new clause in lieu – Acquisition by registration: nationals for purposes of the Community Treaties – Lords **amendment** No. 29 and Government motion to disagree, together with the Government **amendment** in lieu.

Mr William Whitelaw: The amendments are concerned with access to British citizenship by the people of Gibraltar. As the House knows, Gibraltar is the only British dependent territory whose people are treated as our nationals for the purpose of the Community treaties, and it was agreed in another place that, by virtue of this status, people from Gibraltar should be entitled to British citizenship on application. An amendment on those lines was moved by my Hon Friend the Member for Aberdeenshire East (Mr McQuarrie) on Report on 2 June. I explained then that I could not advise the House to give Gibraltar a special position under the Bill. Whilst we fully understood the views put forward on behalf of the people of Gibraltar, specific assurances had been given to them about arrangements for their entry to the United Kingdom. The House decided by a majority of 25 that special access to British citizenship should not be given to the people of Gibraltar.

61. The New Gibraltar

It was, however, clear that there was a large body of opinion in this House and elsewhere who continued to hold the view Gibraltar's position merited special treatment in the Bill. This was emphasised again when an amendment similar to that moved by my Hon Friend the Member for Aberdeenshire East, (Mr

McQuarrie), was moved in another place on 22 July. Again very strong pleas were made that the situation of Gibraltar, the nature of its ties with the United Kingdom and its position within the European Community justified a different approach to British citizenship for its people from that available to other citizens of the British Dependent Territories. The opposing arguments were formidably displayed, but, by a majority of 38, the amendment was agreed. Subsequently on Third Reading the wording of the amendment was somewhat modified, but its intention remains the same – to confer on the people of Gibraltar, as nationals for the purposes of the Community treaties, an unqualified entitlement to British citizenship.

The Government carefully considered what response they should make when the amendment passed in another place came to be considered by this House. We have to reckon with the fact that, though these arguments against the amendment were fully set out in another place, they did not win the day there. Moreover, though this House voted against giving people of Gibraltar special access to British citizenship, it did so only by a relatively slender margin. It is therefore clear, after hearing all the arguments, a considerable body of opinion in this House and another place remains convinced that special access to British citizenship for the people of Gibraltar is amply justified. The Government have therefore concluded that they should not ask the House to disagree with the Lords over this principle of their amendment. Accordingly we do not seek to oppose the principle that lies behind the amendment. I am afraid that we must oppose the amendment as drafted since it fails in our view to achieve its objectives.

We propose that the Lords amendment should be replaced by a simpler provision which will benefit solely those whom the movers of the amendments both in this House and in the Lords clearly intended to help. The new provision confers an unqualified entitlement on those British Dependent Territories Citizens who are United Kingdom nationals for the purposes of the Community Treaties. British Dependent Territories Citizens who derive that status from their links with Gibraltar are the only category of such citizens who fall to be United Kingdom nationals for the purposes of the Community Treaties.

Lords amendment No. 29 would mean that those registered under the Gibraltar amendment, if this House sees fit to accept it, would be British Citizens by descent. They would, therefore, be unable – unless they were in Crown service or other service relevant for the purposes of Clause 2 – to transmit their British citizenship automatically to a further generation born overseas.

The principle that lies behind this is surely right. After all, those who are registered under the Gibraltar amendment will in most, if not all, cases be born outside the United Kingdom. They will also normally be resident abroad, since the entitlement does not depend on a period of residence in this country, and need have no intention of coming to this country at any time during their lives. Their links with the United Kingdom are therefore comparable with those of other British citizens born abroad, and it seems logical they, like these other British citizens, should be British citizens by descent and should be able to transmit their citizenship.

We have decided to accept the principle of the amendment proposed and carried substantially in another place, and we have made the necessary technical adjustments to make sure that the amendment does exactly what the movers of it and those who voted for it in the House of Lords wished. This is the position, and I hope the House will accept it.

I was fortunate to be called by Mr Speaker after the speech made by Mr Whitelaw.

Mr Albert McQuarrie (Aberdeenshire East): I am sure in Gibraltar, a territory many thousands of miles away from Britain, there would be no radio not tuned in to this debate. I should like to make some comments on the new clause. Many of us in all parts of the House attempted to make the amendment before the Bill went to another place. In that respect we were unsuccessful (by just 25 votes). When the Bill reached the other place an amendment was tabled by Lord Bethell. The Government, in their wisdom, thought it necessary to bring in the heavyweights. Indeed, they brought in Lord Soames, who was then the Lord President of the Council, and no less a person than the Lord Chancellor, who replied to the debate. The Government failed. Indeed, they failed to such an extent the amendment is now brought back into this House as an amendment to the Bill.

I pay great tribute to the Home Secretary and to the Minister of State for the way in which they have handled the matter. I agree when it was debated in another place certain drafting amendments were necessary. They were accepted by my noble Friend Lord Bethell. My Right Hon Friend's new clause seeks to make it perfectly clear that the people of Gibraltar will be given the right on application for registration as British citizens. In my view, it has been a wise decision. The most important aspect of the new clause is the people of Gibraltar are United Kingdom citizens for Community purposes, and no other Territories have the right as of now.

It was therefore proper my Right Hon Friend should take cognisance of the decision taken in another place because the people of Gibraltar have suffered badly for eighteen years. They did not expect the British Government to let them down in their appeal. All Hon Members – even my Right Hon Friend the Prime Minister – were aware of the many thousands of petitions which were sent by the people of the Gibraltar pleading for a new clause to be inserted in

THE BRITISH NATIONALITY BILL, 1981

the Bill to permit the registration, which my Right Hon Friend has now conceded. It is a great moment for the people of and I assure my Right Hon Friend that there will be great joy in Gibraltar this evening. I thank my Right Hon Friend on behalf of the people of Gibraltar. If he ever finds time to visit Gibraltar, he will be more than welcome because its people have got what they wanted, to be British. In this respect, nothing better could have come out of the House this evening than the message to Gibraltar.

I sat down to wide acclamation from all sides of the House who welcomed this stunning victory on behalf of the people of Gibraltar.

When I returned to my office after the debate the telephone line was 'hot'. Sir Joshua Hassan, the Chief Minister for Gibraltar was first to congratulate me and all supporters for such a magnificent victory. I was humbled at the sincerity of his appreciation for helping to maintain Gibraltar's links with Great Britain and ensuring they would continue to be British citizens for all time.

On returning to my office in the Commons the next day the telephone calls kept coming. Notable of these was from Major Robert Peliza, a former Chief Minister of Gibraltar, who played such an important part in gathering support for our cause from the many Gibraltarians who either lived in the United Kingdom or other parts of the world. Sadly Major Peliza who later became the Hon Colonel of the Gibraltar Regiment and Speaker in the Gibraltar House of Assembly (now the Gibraltar Parliament) is no longer with us.

I was glad this battle was over successfully. My time was then devoted to the matters concerning the farmers, fishermen and all my constituents in Aberdeenshire East.

Some months into 1982 I received a letter from the Office of the Chief Minister of Gibraltar to say I was to have the Freedom of the City of Gibraltar conferred upon me for my efforts with the Nationality Bill. I was overwhelmed and excited at the news. I travelled to Gibraltar accompanied by Lord Bethell, Lord Wigoder QC, Lord Hughes, Rt Hon Denzil Davies MP and Mr Michael Latham MP, all members of the All Party Gibraltar Group, for the Ceremony on Saturday 23rd October 1982. I had requested the Chief Minister to issue an invitation to the Group as its members did a tremendous amount of work to ensure the passing of our Amendment and Group, for the Ceremony on Saturday 23rd October 1982. I had requested the Chief Minister to issue an invitation to the Group as its members did a tremendous amount of work to ensure the passing of our Amendment and also for him to recognise their contribution during the Ceremony.

62. Signing the Freedom Register

At the City Hall in front of a large crowd and in the presence of the Hon Abraham Serfaty, the Mayor of Gibraltar and a Member of the House of Assembly, I was sworn in as a Freeman of the City of Gibraltar. The scroll which was presented to me by the Mayor was enclosed in a piece of an olive tree grown in Gibraltar. At one end there is a silver medallion of the Coat of Arms of the City of Gibraltar and at the other is a silver medallion of the House of Commons Portcullis. Inside the piece of tree is the scroll which records the granting of the Freedom of the City on day. The 'tree' is mounted on a beautifully carved stalagmite which is millions of years old and was cut from an area in St Michael's Cave in Gibraltar. The piece was carved by a local marble manufacturer. His name was Anis. This was one of my most treasured memories.

There is however a sad part to the story. On my return to the House of Commons I placed the casket with the Scroll in the office of the Commonwealth Parliamentary Association in Westminster Hall in order that other Members could see this magnificent piece of work. It was much admired and for years I visited the CPA Office just to view it. After I lost my seat in 1987 I was seldom at the Palace of Westminster and over the years assumed the Casket and Scroll would still be safely in the hands of the CPA staff. On making contact with the CPA I was dismayed to learn that it could not be found. How such an important piece of history could be lost in

THE BRITISH NATIONALITY BILL, 1981

an Office is beyond me. I am still trying to trace it. If anyone reading this book can throw any light on its whereabouts I would be most grateful. In the meantime this most precious item can only be a memory for me. Fortunately I have a photograph of the Ceremony which shows the Scroll and Plinth placed on the table.

This part of my memories sets out how Members of the House of Commons can win the day against a Government proposal provided there is a justifiable case presented. In this instance the people of Gibraltar were to be denied the right of British Citizenship they had held since 1704. No wonder Westminster Members of Parliament, particularly those from the British Gibraltar All Party Group of which I had the honour to hold the Chairmanship from 1979 to 1987, are very welcome when visiting Gibraltar.

Opening of the Border Gates between Gibraltar and Spain

In mid-January 1985 Sir Joshua Hassan, Chief Minister of Gibraltar, advised me by confidential letter of a rumour that the Spanish Socialist Government had it in mind to open the border between Gibraltar and Spain. It had been closed since 1969. Over the years there was only one occasion when a border gate was opened. It was December 1982 when a small side gate was opened 'for humanitarian reasons'. From that time there were a number of occasions when people requiring hospital treatment at St Bernards Hospital were carried through the gate on a stretcher from an ambulance on the Spanish side and into an ambulance on the Gibraltar side.

At the end of January Sir Joshua advised me the border gates would be re-opened on 4th February 1985. He invited Roseleen and me to travel to Gibraltar from the UK to attend the opening. We were pleased to accept. Thousands of people were gathered at the gates on the Spanish and the Gibraltar sides when the official Gibraltar party arrived. The official Spanish party were there. At the agreed time and when everybody was in position the Spanish representative stepped forward and unlocked the gates. The gates would not move as over the years tarmacadam had been laid up to the gates. Panic set in. Spanish soldiers appeared with picks, shovels and hammers to break up the tarmacadam to allow the opening of the gates. Eventually both gates were swung back to a great cheer from the assembled crowd. The Chief Minister and I shook hands with the senior Spanish Representative and Military Officers, and also the Mayor of La Linea.

There was a surge on both sides to be the first to cross the Border! Roseleen and I were not slow. We, like many, wanted to be able to say we were among the first to cross the border from Gibraltar into Spain after a period of sixteen years. It was a great feeling and a memorable occasion.

63. Spanish officials opening the border gates

We were delighted to be present and to see the joy of the Gibraltarians at being able to travel into Spain once more, free of all restrictions.

We returned to London where I called a meeting of the British Gibraltar All Party Group with a plan for a delegation to visit Gibraltar and Spain. The trip would include a visit to the Mayor of La Linea, the town immediately over the border, to offer the hand of friendship. The members were enthusiastic and at Easter Recess a very successful and enjoyable visit was made.

Honoured by the people of Gibraltar

After the victory gained in 1981 when the Government had to concede the proposal to make the people of Gibraltar Dependent Territory Citizens and bowed to the pressure from back-bench MPs to allow the Gibraltarians to remain as British Citizens I maintained a very active relationship with Sir Joshua Hassan the Chief Minister. I raised matters concerning Gibraltar both with Ministers of the Government and in the Chamber of the House of Commons to such an extent over the years I was often referred to as Gibraltar's MP! There was genuine sadness amongst the Gibraltarians. Their voice in the UK Parliament was lost to them when I failed to be re-elected in 1987 due to tactical voting.

THE BRITISH NATIONALITY BILL, 1981

Shortly after Her Majesty The Queen conferred a Knighthood on me, I received an invitation from Sir Joshua Hassan to visit Gibraltar and attend a reception in the City Hall in my honour. I was delighted and proud to receive an invitation of this nature.

Attending the reception was Sir Joshua Hassan and all his Ministers, Civil Servants and representatives of many Organisations and Groups. Included were other members of communities in Gibraltar, all showing their appreciation for what I had done for Gibraltar during the years between 1969 and 1975 and when I supported them as a Member of the UK Parliament from 1979 to 1987. In all over 200 people were present. I was deeply moved. Sir Joshua delivered his speech in which he praised me for all I had done for the people of Gibraltar over the years. He recounted the battle in the House of Commons when we fought to retain the right of the Gibraltarians to have a British Passport on application – something which had existed since 1704. Sir Joshua concluded by saying the people of Gibraltar would never forget what I had done for them and he was proud to have had the honour of approving of my being granted the Freedom of the City of Gibraltar in 1982.

64. Print of Gibraltar presented to me after the Commons victory. Inscription reads 'Presented to Sir Albert McQuarrie in Gratitude from the People of Gibraltar'

He presented me with a beautiful framed print of Gibraltar with the words **'Presented to Sir Albert McQuarrie in Gratitude from the People of Gibraltar'** printed on the attached brass plate. I admit to being overcome with equal measure of delight and emotion and somehow was able to thank Sir Joshua, his Ministers and the people of Gibraltar for this wonderful gesture. The print hangs proudly in my home as a constant reminder of the efforts I made to help and support the citizens of Gibraltar in their time of need.

CHAPTER TWELVE

The 1981 Budget Fuel Price Crisis

IF THERE IS ONE THING which can raise the temperature of debate in the House of Commons it is an attempt by any Chancellor of the Exchequer to raise the price of diesel or petrol. This happened in 1981 when the then Chancellor Geoffrey Howe, in his Budget speech, stated there would be a 20p increase in the price of derv and petrol.

There was an immediate outcry not only from Members of Parliament but from hundreds of people all over the country protesting at the proposals. In view of the fact they would have a devastating impact on my constituents of East Aberdeenshire I decided there was no way I could accept these penal increases. I led a group of Scottish Tory MPs to a meeting with the Chancellor of the Exchequer demanding a further think on the proposals. I made it clear to him there would be a revolt in the Chamber when the vote on these proposals took place. As he was not prepared to change his mind I warned him there was trouble brewing for the Government.

The following day the *Buchan Observer* had a headline 'Albert MP throws down the 20 pence petrol gauntlet'. The article reported the meeting I had with the Chancellor threatening to vote against the proposals and encouraging other Hon Members to do likewise. I conducted a campaign against them and made sure my name was given to Mr Speaker as one of the Members who wished to address the House when the debate on the Budget Resolutions commenced.

In my drive I secured support from other Members of Parliament who, like me, were opposed to the proposed fuel increases. There was no difficulty as many Members had been inundated with protest letters from constituents, and so the campaign started to force the Chancellor to change the proposals. From then on I led the campaign until we had a 50 per cent victory when the Chancellor bowed to pressure and reduced the 20p proposal on derv to 10p. While total success was not possible there was widespread satisfaction in the country at what had been achieved. I considered the revolt I led on this matter worthwhile.

On 16th March 1981 the first day of the debate on Budget Resolutions and Economic Situation took place in the Commons Chamber. The House was full. Many Members had submitted to Mr Speaker their wish to take an active part in the day's proceedings. I had submitted my name early in the day to Mr Speaker's office in an effort to ensure I would be called. Even with my early notice to speak in the debate, it was 9.45 p.m. that evening before I could 'catch the eye' of Mr Speaker. Here are some extracts of my speech:

'Mr Albert McQuarrie (Aberdeenshire East): I am most grateful for this opportunity to address the House today, because this is the first occasion on which a Member from Scotland has been able to say something in the Chamber about the Budget.

> The decision to increase the cost of petrol and derv by 20 pence per gallon will have a devastating effect on all of the rural Constituencies and the islands of Scotland. If 20p is added, it will mean not 149p per gallon, as is seen in London, but 165p a gallon in my area of Scotland, and in other parts it will mean 180p and 192p a gallon. This is if the minimum figure is added, although I suspect that the operators will need to add another 2p on to the price. In some cases one will find many of the smaller service stations will go out of business altogether.
>
> Minibus operators in Scotland who take children to school will be seriously affected. They take a contract from the local authority for a period of three years at a fixed price, after a tender. One of my Constituents, to whom I spoke over the weekend, advised me the increase would amount to £500 in the year. This is much more than the profit he would estimate making as a result of a competitive bid to the Local Authority. This will mean a number of these small operators will go out of business altogether. Then the danger will be the children will not be taken to school, or their parents will be put to great bother in order to try to ferry them forwards and backwards at inconvenient times for them.
>
> The farmers in Scotland had a very difficult year, unlike farmers in England. I have heard from Members of the Back Bench Agriculture Committee that last year English farmers never had it so good. I can speak for farmers in Scotland, whose incomes, in real terms, fell by 52 per cent last year. This increase in fuel duty will be the last straw.
>
> The fishing industry, both offshore and inshore, of which we have heard much in the House recently, will not be able to withstand the increase. This House is well aware of the desperate state of the fishing industry. Many of its problems

THE 1981 BUDGET FUEL PRICE CRISIS

can be laid at the door of fuel costs. To add a further burden to the industry will lead to massive bankruptcies at a time when we who represent fishing Constituencies are trying desperately to save it from extinction.

Industry and commerce in the rural areas will suffer considerably as the impact of the 20p a gallon leads to increases in the price of all commodities and of services coming from and going into the rural areas. For many years, great endeavours have been made to repopulate the rural areas. Sadly, this crippling blow will do just the reverse. With no public transport to speak of, the loss of the minibuses and the inability of people living in rural areas to pay the increases which will be forced on them from all quarters, we shall soon begin to see an exodus from the rural areas and islands far greater than the Highland Clearances ever created.

There must be some way that relief can be granted. It is ironic that gas and oil from the North Sea to the mainland arrives in my Constituency to supply the rest of the United Kingdom yet my Constituents will be the most adversely affected by this penal tax.

The imposition of an increase of 20p will have a devastating effect on the cost of freight in rural areas. Vehicle excise duty will be increased by £58 million and the fuel duty by £290 million. It represents a total of £348 million, and is to be imposed on the rural areas and the islands. Already in my Constituency it costs an extra 5 per cent to bring goods by road. This is one of the main reasons which justifies a reduction in the tax.

I received a letter from Lord Boothby, former Member of Parliament. He said: If I had still been Member of Parliament for East Aberdeenshire I should have no hesitation in voting against the increase in the oil duty, and I entirely approve of what you are doing.' If my Right Hon and Learned Friend the Chancellor cannot come to the Despatch Box this evening and say he will introduce an alternative to the 20p increase in the oil duty I shall follow the Noble Lord's advice and vote against the measure.

This is exactly what I did. I was delighted that of the Members whose support I sought, twenty-seven followed me into the Lobby to vote against the Government on two different votes. We failed to win the vote of the majority of MPs but it was a clear indication to the Chancellor we were not giving up and would continue our attack against the proposals in a later debate. We felt certain the Chancellor was shocked when he realised the extent of the opposition to his proposal on the Tory Back Benches and would be looking hard at what could be done to gain our support for his Budget.

Why I voted against dearer petrol: by Albert McQuarrie MP

Glasgow Herald 25th March 1981

I voted against the Chancellor's decision to increase the fuel tax on petrol and derv by 20p because I had the courage of my convictions and voted according to my conscience.

In East Aberdeenshire there are thousands of Margaret Thatcher's most loyal and staunchest supporters. This was proved at the last General Election when the Conservative Party regained the Seat from the Scottish Nationalists and I was elected to represent them at Westminster.

I do not consider that my action in voting against one section of the Chancellor's Budget proposals was in any way disloyal to my Party. After all, we are the Party of freedom and the one which cares for all. This is why I had the freedom to make my own decision about the petrol and derv increases.

As I sat in the House of Commons on March 10th, listening to the Chancellor delivering his Budget proposals, I gasped in horror when he announced the 20p increase on fuel tax.

My immediate thoughts were of deep concern for the rural areas like East Aberdeenshire and the impact it would have on those who use a car for necessity rather than for pleasure. I was aware even before the new increase was imposed, that petrol and derv were already 10 to 15p more expensive in the rural areas than in the cities and urban areas.

Everybody expected a tough Budget. For the past 18 months we have accepted the need to tighten our belts because of the world recession which has hit Britain so badly and also the need to give massive sums of aid to firms such as British Leyland, British Steel and the Mining industry.

On top of this we had to meet some dreadful debts left behind by the last Socialist Government. All along I have fully supported the Prime Minister and her Government on the broad policies to get Britain back on its feet, and will continue to do so as I believe this country could have no better person than Mrs Margaret Thatcher leading us in the fight which we had to face since May 1979.

Cigarettes and liquor have always been a target for successive Chancellors and the people have come to accept this. However, I think the Chancellor could have put more money on the cigarettes, if they are such a health hazard. Any increase on spirits could do great damage to rural areas which depend on their livelihood from distilleries.

THE 1981 BUDGET FUEL PRICE CRISIS

Many of these small areas will suffer greatly as there is no other form of work and in these circumstances they will quickly become depopulated.

My personal rejection of the Chancellor's proposal for the 20p increase in fuel tax was more than justified by the incalculable number of telegrams, letters, telephone calls and personal approaches of support which I received endorsing my action.

I made a tour of my Constituency on the previous weekend sounding out the views of many people. Only one couple did not approve of my decision, but as the comments from my Constituents overwhelmingly supported the stand I was taking my mind was fully made up. I could not abstain on this particular vote, but would enter the lobby to vote against the Chancellor's proposals.

As I read comments in the newspapers about those voting against the petrol increases being called 'rebels' and part of a threat to topple the Prime Minister. I thought these people should get their facts right as nothing was further from the truth.

What I wanted was for the Chancellor to have second thoughts on this fuel tax before the Finance Bill is debated next month, and bring forward proposals to reduce or remove it and turn his attention to collecting the money from some of the sources I have mentioned.

If he does this he will have my support, and the vote I made against his original proposals will have been justified and will also be a great relief to my Constituents and those in the many rural areas which will suffer if the fuel tax remains.

As there were six weeks before the debate in the Chamber re-commenced I arranged meetings with Finance Ministers to negotiate an undertaking these huge increases would either be reduced or wiped out altogether. At these meetings I set out where the Government could make up the funds if the petrol and diesel increases were cancelled. They listened but could give no guarantee the wishes of the backbenchers could be granted.

In an effort to press the matter, along with the twenty-seven Members who voted against the Government, we planned two Amendments which could possibly be acceptable to Mr Speaker as part of the debate.

The first Amendment – No. 1 sought to reduce the increase on derv to 10p per gallon from the 20p proposed.

The second Amendment – No. 2 sought to reduce the increase on petrol and derv by 10p per gallon on each from the 20p proposed by the Chancellor.

The two Amendments were presented to the Table Office in the Commons and from there to Mr Speaker for his decision whether to allow them as part of the debate or not.

On 30th April 1981 the Committee of the entire House sat again to debate further Budget Resolutions and Finance which included the increases proposed on hydrocarbon oils etc. Before the debate commenced Mr Speaker Thomas announced the Amendments submitted had been accepted for discussion.

I was pleased as I felt the Chancellor would be having some concern knowing the strength of feeling in the country against the proposed increases, as more Members would support the two Amendments on the vote. There was no indication from Ministers the Government was considering any changes to the proposed increases. We were determined to push these Amendments to a vote and had advised the Finance Minister of our decision.

A most pleasant surprise was in store for us after the Chancellor entered the Chamber on 30th April 1981. He was in his place for only a few minutes when, after the Member speaking sat down, Mr Speaker called the Chancellor. Geoffrey Howe stepped up to the Despatch Box and after covering a number of matters made several remarks about the proposed increase of 20p per gallon on petrol and derv. He highlighted the fact he had received representation from the Freight Transport Association, the Road Haulage Association and representations from many industries. He accepted the duty on derv accounts for eight per cent of road freight transport costs which in turn fed through to other business costs and ultimately retail prices. The whole House waited with baited breath as to what would come next! The Chancellor continued by saying:

> I propose to accept Amendment No. 1 in respect of derv. The duty reduction will be of particular benefit to rural areas because transport costs play an important part. Although the reduction does not meet all the points which have been urged on me by Hon Friends, it will be of particular benefit to rural areas and to the Scottish economy. It will also meet the concern widely expressed about the distribution cost of many commodities.

There was a cry of 'Hear, hear' from every part of the House immediately he announced the Government's acceptance of our Amendment No. 1 to reduce the proposed increase of 20p per gallon for derv to 10p a gallon. All of us who had spent countless hours gaining support for the two Amendments were elated at the 50 per cent victory for the people of the UK. The position I took at the last sitting of the Committee backed by my twenty-seven colleagues was not so much a revolt as a matter of courage of conviction and a determination to secure a more satisfactory outcome on fuel taxation. I certainly liked the words the Chancellor used when he said 'It will be of particular benefit to rural areas and to the Scottish economy'. He obviously recognised the head of steam for the protest in the House of Commons had been led by a Member from Scotland!

The battle was not over. We decided to forge ahead with Amendment No. 2. I caught the Speakers eye at 8.00 p.m. that evening and delivered my speech – extracts are included with thanks to Hansard.

Mr Albert McQuarrie (Aberdeenshire East): The reduction in the tax on derv announced by my Right Hon and Learned Friend the Chancellor of the Exchequer will be welcomed by industry in general, and especially by the rural areas who are fighting desperately for survival. However, it does not go far enough, which is why I want to deal specifically with Amendment No. 2.

The Amendment would reduce the price of both petrol and derv by 10p per gallon. My Right Hon and Learned Friend's decision to increase the duty on fuel as proposed in Clause 4 will result in an increase of 20p per gallon on both derv and petrol. Since the announcement in the Budget statement of 10 March, there have been an overwhelming number of protests from the rural areas. It applies not only to industry but to farmers, fishermen and the local communities who are entirely dependent upon their own transport to travel to work.

No one in my Constituency considers the ownership of a motor car as a luxury. It is regarded as an essential mode of transport. The increase imposed by my Right Hon and Learned Friend is regarded as a punitive tax, especially when often the cost of a gallon of petrol in my Constituency is from 15 to 20p greater than it is in the cities of Aberdeen, Glasgow, Edinburgh and London.

I must warn my Right Hon and Learned Friend he should not underestimate the hostility to the increases which have been forced upon rural areas since 10 March. He should not imagine the original antagonism to the 20p increase is beginning to fade. I assure him he has witnessed only the early warnings. Such increases add to the price of every commodity, which is delivered into rural areas or sent out from them. It makes manufactured goods and agricultural and fishing products more expensive.

These penal increases are forcing many small businesses to close. In my Constituency this week a firm operating 14 vehicles is to close with the loss of employment for the drivers and the clerical staff. This is only one of a number of firms which cannot continue because of increases like these being imposed by the Chancellor.

There are no buses in many parts of my Constituency and Constituents have to travel great distances. This morning I received a letter from one of the social service councils. One paragraph states: *'As there is very little public transport in our area it is essential for most households to own a car. Only this month the Education Authority has withdrawn school transport in some areas making it necessary for some children to walk almost three miles to the collection point for school transport at 8.05 with a similar walk home in the evening at 16.30 – a working day that many adults would claim to be excessive'.* It seems that the 20p increase in petrol and derv prices is expected to yield an extra £1,180 million in 1981-82, made up of £900 million from petrol and £270 million from derv. On the basis the 20p increase has been paid since 10 March and the Amendment is accepted by the Chancellor of the Exchequer, the £1,180 million will be reduced to £600 million. Any reduction of the present prices will probably not be operative until 1 August 1981.

If on that data the 20p was reduced to 10p, the total amount required would be about £340 million up to the financial year 1981-82. The realisation of such a sum should not be insurmountable. There are some alternatives which would allow my Right Hon and Learned Friend to obtain the necessary amount to make up the shortfall. I shall suggest once more to my Right Hon and Learned Friend from where they could come.

First, there is the dog licence. I know this will attract some interest. The charge for keeping dogs was first devised in 1796. The rate varied from time to time until 1867 when it was replaced by the existing licence, which is now 37½p. At today's prices the cost of the licence should be about £9. The taxpayer lost £1 million last year in the collection of dog licences. This is one area in which there is considerable scope to bring in extra revenue.

There are estimated to be at least 6 million dogs in the United Kingdom. If the fee was increased to £10, the revenue would be about £60 million a year. The money could quite easily be raised; the Minister of Agriculture, Fisheries and Food is merely required to lay a Statutory Order as he has responsibility for the issuing of dog licences.

I would accept that guide dogs for the blind, the handicapped and the elderly and other work dogs should be exempt.' As several Hon. Members have illustrated in the debate, there is the gaming and betting tax, which is forecast to raise £510 million in 1981-82. If the duties were raised by only 20 per cent, the additional revenue would be £90 million.

I should also like my Right Hon and Learned Friend to take account of the space invaders machines which are flooding the country and which I mentioned during the Budget debate.

There are other alternatives which are open to my Right Hon and Learned Friend such as another 1p on cigarettes, which would bring in £35 million and a further 1p on beer which would bring in £95 million. An increase of 10p on a bottle of wine would bring in £50 million.

At this point I was interrupted:

Mr Dale Campbell-Savours (Workington)
What about whisky?

Mr Albert McQuarrie (Aberdeenshire East)
The Hon Gentleman and others mention whisky. With respect, many Hon Members are ignorant because they do not realise in most rural areas, were it not for the whisky distilleries, there would be no rural communities. Therefore, we must try not to overdo the tax on whisky. We must ensure we maintain the rural areas where the distilleries produce whisky.

I am sure many other options are open to my Right Hon and Learned Friend. I have only illustrated enough to him to show that the £340 million which would be required in order to reduce the 20p on petrol and derv to 10p, which is the subject of the Amendment, can be raised. The Chancellor of Exchequer should have a close look at those alternatives, even if it means coming back to the House in some cases to seek a new money resolution on the Budget.

Even if the Chancellor of the Exchequer cannot take the whole Amendment on board, I sincerely hope he will be able to give some hope to the people who cannot fight back and who are totally dependent upon what he can offer. I am aware of the need to control inflation and to conserve energy. The people in rural areas are not the ones who should be penalised, or who should have to pay the penalty of the failure of the large industries which are bolstered up by the Government.

It gives me no pleasure to be opposing the proposals of my Right Hon and Learned Friend because I believe in the Government's present strategy and I fully support their aims. However, I believe the Chancellor of the Exchequer was ill advised to place such a heavy burden on all those who live and work in the rural areas. I appeal to him to grant some relief by making the reductions which are called for in the Amendment which I commend to the Committee.'

Despite the most strenuous efforts by me and others to persuade the Chancellor to reduce the petrol increase we failed. At the end of the debate the Amendment No. 2 failed to be passed and we just had to live with it. There was some consolation in having gained the reduction in derv which had been well received all over the country and particularly in my constituency of East Aberdeenshire where the news was most welcome.

Having secured an acceptable result on an issue in the 1981 Budget

Speech in which I had a sincere belief, my attention was then entirely focused in representing my constituents to the best of my ability, handling the many queries raised by them which I was able to do as their Member of Parliament.

CHAPTER THIRTEEN

Parliamentary Delegation to Australia

BEING A MEMBER OF THE Commonwealth Parliamentary Association allowed me to apply for my name to be considered as part of a Parliamentary Delegation to a Commonwealth Country.

An opportunity arose in October 1981 when it was announced a delegation would be visiting Australia from 11th to 20th November. I submitted my name to the CPA office pointing out a forebear, Major General Lachlan Macquarie was the first Governor General of New South Wales and was deemed to be the Father of Australia. It is understood he changed the spelling of his name while he lived in Australia.

Within a week I was notified my name was on the list of successful delegates. The other members were the Rt Hon Denis Howell MP, Mr James Dunn MP, Sir John Langford-Holt MP and Mr William Ross MP. I knew those Members well and looked forward to working with them on the visit to Australia.

I arranged to travel out ahead of the delegation as it was an opportunity to see some of the buildings in Sydney which had been built during the time of Governor Macquarie.

On 3rd November I left the House of Commons after a 10 o'clock vote which was a 'three line', meaning I had to be present to record my vote. I travelled to Heathrow Airport for the flight to Australia. I decided to pay the excess and treat myself to First Class travel. After a very fine meal – and a little wine – I slept the entire journey and only wakened when I heard the voice of the Flight Attendant saying to me 'Good Morning, Sir, we are about to land at Sydney Airport'. I was amazed to learn there had been a re-fuelling stop at Azerbaijan. I must have been tired – or was it the wine!

Having collected my bags on arrival at the airport, I took a taxi to the Royal Australian Automobile Club where I had reserved a room under the reciprocal arrangements of the Royal Automobile Club in London where I was a member. The very comfortable room I was allocated was most suitable for my stay. I had noted the Club was located on Macquarie Street –

171

the main street in Sydney. After a good night's rest I was ready to get out and about. Before doing so I took a call from the Editor of the *Sydney Morning Herald* who had been made aware of my arrival from their London correspondent. An interview about my visit was arranged for the following morning. I spent the rest of the day exploring the heart of Sydney. It was then on my return to the Club I noticed with amazement not only was the Club situated on Macquarie Street but the Street in the gable end of the building was called Albert Street!

The following morning a journalist and photographer arrived at the Club where I was queried on matters general and political. I was asked about Clan McQuarrie in Scotland and how I felt about visiting a country with the name Macquarie popping up in so many places. The journalist told me there was a constituency named Macquarie and suggested if I came out to Australia and stood for election in that constituency I would win hands down! It was an interesting thought but not one I could think of seriously when I was so entrenched in British politics. The photographer asked to take some shots of me standing at the junction of Albert Street and Macquarie Street – this photograph I have used for the back cover of the jacket of the book. (I emailed the *Sydney Morning Herald* for permission to use the photograph) He also took a photograph of me standing beside the bronze figure of Governor Macquarie just opposite Parliament Buildings.

65. Standing beside the bronze figure of Governor Macquarie

I made my way to Parramatta where Old Government House, one of Australia's most outstanding buildings is situated. When Governor Macquarie arrived at the house it was almost uninhabitable. He decided to restore it to the former grandeur it enjoyed when first constructed. In 1815 he enlarged the building adding new wings and creating a new covered walkway with columns which gave the building a stately appearance. When the work the Governor had directed was completed it was said by many to look like a palace. Old Government House was still in that category when I made the visit to it in 1981, having been refurbished and officially opened to the public in 1970 by Her Majesty The Queen of the United Kingdom and the Commonwealth.

I toured Old Government House and as I wandered around this magnificent building I thought – what a wonderful tribute to the foresight of Governor Macquarie. Old Government House is recognised as the oldest building in Australia. During my visit I was thrilled to be invited to sit in the Governor's Chair which was made especially for him. It has the Governor's Coat of Arms carved out on the back. I was delighted to see his Coat of Arms had the machete arm figured at the top exactly as I have in mine. The Chair is a companion to that at Macquarie University with the same feature. I came away from Old Government House very satisfied at seeing this imposing building.

On the following day I visited Macquarie University set within 135 hectares at North Ryde in the north-west suburbs of Sydney. The University was established by an Act of the New South Wales State Parliament in June 1964. The enrolment of students in 1981 was estimated at 10,000 making it the sixth largest University in Australia. I was greeted by Vice Chancellor Emeritus Professor Edwin C Webb and Mr Walter Abraham. These two fine gentlemen guided me through some of the Departments of the University where an extensive range of subjects were available to the students.

It was during this visit I learned of the launch of the Macquarie Dictionary. At the launch Professor Manning Clark, Australia's leading historian, opened his speech with the remarks 'Without apology and without embarrassment or shame I take pride and pleasure in launching the Macquarie Dictionary because, as I see it, it's a dictionary of Australian English – the language we use, it's the one language by which we Australians can speak to each other'. The Professor made the point that it had taken a team from Macquarie University eleven years to produce the Dictionary. In the course of his speech Professor Manning Clark also stated it was appropriate the Dictionary of Australian English should be called the

Macquarie Dictionary and for it to be launched at the Macquarie University. He recalled how in 1817 Governor Macquarie sent a Despatch to London Foreign Office recommending Australia should be the name for the country instead of New Holland. I was immensely proud to know it was a Macquarie who gave Australia its name, and to return to Scotland with a copy of the Australian Macquarie Dictionary.

66. Sitting in Chancellor's Chair at Macquarie University

My thanks to Macquarie University News of October 1981 for the information on the Macquarie Dictionary.

The Chancellor's Chair used at graduation Ceremonies at Macquarie University was made for Governor General Macquarie during his term of Office in New South Wales. It was presented to the Macquarie University by Mrs J.E. Taylor of Edinburgh, a descendant of Governor Macquarie's brother Colonel Charles Macquarie. It has the Governor's Coat of Arms carved out on the back of the chair – as in the Governor's chair. I had the honour of sitting in the chair dressed in my McQuarrie kilt.

The Bank of New South Wales regarded Governor Macquarie as its founder and was investigating ways of commemorating its 150th anniversary in 1968. It entered into discussions with the Macquarie University Council to find something appropriate to mark the occasion. Following discussions it was agreed to approach the owner of Gruline House, the Governor's home on the Isle of Mull off the West Coast of Scotland, with a request for the panelling of the parlour to be used in the creation of a Macquarie Room at the University. Mr E.H. Mather MBE generously agreed to donate the panelling for the benefit of the people of New South Wales. This was greeted with much satisfaction by the Bank of New South Wales Executives and the Council of Macquarie University. The panelling was removed and transported to Australia in 1967. The installation of the panelling took place in 1978. During my tour of the University I was shown the Lachlan Macquarie Room which was opened by His Excellency the Governor of New South Wales Sir Roden Cutler VC, LCMG, KCVO, CBE on 24th September 1978.

67. Laying Wreath at Cenotaph

My day at Macquarie University was certainly memorable. The name Macquarie is still used with much affection at the University and in Sydney.

Prior to leaving the UK, I had made arrangements to visit the Sydney Parliament through Mr D.L. Wheeler of the Australian Parliamentary staff. When I arrived at the appointed time Mr Wheeler escorted me to the office of the Premier and Minister for Mineral Resources The Honourable Neville Kenneth Wran QC, MP who welcomed me warmly. After chatting about our respective Parliaments, Mr Wran invited me to accompany him into the Chamber and address the Parliament Members. It was a thrill for me to realise another McQuarrie was addressing the New South Wales Parliament just as the Governor Lachlan Macquarie had done in his day. After I had spoken I received a cordial acclamation from the members. In thanking Mr Wran for meeting me I told him I would look forward to seeing him again when my colleagues from the United Kingdom arrive on 16th November.

As arrangements were being made for the Armistice Day Service at the Sydney War Memorial for the fallen in the two World Wars, I was invited to lay a wreath. There were a large number of organisations represented at the impressive Service and it gave me pride to be honouring the lost servicemen and women in Australia.

The following day I met up with Dr John Whyte, a Medical Practitioner who had emigrated from Fraserburgh in my constituency, to set up a Practice in Sydney. He was accompanied by his wife, Flora, and Don and Maurine Champion, two of his close friends who were to show me around Sydney while he attended to his patients. They gave me a most enjoyable day with visits to Mrs Macquarie's seat, the Insurance Building in Macquarie Street where a life-size bronze statue of Governor Macquarie stands. Then it was on to the barracks and church buildings where the Governor had laid the foundation stones. We also visited the Court House where I noted hanging on the wall behind where the Judge would sit, was an oil painting of the Governor. I wondered why it was not Her Majesty The Queen, but was still proud it was a Macquarie!

No tour would have been complete without a visit to the Sydney Harbour Bridge and to the Sydney Opera House at the side of the river where there was an abundance of restaurants and pubs serving the most delicious food to end what had been a great day. I retained my friendship with Dr Whyte until his passing and continue my friendship with his widow, Flora, and Don and Maurine.

The arrival of the delegation from the UK meant the beginning of the Parliamentary visit to Australia. Plans were laid for a series of meetings with Australian Parliamentarians in various centres and these meetings involved considerable travel. It was to Canberra we travelled first where we visited Australia's new Parliament House on Capital Hill. There we were met by Prime Minister the Rt Hon Malcolm Fraser CH, MP. We toured the impressive building which was seen by all to be a very fine building for the Parliament of Australia. Before leaving we were presented with very nice boxed engraved cufflinks.

From Canberra we flew to Melbourne where an extensive tour of the countryside was undertaken. General political matters including agriculture, local government, sport and leisure were discussed with the State Premier and other Members of Parliament at Parliament House. This tour extended to include a Kangaroo Park, and a sight of many huge ant hills from which we kept our distance. Before continuing on our trip to Brisbane, the State Premier held a fine dinner for the delegation. Each of us at the end of the dinner received cufflinks in a nice box!

The following day we flew to Brisbane where we were met by the State Premier the Honourable Robert (Bob) Borbidge and several of his Ministers. Mr Borbidge's office had arranged a series of meetings on various matters pertaining to both our Parliaments, in particular the economies of the State of Queensland and the United Kingdom. We were entertained at the Premier's home where he and his charming wife Jennifer were splendid hosts. A dinner had been arranged for the evening when each member of the delegation received a pair of engraved cufflinks in a very nice box!! The few days spent on the Gold Coast were enlightening, interesting as well as relaxing. We returned to Sydney by air for the final part of the visit.

On arrival we were met by the joint Presidents of the New South Wales branch of the Commonwealth Parliamentary Association, Mr John Johnson MLC and Mr Lawrie Kelly MP at Parliament House along with Ministers from the Departments. We entered into frank discussions on the importance of maintaining links between the United Kingdom and Australia and the benefit to one another of membership of the Commonwealth Parliamentary Association. The two groups were firm in their belief that the strong bond which exists between our two Nations is in no small measure as a result of the importance of the work of the CPA.

After a tour of Parliament House and a meeting with the Premier the Honourable Neville Kenneth Wran QC, MP followed by lunch in the House we moved on to the Sydney Opera House where we were met by the General Manager, Mr Lloyd Martin who gave us a tour of the world famous Opera House. Later that day we attended a reception hosted by the Acting British Consul-General. Mr Donald Pragnell. A splendid day.

The following day it was arranged to meet the Lord Mayor of Sydney,

Alderman Douglas Sutherland, and Officers of the Sydney City Council in their Chambers. On this occasion, as happens often, the political discussions were more of a local nature and we found the issues which are common in the UK Local Authorities are little different from those in Australia. As guests of the Australian Commonwealth Association, lunch was provided again at Parliament House hosted by the joint Presidents. Denis Howell, a former Minister for Sport in the UK, had made arrangements for the delegation to meet the Minister for Sport, Recreation and Tourism, Hon M A Cleary MP for talks on his portfolio. This was a most fruitful meeting particularly on the subject of tourism.

After leaving the Minister for Sport the rest of the day was free. I suggested we could have dinner at one of the Warehouse Restaurants by the river which I had visited with Dr John Whyte and Don and Maurine Champion. I would make the arrangements and would invite my friends to join us. This I saw as an opportunity for my colleagues to meet Australians who were not connected with politics. It was a great idea as it turned out. The evening was a great success when all of us 'could let our hair down' and not be inhibited by political protocol.

The next two days were planned to show us the importance of the land and sea in supporting lives in Australia. We visited the Food Research Division at North Ryde, the Port facilities at Fort Denison, had a drive into the countryside as well as a sightseeing tour of the Northern Suburbs and beaches of Sydney. These two days together with the visits to the other States gave us a valuable insight into life in this part of the vast country. I recall the afternoon we boarded a Police Launch for a river cruise sailing under the Sydney Bridge and as the Launch sailed up the river how the other craft kept well out of the way. The delegation members were delighted to have the opportunity to see the city from the river and were extremely grateful to the Commonwealth Parliamentary Association for making all of this possible, albeit as a fact-finding excursion for the UK Government.

No visit to Sydney would be complete without taking in a performance at the Sydney Opera House. On our penultimate evening of this part of the visit we were entertained to dinner in the Bennelong Restaurant at the Sydney Opera House. An excellent dinner was followed by a splendid performance of Myron Fink's opera Chinchilla.

On the final day of the trip a sightseeing tour of Sydney which included the main thoroughfares and shopping centres of the City was organised.

A farewell dinner was hosted again by the joint Presidents of the Australian Commonwealth Parliamentary Association in Parliament House. After being entertained by the Association on many occasions during the entire tour it was Denis Howell who made a presentation on our behalf to the two gentlemen who had been such wonderful hosts. Each received a bottle of House of Commons whisky. The gentlemen in turn presented each of our party with a pair of engraved cufflinks!! It was interesting that at each stage of our visit the gift should be a very nice pair of cufflinks. Whether this was chance or whether cufflinks are a classic memento I did not seek to enquire. They were much appreciated and have been worn by me on many occasions over the years. When not in use they are returned to the boxes which are memories of my visit to Australia. This was a happy evening – good food, good wine enjoyed during a relaxed evening when all of us thanked our hosts in our own different ways for making the visit such a memorable one.

For me it was marvellous to be in Sydney where the name of Governor Macquarie is still held with respect as the Father of Australia. The Governor left New South Wales in 1822, and died two years later. Never would he have imagined 159 years later, for the first time ever, someone bearing the name McQuarrie would be elected as a Member of Parliament in the United Kingdom Parliament and as an MP be visiting New South Wales where Governor Macquarie ruled. He would have been intrigued that, also, for the first time, a member of the McQuarrie Clan had a Knighthood conferred upon him, in 1987, by Her Majesty The Queen of the United Kingdom and the Commonwealth, an honour which was apparently denied Governor Macquarie when he returned to London after he was replaced. It was with great pleasure and much pride during my visit to Australia I learned of the wonderful service Governor Macquarie had given to New South Wales. As I stood at the junction of Macquarie Street and Albert Street, before taking my leave of Australia, wearing my McQuarrie tartan kilt as Major General Macquarie would have done in his day, I was proud of the achievements he had secured during his term as Governor of the State.

When I returned to the House of Commons and reflected on being part of the Commonwealth Parliamentary Association delegation to Australia in 1981, I was so grateful to the CPA for the opportunity to be a part of an interesting and enjoyable group tour.

CHAPTER FOURTEEN

Common Fisheries Policy, 1983

THE YEAR 1982, LEADING UP TO THE Common Fisheries Policy and the surprise General Election in 1983, was a busy one in Parliament and in the constituency.

I had achieved considerable success in gaining funding from the FEOGA grants from Europe for the fishing industry in the constituency which was greatly appreciated by the fishermen.

I worked closely with the National Farmers Union Officials and promoted the importance of the agriculture industry in the House of Commons.

Correspondence from constituents kept arriving on my desk at the House of Commons and there were many ongoing cases which, in the main, I was able to resolve. Consultation sessions with constituents were held regularly in the offices of the Conservative and Unionist Association as well as in the larger towns, and during the summer recess in my mobile office. This service was worthwhile and proved how vital it was for the Member of Parliament to make himself/herself available to all at any time.

On 28th January 1983, Rt Hon Peter Walker, Minister of Agriculture, Fisheries and Food made an announcement to the House of Commons that the Council of Fishery Ministers in Europe had passed the Common Fisheries Policy (CFP). Mr Walker stated this unqualified agreement had been reached after four years of discussions between the Fishery Ministers of the ten European Nations. He praised the work done by the Minister of State (Mr Alick Buchanan-Smith) who had been the instigator of the Policy and who presented the Policy in such a manner it was acceptable to the other Nations. An official announcement was made that the Common Fisheries Policy would be in force for a term of twenty years or thereby.

Mr Walker also placed on record his thanks to the leaders of the fishing industry from the United Kingdom who, having attended every meeting with him, had taken part in the discussions and negotiations. In welcoming the eventual agreement, he made clear the leaders, who were pivotal in the agreement, shared with the Government his view that it provided the basis upon which the industry would obtain a secure future and also be of benefit to the United Kingdom.

The announcement was greeted with acclaim by all on the Tory side of the House. In the country as a whole it was seen, at last, that the CFP would safeguard the livelihood of fishermen and processors of the fish landed on the shores of the United Kingdom.

Following the announcement in the House of Commons, the Secretary of State took questions. I caught the 'eye' of Mr Speaker and was called to put my question when I said 'May I add my congratulations to my Rt Hon Friend the Secretary of State, the Minister of State and the Prime Minister on the resolute stance they have taken in negotiating this Common Fisheries Policy which is acceptable to British fishermen. Will the structure package be run by the Department of Agriculture Fisheries and Food in Scotland or by the Sea Fish Industry Authority? If it is the latter, will he take steps to ensure every application is treated with the utmost urgency?'

The Secretary of State replied 'Responsibility for the structure package will be with the Secretary of State for Scotland and myself. Responsibility for the detailed arrangements of the grants will also partly rest with the European Commission. In operating such schemes we shall see they are conducted as speedily and as efficiently as possible'. I was grateful for the reply as I knew this would please the fishermen in my constituency who would be applying for grants.

Sadly this was not to be. After several years when the Policy operated very successfully several Nations in Europe started to break the regulations on quotas. Some of these Nations fishermen invaded our waters and were catching cod and haddock to such an extent there was a grave danger the stocks in the sea would be depleted to a dangerously low level. The once heralded Common Fisheries Policy was beginning to be seen as a disaster for our fishermen. In my latter years as a Member of Parliament I fought many battles in the House of Commons for a new Common Fisheries Policy but had no success as the Nations who had broken all regulations and refused to agree a new Policy were well aware it would place them under restrictions preventing them from plundering our fishing stock. The battle went on for years at the European Parliament with bureaucratic dictation from Brussels causing considerable damage to the ability of the fishermen to earn a living to such an extent in the years from 2001 to present time the fleet operating out of Scottish Ports had fallen by 69 per cent. No amount of oil and gas production from the North Sea can provide alternative employment to those in the fishing industry who accepted the ravages of the sea to support their families.

Now, as I write this thirty years on since the Common Fisheries Policy of 1983 was brought into force, a breakthrough has been made in the recent negotiations which may help to maintain the future of what is left of the Scottish fishing fleet. A successful future for our fishing industry is vital for the numerous communities around the coast of Britain which have produced generations of fishermen who bravely go to sea not only to earn a living but to provide the fish for the processors who give employment to the local communities.

68. At Fish Processing Factory in Fraserburgh

On 7th February 2013 a vote was taken in Strasbourg which could lead to a new Common Fisheries Policy. The terms of the proposals are intended to protect endangered stocks with control of the quotas dealt with at regional level rather than from Brussels. There is an important measure within the proposals to ban the discarding of fish back into the sea as early as 2014. As fishermen have witnessed fish discarded over many years, this measure if adopted will allay fears for the future livelihood of fishermen who will feel their complaints have been taken notice of at last.

The package has been given a cautious welcome by the Fishermen's

Organisations who have warned of the usual bureaucratic hurdles. In addition the Council of Ministers in the European Parliament have a part to play in approving the new measures. It is right these two bodies must not be allowed to jeopardise something the fishermen have been crying out for and which is now within sight. These are measures I campaigned for during my time as a Member of Parliament in the constituency which has the largest fishing industry in Europe.

I sincerely hope in a short time a comprehensive Common Fisheries Policy will be produced by the European Parliament which will be legally binding on all Nations in the European Union – one which will secure the Scottish Fishing Industry both offshore and onshore. It is satisfactory that the present EU Fisheries Commissioner, Maria Damanski, has urged MEPs to help bring about the ambitious reform of the Common Fisheries Policy. She has said 'Your Fisheries Committee has put down the right foundation to increase by 2020 the fish in our seas to 15 million tonnes and the fish landed by our fishermen by 500,000 tonnes'. Mrs Damanski said the proposed changes would lead to a 25 per cent rise in fishing incomes and a 30 per cent rise in new jobs by 2022.

These are most encouraging words. The changes must be implemented and not impeded in any way in Europe. It is the culmination of many years work by the representatives of the fishing industry who deserve great credit for their perseverance over the years to secure a Common Fisheries Policy to guarantee the future of the industry and food for the ever growing world population. I will follow events carefully and will look for details of the proposals as early as possible.

1983 General Election

Just as everything seemed to be going smoothly, the Prime Minister shocked Members of Parliament by calling a General Election to take place on 9th June 1983 – a full year shorter than a normal Parliamentary term. I must say the news did not please me and I made my views known to the Chief Whip.

An upheaval had already taken place in March 1983 when the recommendations of the Boundary Commission were debated. I was one of the Members who was particularly affected. My constituency was to disappear in name and a new one encompassing different areas creating a new constituency.

At first I resented the changes very much and in a speech on the matter I complained the Boundary Commission should have taken account of the future growth in areas like Grampian. I suggested it was wrong to take the 1978 figures as the basis for the re-organisation of the boundaries for the next General Election when it was obvious there would be considerable growth in the Grampian Region which covered East Aberdeenshire. Growth was such since 1978 that by the next election the Boundary Commission figures would be totally out of proportion. In the course of a speech I made at the time I stated:

> My constituency of East Aberdeenshire was ably represented by a Conservative and Unionist Member of Parliament for thirty-four years in the person of Bob Boothby (later Lord Boothby) and a further twelve years by Mr Patrick Wolrige-Gordon. Unfortunately the name would now disappear into Banff and Buchan, carving up East Aberdeenshire and, worse still, the loss of Banffshire as a constituency and with it the loss of a Member of Parliament.

I sought an assurance from Ministers that in future the Boundary Commission would take cognisance of the growth in areas like the Grampian Region so that we do not only lose a Member of Parliament and also an entire constituency when the population was increasing rather than decreasing.

In assessing the situation I found the new constituency boundary removed the town of Ellon, the villages of Newburgh, Tarves and Methlick along with areas of rich agricultural land maintained by farmers and their families who had supported me in 1979. The boundary of the new constituency would be formed from a large part of the previous East Aberdeenshire and a smaller part of Banffshire. The constituency of Banffshire was completely wiped away after many years as a county with its own Member of Parliament serving in the Palace of Westminster. Thus, a Candidate had to be selected to contest the new constituency of Banff and Buchan for the Conservative and Unionist Party, as laid down by the Rules of the Scottish Party, for the forthcoming General Election on 9th June 1983.

As I wished the opportunity to continue serving as a Member of Parliament I decided to make it known I was interested in applying for the Candidacy of Banff and Buchan. I knew others would put their names forward but I hoped my service as a Member for the last four years would serve me in good stead at the Selection Meeting.

The Office Bearers and Executive Members of the newly created Association gave me a good reception at the Selection Meeting. When the Chairman announced I had been selected as the Prospective Parliamentary Candidate for the Conservative and Unionist Party at the General Election I was elated at the confidence shown in me. I was particularly pleased the Office Bearers of the former Banffshire Constituency gave their support to my candidacy despite the hurt they felt at the loss of the constituency of

Banffshire and their Member of Parliament. I assured them of my sincere regret in the loss of their Member.

Having been selected to contest Banff and Buchan my campaign started immediately knowing the Candidate of the Scottish National Party would be my main opposition. The Candidate was the one I had defeated at the General Election in 1979 when he was the Sitting Member. Due to the redistribution of the Parliamentary Boundaries, he had to contest the new seat.

The active campaign got under way after Parliament was dissolved. It was hard work delivering leaflets, knocking doors and visiting numerous businesses throughout the constituency. The Opposition Parties were active and I knew it was necessary to keep up the pressure, to leave nothing to chance in seeking the votes of the electorate on Polling Day. As it happened, the hard work paid off as the people voted for me. At 2.10 a.m. on 10th June I was declared the first Member of Parliament for Banff and Buchan Constituency having almost doubled the majority I had in 1979. My Office Bearers and Election Committee Members were ecstatic outside the Macduff Town Hall where the count took place. With bottles of champagne at the ready their cry was 'We won, we won'.

69. Prime Minister surrounded by supporters in Strichen

My supporters, in great spirits at the victory, took Roseleen and I off to a nearby hotel for a celebratory party. At 4.00 a.m. we broke up to go home for a well earned rest, knowing the media would be seeking me out in the morning for comment on the result. Over the next few days I toured the constituency thanking the people who had given me great support during the campaign and those who had burnt the midnight oil to secure success for me. I was determined to serve my constituents in Banff and Buchan with the same dedication I gave to the Constituency of East Aberdeenshire.

On 11th June 1983 an article was published in a local newspaper covering Banff and Buchan carrying the banner heading 'Buchan Bulldog's Thanks to Thatcher'. The article recorded my success as the first Member of Parliament for the new Constituency of Banff and Buchan to serve at the Palace of Westminster. By courtesy of *Aberdeen Journals* I am copying some of the comments from the article.

The Buchan Bulldog is still in business!

And according to Albert McQuarrie, who grabbed the Banff and Buchan Seat for the Tories, his victory was as much due to Mrs Thatcher as himself.

As his delirious supporters celebrated his win, the ebullient Mr McQuarrie claimed the result was a "vindication" of the Prime Minister's policies.

Sixty Five year old Mr McQuarrie, who was East Aberdeenshire MP in the last Parliament, polled 16,072 votes to secure a majority of 937 over his old rival from the SNP, Douglas Henderson, who was runner-up with 15,135 votes.

As a happy band of Tory supporters organised a celebration party after the 2.10 a.m. declaration at Macduff Town Hall, Mr McQuarrie reflected on his win.

I am delighted with the majority and greatly honoured to represent this Constituency. I was the last MP for East Aberdeenshire and I am the first for Banff and Buchan.

Mr McQuarrie had a double reason to celebrate for today is his wife Roseleen's birthday – an occasion which prompted a chorus of Happy Birthday at the post declaration party.

SNP candidate Douglas Henderson, who has now lost twice in a row to Mr McQuarrie could not hide his disappointment in failing to capture a Seat in which his Party had high hopes.

Bottom of the poll with a lost deposit was Labour hopeful Ian Lloyd who secured 3,150 votes.

Back in the House of Commons the Prime Minister called me to offer her congratulations on my re-election. I told her it was the policies provided by her Government which had helped me towards success.

COMMON FISHERIES POLICY, 1983

70. Prime Minister signs visitors book at Party HQ in Mintlaw

With the 1983 General Election behind me I set about being a member of the Governing Party in the House of Commons, occupying my seat in the Chamber two rows behind the Prime Minister from where I played a part in the 'heckling' battle each week with the full support of the Prime Minister and her PPS the late Ian Gow MP.

CHAPTER FIFTEEN

St Fergus Gas Terminal

THE WORK OF AN MP IS very much varied. All sorts of issues arise for the Member to deal with by correspondence, often by meeting those with problems and seeking meetings with Ministers at the House of Commons. Visits to businesses in the constituency keep the Member in touch with management and staff. This Chapter reveals examples of things I became involved in during my time as a Member of Parliament. One is the development of a vital industry, the other a Prison Riot - varied indeed!

In the course of my election campaign, I visited the St Fergus Gas Terminal, located between the towns of Fraserburgh and Peterhead near the village of St Fergus. Shortly after the election I made arrangements to visit the Terminal to acquaint myself fully with the operations. These were carried out by a number of companies within a vast area adjacent to the fine golden sand dunes associated with the coastline of Buchan. The development of massive buildings and huge chimney stacks pouring out gas flares was awesome.

Construction began at the St Fergus site which had been selected as an appropriate location for a Gas Terminal in the mid 1970s. The first of the Terminals was occupied and operated by Total Oil Marine and British Gas. The TOTAL Terminal received hydrocarbon via two No. 32 pipelines from the Frigg Field which straddled the Norwegian and UK continental shelf. After treatment the Gas was exported to British Gas (now National Grid) where it was compressed and sent throughout the UK via the Gas Network with the condensates being exported to Peterhead Base. The St Fergus Gas Terminal and its structures were officially opened by Her Majesty the Queen in 1978.

In the mid 1980s TOTAL were joined by Shell and thereafter Exxon Mobil (now Apache). TOTAL E&P UK is the largest operator within the St Fergus complex where it covers 220 acres of land and employs 1200 people onshore and offshore. At the St Fergus Terminal TOTAL Oil receives and processes 20 per cent of the UKs natural gas requirements from twenty

ST FERGUS GAS TERMINAL

fields in the UK and Norway. TOTAL owns 100 per cent of the Terminals' facilities and 50 per cent of the Common Facilities which is a substantial investment of the site. Today there are four Terminals operating within the entire site – TE&P UK, National Grid, Shell and Apache.

The St Fergus Gas Terminal has been of tremendous value to the economy of the north east of Scotland. The four operators at the Terminal have been extremely generous to the local community in funding various projects. These continuing gifts are greatly appreciated by the community and particularly in the villages of St Fergus and Crimond. It is fitting on the completion of a Sheltered Housing Complex in 1990 at St Fergus it was named after the Managing Director of TOTAL Mr Dominic Renouard. It is known as Renouard Court.

71. St Fergus Gas Terminal

After my first visit and subsequent visits to the Terminal, I always came away in the knowledge this Terminal in the north east of Scotland was playing a large part in providing gas for the United Kingdom and overseas. As long as there is gas in the North Sea there will be employment for many people at the St Fergus Gas Terminal – long may it continue.

My association with TOTAL continued for a number of years through my friendship with Mr Dominic Renouard, Managing Director of TOTAL and his wife whom Roseleen and I regularly met socially in London where he had an apartment. Our visits to Glyndebourne Opera Concerts with them were most pleasant times.

Early in 1984 I read a prominent article in a local newspaper of a proposal by British Gas in co-operation with the Norwegian State Oil Company – Statoil – to build another plant at the St Fergus site which could lead to the employment of up to 1,000 people. This news was most welcome to me as the fishing industry, which was a mainstream employer of labour in the north east of Scotland, was suffering a recession resulting in a loss of employment of many workers in my constituency.

The proposal was to build a Plant to take gas from the Norwegian Sleipner Field through a 128 mile pipeline. I saw this as a boost to employment in the area and arranged a meeting with the Executives of British Gas for project discussions so I became fully aware of the proposal and ascertain the areas where I could give help. I learned the negotiations between the two companies were progressing well and in the region of 1,000 new jobs would be created in the construction of the Plant including permanent jobs. Having satisfied myself the companies were sincere with the proposal I sought a meeting with Mr Alick Buchanan-Smith, Minister of State at the Department of Energy, drawing his attention to the matter. He told me he had spoken with the Norwegian Executives and assured me the Norwegians involvement was genuine and he was keeping an eye on the matter hoping it became a reality. The Minister advised me the cost of the 129 mile pipeline and the onshore facility at St Fergus was estimated at £500 million with the prospect of the first gas coming ashore in 1990.

Sadly this proposal did not proceed in any form at all. After protracted negotiations the decision was taken to abandon the plan. I was bitterly disappointed but consoled by the fact that TOTAL E&P UK and the other operators at St Fergus Terminal would continue to develop at the site and create employment onshore and offshore.

Peterhead Prison Riots

Visiting establishments within the constituency is not unusual. One of the establishments from where I received many letters was Peterhead Prison. As prisoners have a right to request a meeting with the Member of Parliament – although they have no vote while serving a sentence – I made many visits to Peterhead Prison to interview prisoners who had indicated a problem. The problems were many and varied. The interview was conducted with the prisoner sitting behind a glass screen while I was in another room looking through the screen. In many cases the complaints had no foundation. Tensions existed within the prison continuously. Prison Warders were doing a marvellous job and received whole-hearted co-operation from all sources in the Peterhead community.

On 20th August 1979, during the summer recess, the Peterhead Police Office advised me a riot had broken out at the prison. Eighteen prisoners had gained access to the roof of the building, and were removing the slates and smashing skylight windows. I drove from my home to the prison to meet with the Governor who appraised me of the situation. Soon television crews and many reporters arrived at the scene seeking news.

I was told the prisoners had managed to secure food from the prison to give to the rioters. From time to time a few of them appeared on the roof in defiant mood. This was halted, to a degree, when the Fire Service used jet spray hoses. While the jet spray kept them from appearing on the roof as often, they re-appeared wearing yellow oilskins which they had removed from another prison store.

This incident involved only a few inmates but it meant the remainder of the 300 prisoners were locked in their cells. They were angry and kept banging on the cell door to the extent that the noise could be heard outwith the prison walls.

The riot continued into the following day. There was no sign of it ending while the situation was attracting the nation's media. Television news and the nation's press showed graphic photographs of the riot.

I seldom left the area. I was receiving regular updates from the Governor and the Police. I had telephone conversations with Mr Malcolm Rifkind MP, Scottish Office Minister for Home Affairs. There had been adverse comment that the Minister had not come to the prison to see the situation as had been planned. He explained to me the visit had been cancelled because of the additional strain it would put on the overstretched resources of the prison and Police staff. I advised the Governor and the Police that Mr Rifkind was to make a statement from his Edinburgh office that day. In the event, the statement was well received satisfying the people who had been calling for a visit by the Minister.

The following days were wearying as there was no progress. After ninety-six hours Prison Warders gained control. The prisoners from the attic were taken to their cells and so ended my first experience of unrest at the prison. I was only sorry that a number of Prison Officers had been injured and also some of the prisoners.

More was to follow although three years had passed before another riot. On 9th January 1984, fifty-six prisoners took over the 'A' Hall at the prison forcing the Officers out and then barricading themselves in. Some climbed on to the roof of the hall, stripped off slates and broke the glass of the skylight windows. They then systematically smashed up 'A' Hall which had recently undergone a £1 million refurbishment. Considerable damage was done to toilet facilities and furniture fittings at an estimated cost of £60,000. 'A' Hall housed some of Scotland's most violent offenders who did not care how much trouble they caused.

During the night the prisoners set fire to another part of the roof. Fire Brigade Units were called. At the same time Prison Officers directed water hoses on to the area of roof which the prisoners had cut open, in an effort to dissuade them from coming on to the roof. Prison staff had been issued with helmets and shields. Police were drafted in to the area, some with dogs, and were ready if action was required. The following morning Prison Officers broke through the barricade in 'A' Hall. After a short time they were able to remove forty-four of the rioters back to their cells. The remaining twelve escaped to the other end of the roof and once more barricaded themselves in. It was generally accepted they would not remain there as it was bitterly cold and they had no means of heating.

In the afternoon eight of the prisoners were persuaded to come down from the roof. The remaining four were defiant, kept shouting and tearing more slates off the roof. After a time these four were taken down and the riot was over. No Prison Officers were injured. The following day I travelled to London and to the House of Commons where I made a full report of the riot to Scottish Ministers and the Prime Minister who called me into her office in the Commons for an update on the situation.

Three years later on 11th November 1986 another riot broke out – this time even more serious as a Prison Officer was taken hostage. I had returned home from an Armistice Day Church Service expecting a quiet few hours before returning to London. I abandoned earlier plans and drove to Peterhead Prison where I met with the Governor. He explained three prisoners in 'A' Hall had overpowered a young Prison Officer, taking his keys which gave them access to all parts of 'A' Hall including doors to other parts of the prison. By opening other doors they were able to release another fifty inmates from their cells. The prisoners then congregated in 'A' Hall and systematically destroyed as much of it as they could.

I returned home late in the evening having assured the Governor I would be back next day. After a very restless sleep I rose before dawn to drive back to the prison to find the riot still active. Many media reporters had gathered. Several asked me what I could do to help the besieged Prison Officer. I replied there seemed little other than offer to go into the prison and take the place of the Prison Officer. This response was relayed and reported on news bulletins. Several hours later a banner appeared on the roof of the prison which read – **ALBERT WHO?** Naturally the radio and television reporters on the street by the prison were anxious to know my reaction to the banner. I told them 'These prisoners have a sense of humour. They know fine who I am. I have made visits to the prison on many occasions since 1979 and the majority of these were to speak with prisoners at their request'. My well intended offer was turned down by the Authorities.

No progress was made over the next few days to end the riot. The Prison Officer taken by the rioters was 'paraded' several times on the roof of 'A' Hall to let the Authorities see he was well. On these occasions he was surrounded by around thirty rioters on the roof. He was seen to be extremely nervous which was of some concern to the Governor.

On Thursday 15th November around 9.30 in the morning, ninety-one hours after the riot started, it ended. The first of the rioters to surrender rushed over the roof to a point where Prison Officers were on guard. He was followed by another. Soon flares were seen to rise from the roof of 'A' Hall. The prisoners began to leave the area to give themselves up. By the time the last prisoner had been 'captured' the roof of 'A' Hall was a blazing inferno. It was completely destroyed. Once calm had settled in the prison I met with the Prison Governor to thank him and his staff for the efficient manner they dealt with the riot. I was grateful the young Prison Officer who was taken hostage was unharmed although deeply shocked at such a dreadful experience so soon into his career as a Prison Officer. He was re-united with his family and given a medical check-up by the Prison Doctor.

As this was a serious incident I demanded an inquiry had to be made into the circumstances surrounding the riot. There were suggestions the reason for the riot was due to brutality and bad conditions within the prison. Certainly I had not seen any evidence of this during visits, nor had I received communication from any source to that effect. On returning to the House of Commons I sought a meeting with the Secretary of State for Scotland insisting an early inquiry be held with the findings made public. The Secretary of State advised me an inquiry would be held led by Her Majesty's Chief Inspector of Prisons. When the Report was issued it clearly stated there were no grounds for the allegations of brutality for which I was glad as it vindicated all the Prison Officers. The claim of bad conditions was given a qualified acceptance. The report also contained information that a new prison would be built at Peterhead as soon as possible. Sadly this did not happen and yet another riot took place in 1987 when a similar situation arose as had been seen in the riots of 1979, 1984 and 1986.

It is only now, in the year 2013, the new prison is being built in Peterhead, adjacent to the existing Victorian building. I sincerely hope when it is occupied and operational there will be no more sieges at Peterhead Prison.

CHAPTER SIXTEEN

A Holiday in South Africa

EARLY IN 1985 ROSELEEN AND I WERE having lunch in the House of Commons with a good friend Andrew Gay who held the position of Managing Director of Marples-Ridgeway International Limited – a large Building and Civil Engineering Company. Throughout the conversation we talked about what we did and where we travelled to on holiday. Andrew told us he returned to South Africa as it was where he was born. We said our holidays now were mainly spent in Spain or at home in Teuchar Lodge with the grandchildren.

Andrew was also a Director of LTA Building International, a company operating in South Africa. The conversation moved to that country and I indicated it would be fine to visit South Africa to which Andrew said we should do so in the autumn when the weather would be good. He would organise the trip drawing on his friends at LTA to help. We were delighted and within a few weeks a programme was arranged.

Excited at the prospect of the trip, plans were made to take account of matters, which may arise, with my Parliamentary Secretary, Barbara, at the House of Commons and with the Constituency Office Secretary Miss Rhoda Gall, during our absence from the country.

I notified the Foreign and Commonwealth Office giving full details of our itinerary. A response was received to the effect that Her Majesty's Consul-General in Johannesburg, Mr C.T. Brant, had been notified and would render any help we may require during our visit.

As this trip was over four weeks I decided to keep a diary of each day's activities. Over the next pages I write about our journeys and highlights of the holiday.

On 31st August 1985 our son Dermot drove us from home to Aberdeen Airport for the flight to London. That evening we flew in the luxury of a First Class Cabin, as this was a special holiday. The flight by South African Airways to Johannesburg Airport arrived early the following morning. I was relaxed after the excellent attention of the Flight Attendants. We were met by the Private Secretary of an LTA Director. On the drive to our hotel where we stayed overnight she told us how she arrived in South Africa two years earlier from Zimbabwe where her husband had been an Advocate in Salisbury. One evening, in a telephone call to her from South Africa where her husband was on business, he said her mother was very ill in South Africa and that it was imperative she come to South Africa as quickly as possible. She told him this could not be as she had spoken to her mother that day. He replied to her 'you must come at once'. She realised her husband was anxious to see her out of Zimbabwe. She packed everything she could into her car, handed the keys of the £150,000 house to the black servant and drove the long journey to meet her husband in Johannesburg. It was impossible to do anything about access to their joint bank account in Zimbabwe. On meeting her husband he told her there was a threat to oust them from their home and a danger of being murdered. They were now making a new life in South Africa having lost everything they had worked for in Zimbabwe. We were shocked and wished her well for the future.

The following day we flew to Durban where we hired a car and drove to the San Lameer Complex near Durban where we relaxed for six days in a luxurious lodge within a secure and guarded development. We enjoyed playing golf, drives in the countryside, the sandy beaches and swimming in the sea water pools as well as swimming in the Indian Ocean. During the evening, in the tranquil surroundings of the complex and far from the hustle and bustle of our normal lives at home, dinner and a glass of wine was the best way to complete each day at San Lameer.

Soon we had to leave the complex and return to Durban for the next stage of our trip. We decided to drive ourselves there passing through a number of Black and Indian townships. We could see, in these townships, the houses were nothing short of mud huts with no apparent sanitation. These townships appeared in the countryside. There was no form of transport, forcing the people to walk many miles to collect food for their families. Those who found work on a seasonal basis were employed cutting sugar canes when the crop was ready. There were no machines capable of doing the job. In contrast to the undeveloped countryside we had driven through we arrived in Durban where there were obvious signs of massive developments taking place. We saw a huge Oil Refinery and the sugar Terminal both of which were employing black and white people seven days a week.

Durban was our home for a few days and it was while there we strolled along the beach to find only white people were allowed in a specific marked area. We further found that there was a section for Indians and one for the black population. This was a clear indication to us that in 1985 segregation still existed. The research I made before leaving the United Kingdom was that the populations comprised the native Africans, 900,000 Indians and 11 million black people showing that there were grounds for the demand by the Blacks for more power.

On our second Sunday in South Africa we decided to find a Church. The Hotel Receptionist directed us to the nearest which was Episcopalian. We received a warm welcome from the Minister at the door where he was welcoming all worshippers. He enquired where we came from and why we were in South Africa. During the service he announced there were a number of visitors in the congregation from various parts of the world and to our astonishment then added there was a couple from the United Kingdom and the gentleman of the name McQuarrie was a Member of Parliament – shades of what happened in church at home in Aberdeenshire each Sunday!

72. A Helicopter trip to the Gold Mines

Visiting the Gold Mine

We flew from Durban to Johannesburg to prepare for the visit to Western Deep Levels Gold Mines. Next day we were taken in a helicopter to the Mines – a thirty minute flight. On arrival we met the Managing Director who gave us a briefing on the operations carried out at the mines and how we would have a complete change of clothing before the adventure into the mines. It was explained to us the temperature could be 89°C. When we were ready, we boarded the lift which took us down 6,000 feet to the working area in four and a half minutes. The mine used 383 megawatts of electricity per day, equal to the needs of the entire City of Johannesburg. After a long walk we reached the area where I was invited to drill a section. I accepted at once and was given the great pleasure of drilling for gold. After a few minutes I did see some which was swiftly taken by the operators and placed in the melting pot. Following this adventure we visited the Underground Training Centre. This Centre had a sign at the entrance which read – *Welcome to B.B. and S Bar*. It was explained to us that the sign meant Bun, Bacon and Steak Bar! After an enjoyable snack at the Centre we took the underground train to the lift which took us back to the offices and reception. We were amazed how the workers could operate at such depths and in high temperatures. Before departing we were shown a bar of gold in the Melting Shop which had a value of £150,000. It was there I spotted a sliver of gold on the floor. I picked it up and put in the palm of my hand. I was just thinking what a nice souvenir this would be when one of the security men took it from me placing it in a container – so no souvenir, only a memory!

73. Drilling for Gold at the Nibe

The Black Township

The second part of this day's trip was a short helicopter flight to a Black Township and to the school built and supported by the Western Deep Levels Gold Mine, for the children of the mine workers. It was here we were made aware of the huge effort by the owners of the Gold Mine to educate the children of the workers in the skills required for working in the mines while at the same time giving the pupils a good all-round education. I will never forget seeing, for the first time ever, a classroom where each and every pupil sat at a desk with a computer. The school was equipped with the tools of all trades including joinery, plumbing, welding, electrical and general engineering while the company ensured there were opportunities for girls to further their education also. This was a really fascinating day and a wonderful experience ending with a helicopter trip back to Johannesburg.

74. With children at the Mine School

A new Golf Experience

I was invited by the Managing Director of LTA to play golf at the River Road Golf Club – a most exclusive Golf Club with a maximum of 200 members at any one time. The joining fee is very high and restricted to extremely wealthy South Africans. At the end of each year the total costs incurred, which were substantial were equally apportioned and paid by each member. No trolleys and golf carts were permitted and certainly no member was allowed to carry his clubs. Every golfer had to have a Caddy. With an ageing population even the millionaires in South Africa may request a 'buggy' nowadays. I had a most enjoyable day at the course and a Caddy who kept me out of too many bunkers.

Visit to Londolozi Game Reserve

From Johannesburg we flew to Skukuza Airport which was only a thirty minute drive from the Londolozi Game Reserve where we were to be for four days. Our accommodation in the Game Reserve was a 'hut'. There was a sitting room with a small dining area, a bedroom, washroom and facilities for making tea. It was lit by attractive gas lights. The roof of the 'hut' was thatched. We dined in the restaurant at night. Each morning we rose early as the Land Rover would arrive to pick us up for the adventure into the Game Reserve. We were amazed at the number of species we did not recognise roaming around. 'New' breeds of animal were spotted on each trip. Our driver and guide told us about the work in the Reserve and the efforts made to keep as many species alive as possible. We were fascinated but glad to be in the security of the Land Rover!

Visit to Cape Town

After our stay at Londolozi we flew back to Johannesburg where meetings had been set up for me to have informal talks with a number of representatives of the main political parties. Our overnight stay was in the Sandton Sun Hotel where I met the politicians and had positive discussions.

Next day we flew to Cape Town where we were to spend a few days. We were met at the airport by Mr Jan Van Zyle, Chairman of LTA Cape Town. He welcomed us warmly and told us 'our' car and driver were waiting for us and they would be at our disposal during our stay in Cape Town. The hotel was the President Hotel and our suite had the most wonderful view of the Atlantic Ocean.

Over the next few days Edgar, our driver, a native of South Africa, proudly showed us many of the fine buildings and places of interest in Cape Town. He drove us to the foot of Table Mountain where we took the cable car to the top. We stepped out to a breathtaking magnificent panoramic scene captured on the many photographs we snapped. All too soon it was time to return in the cable car. As we were coming down the white clouds were forming around the Mountain and by the time we reached the ground Table Mountain was entirely covered in white clouds. The contrast in such a short time was incredible.

At the Races

We were guests of Mr & Mrs Van Zyle on a day at the races. They were accompanied by Mr & Mrs Harry McCarthy. Mr McCarthy was a Steward of the Racecourse and Managing Director of LTA Cape Town.

We were directed to the Steward's Enclosure when we arrived at the Kenilworth Racecourse for the day and joined the party. Delicious food and a plentiful supply of drinks were available. A betting area for the Stewards Enclosure was kept busy. We watched the races with great enthusiasm - Roseleen had four winners, I had two. We thanked our hosts for entertaining us and for a splendid day.

The Cape Town Wine Route

We had now reached 17th September. The sixteen days since we arrived in South Africa had flown past. Every day had brought us great pleasure.

Edgar, our driver, took us on a tour of the Wine Route. It was a beautiful drive through the countryside where the vineyards were situated. We drove through acres and acres of vineries arriving at Boschendal Wine Farm at lunchtime. I remember it most for its beautiful restaurant, its hanging baskets of roses and for the perfect lunch. We toured the Old Manor Shop and the Wine Shop before leaving for another Wine Farm. We had a tour of the winery with our guide telling us of the processes of wine making before the bottling which we also saw. Edgar then drove us back to Cape Town by a different route with vineyards as far as the eye could see. As this was our final day in Cape Town we thanked Edgar for making our time in his city so enjoyable and interesting. We were sorry our time in Cape Town was so short as we found it an attractive place with a lot of magnificent buildings.

George and the Garden Route

Having said our farewells to our hosts in Cape Town and to Edgar our driver, he insisted he would drive us to the airport for the short flight to George which was in the constituency of Mr P. (Pic) Botha, the State President. We were met at George by a representative of LTA (Port Elizabeth) who handed me the keys of a BMW. I took possession of the car which I would drive to Port Elizabeth. We spent a splendid day in George before driving to Plettenberg Bay and the Beacon Island Hotel for an overnight stay. The hotel was situated in a most beautiful bay with golden sands.

The following day we drove the scenic Garden Route to Port Elizabeth. This was a delightful drive. The Elizabeth Hotel was our overnight hotel which like all other hotels on the trip was excellent – in comfort and food. It was here that as the temperature was high I swam in the sea again. We left our hotel early next morning for a flight to Cape Town where we were to join the Blue Train for the journey from Cape Town to Johannesburg. Later that day I met with business people and politicians in Cape Town including a meeting with the British Vice-Consul who had been made aware of my visit to Cape Town by the Foreign and Commonwealth Office. One of the projects to which I was taken was a large housing development for black people built by the City Council. The meetings and site visit were most useful.

The Blue Train

The Blue Train (in its various style and name) dates back to 1901. It was in 1937 real luxury was introduced when twelve luxury coaches were ordered from a United Kingdom Company in Birmingham. Prior to these coaches being delivered, another order was placed for two air-conditioned, all steel lounge cars; two air-conditioned, all steel dining cars; kitchen cars and an all steel, luggage van. All of these were delivered in 1939. Due to the Second World War these special cars were withdrawn until 1946 when it was officially named the Blue Train by the Hon F.C. Sturrock, the then Minister of Transport. The Blue Train was regarded (rightly so, as we found out) to be the epitome of luxury train travel.

In 1972 the authorities believed they could improve on the quality of service offered to train travellers. Two new Blue Trains were built in South Africa at a cost of 3 million Rand. No expense was spared to create a mode of travel with the utmost luxury and comfort. It was one of these trains we boarded on 24th September for the twenty-four hour journey covering in total 1608 kilometres from Cape Town to Pretoria.

We had secured Type A accommodation – a private sitting room, bedroom and bathroom. It was delightful. We settled in looking forward to the journey through a large part of South Africa. As the train travelled noiselessly and vibration free through beautiful well maintained regions, we also travelled through 'shanty' towns where the poverty was obvious. Little black children were running around with no clothes – others were scantily dressed. It made us feel sad and we hoped that one day the 'shanty' townships would be wiped away and the poverty stricken areas replaced with a meaningful community for the children to grow up, just as the Gold Mine workers' children were enjoying.

Lunch, dinner and breakfast were served in the dining car. The menu selection for all meals was exceptional. High quality South African wines were served finishing with liquors in the evening. The service was of a very high standard – even breakfast was just as wonderful!

All too soon and after a relaxing and restful twenty-four hours in the Blue Train we arrived in Johannesburg. We made our way to the Sandton Sun Hotel bringing with us the most pleasant memories of a special journey.

The last four days!

Before leaving home several of my constituents gave me names and addresses of relatives living in Johannesburg. We made contact and spent several happy hours in their homes chatting about the farming scene as it was in Aberdeenshire before they left for South Africa and how they had made well in South Africa since moving there.

Arrangements for a visit to Pretoria had been made in advance. Pretoria is the administrative capital of South Africa and it is also the second Terminal of the Blue Train. I arrived by car and soon realised why the city is often referred to as the Jacaranda City. There must have been thousands of Jacaranda trees blooming all over the city. Late September and October are the months to see the blossom which reminded me of my many visits to Marbella in Spain where Jacaranda grows in profusion. The purpose of my visit was to meet politicians along with senior Civil Servants from all parties in the State Government. The Government building where the offices of the Prime Minister are located is estimated to be one of the world's outstanding examples of architecture of the time. It was there I met with delegates from the Political Parties and with Civil Servants who were available. I quickly realised I had to exercise diplomacy as the views expressed by one may well have been the opposite by another. I listened carefully, in the case of the Civil Servants I was looking for answers to matters I raised. On returning to our hotel and reflecting on the day with the politicians it was then I knew how much I had learned about South Africa's problems.

On our penultimate day we drove to Sun City - a holiday town with every imaginable amenity. We played a round of golf on a magnificent course – we relaxed by the swimming pool – I could not resist but to swim under the waterfalls – we had a late lunch and drove back to our hotel.

On 29th September 1985 we spent our final day of the trip to South Africa. Roseleen went shopping while I completed my 'diary' of our month in the country and a report which I had promised Mr Malcolm Rifkind MP Minister of State at the Foreign and Commonwealth Office. At 8.00 p.m. our flight to London departed. We left South Africa with many happy memories of the most wonderful holiday of our lifetime for which we were indebted to Andrew Gay and all members of LTA South Africa for the excellent planning and services provided.

We arrived in Aberdeen to be met by our son Dermot who was anxious to hear of our experiences. On arriving home we were met with a rapturous welcome from our grandchildren. Over the next few evenings at the fireside we reminisced with the family of our month in South Africa. All of them were enthralled. One of my younger grandchildren wanted to know if I had killed an elephant in the Game Reserve!

Author's Note

Readers of the book will appreciate my memories of South Africa go back to 1985. Since then the country has seen many dramatic changes. Apartheid has gone. Segregation is virtually a thing of the past. Black people hold the most senior positions in Government. South Africa is held in high esteem by those countries in the United Nations. In the sporting world South Africa has produced many champions at the highest level and its people have learned to live with each other.

What struck me very strongly was the number of South Africans who were devoted Christians and Gospel followers. There are adult and children's Gospel Choirs performing all over the world with much acclaim. As I ponder on the changes which have taken place since Roseleen and I holidayed in South Africa I find a verse in the hymn - Love Divine all Love Excelling - which epitomises the feelings of those people who live and work in South Africa. I end this Chapter about a holiday full of interest and with memories preserved in my mind for ever.

> *Love Divine, all loves excelling, Joy of heaven, to earth come down.*
> *Fix in us Thy humble dwelling, All Thy faithful mercies crown.*
> *Jesus, Thou are all compassion, Pure, unbounded love Thou art:*
> *Visit us with Thy salvation, Enter every trembling heart.*

I hope readers of the book will enjoy this Chapter as much as I have in writing it.

CHAPTER SEVENTEEN

Peterhead Harbours (South Bay Development) Order Confirmation Bill 1986

PETERHEAD IS ONE OF THE LARGEST, if not the largest, fishing Port in Europe. Over the years its trade increased with the use of the Port by the agricultural industry for the export of grain. The growth of this business, together with the increased use by fishermen and the potential of other business, made it necessary for the Trustees of the Harbours to consider the construction of quays which would be available to meet the additional demands on the Port.

In 1985 the Trustees presented the proposals to the Secretary of State for Scotland which they were obliged to within the legislation. These proposals were in the form of a Bill which was named – Peterhead Harbours (South Bay Development) Order Confirmation Bill. It was presented for approval by Parliamentary Agents who had been appointed by the Trustees.

The object of the Order was to authorise works at the harbours which would calm the waters in the existing harbours and provide additional space for the fishing vessels using the Port. As evidence of the need for these works, it was illustrated that the number of boxes of fish landed at Peterhead had increased from 300,000 in 1970 to 2,109,000 in the years up to March 1985. In addition the Port had become an important one for the export of grain and other bulk cargoes, serving its own hinterland of grain producers in the north east of Scotland.

It was pointed out in the Report included in the Bill presentation, the increase in trade at Peterhead Harbours has led to severe congestion within the fishing vessels' area in the harbours. At weekends particularly, vessels frequently had to berth several deep from the quay wall making the servicing of vessels difficult, inefficient and creating a health and safety hazard. Steel hulled boats had to berth alongside wooden hulled boats which often created considerable damage to the fishing vessels. In effect the harbours were too often crowded resulting in vessels normally using their home Port going elsewhere.

An important factor in the Report to the Bill was Peterhead Harbour Trustees did not engage in any oil related activity at the Port. This was made clear to allay the fears of companies and other harbour authorities involved in the oil industry of a possible threat to their business. Nor was it the intention of the Trustees to engage in this type of business if the Development is approved and constructed.

Following the proposals being deposited with the Secretary of State for Scotland and advertised in the media, there were ten petitions against the Draft Bill. Three were withdrawn before the Public Inquiry and the remaining seven were recorded.

In due course the Government appointed a Panel of Commissioners from both Houses of Parliament to hold a Public Inquiry in Peterhead to examine the proposals and hear evidence from all objectors in addition to examining the proposals at the site. The Panel was chaired by Lord Hughes, an experienced former Scottish Office Minister in a Labour Government. The other members of the Commission at the Public Inquiry in Peterhead were the Earl of Balfour, Lady Sempill and Mr Ronald Brown MP for Edinburgh Leith. In the normal course of events the Bill would have been presented to Parliament and passed through all its stages without a problem. However, it was not to be as the Aberdeen Harbour Board members presented a petition to Parliament hoping that the Confirming Bill be referred to a Joint Committee of both Houses of Parliament. If this had been accepted there would have been an inordinate delay in getting the development started in addition to a further £100,000 of legal fees having to be paid by the Trustees during any investigation by a Joint Committee.

Up to this point I had not been involved in any major way with the proposals of the Peterhead Harbours Trustees. With the advent of the petition from Aberdeen Harbour Board, the Peterhead Harbours Trustees requested a meeting with me, as the local MP. On being appraised of the proposals and the objections to it, I undertook to do my best for the development to proceed as I fully understood and agreed with, the proposals the Trustees were making to improve the harbours at Peterhead.

Within days I received a request for a meeting by the Peterhead Business Association who were urging me to support the efforts of the Trustees to secure approval for the development. The Association members stressed upon me the importance of the proposed extension to the harbours for the future employment prospects of Peterhead. The President of the Association stated he was appalled that rival Ports could meddle in the business of Peterhead officers in an attempt to protect their own interests.

He complained the objectors were not prepared to accept the decision of the Commissioners at the Public Inquiry. I assured them I would fight the case when the Bill came before the House of Commons.

The Bill was called in the Chamber in October 1985. A Member of Parliament for one of the Aberdeen Seats used a Parliamentary procedure by calling 'Object' which he was perfectly entitled to do – much to my regret. This signalled a considerable delay would take place. There was also a danger the Bill would be referred to a Joint Committee of both Houses of Parliament - something the Peterhead Trustees did not want to happen.

On 15th November 1985 Mr George Younger MP the Secretary of State for Scotland dramatically attempted to break the deadlock by introducing a Bill to confirm the Peterhead Harbours (South Bay Development) Provisional Order. By doing so Mr Younger ensured that even if any MP attempted to object to the legislation on its Second Reading, the delay would only be temporary. For me this was a substantial step forward and was pleasing to the Peterhead Harbours Trustees when I acquainted them of the decision of the Secretary of State for Scotland.

As a result of the intervention of the Secretary of State, the Bill came before Parliament for Second Reading. The Debate started immediately after questions to Ministers was completed and continued for many hours into the night. A number of Peterhead Harbour Trustees and Officials were present in the Public Gallery to listen and watch the proceedings. There followed a ferocious battle with claim and counter claim. I was fortunate to 'catch the Speaker's eye' early in the Debate. When he called me I made a plea for common sense.

I explained the Bill was to confirm the Provisional Order made by the Secretary of State for Scotland under the Private Legislation Procedure (Scotland) Act 1936 after a Local Public Inquiry by Commissioners in pursuance of the Act. Continuing to address the House I made clear the Order was promoted by the Peterhead Harbours Trustees who are charged by statute with managing the fishing harbours in my constituency. During my speech there were many interventions which I was able to handle satisfactorily.

Many Members from all sides of the House wished to speak in the debate – some were for and some were against the proposals. All the objectors were Members who had interests in the fishing industry and whose constituencies included harbours in other parts of Scotland. I was challenged on where the funding, which was estimated at £17 million pounds, would be found. On this significant matter I was happy to say the Trustees had adequate provisions to meet the cost and would not be making an application for funding from any Government source received by way of taxpayers.

The media in the north east of Scotland had a few field days reporting the debate in the House of Commons on the Bill. Some of the headlines read:

> Harbour rebels ready for a fight – No Peace in Bill Battle
> McQuarrie in attack on Aberdeen Trustees
> The Peterhead Harbour battle erupts
> Peterhead Setback - MP blocks Harbour Extension
> Harbour Project could be scuppered
> McQuarrie blast at Intransigent
> Almost Floundered but not yet says MP McQuarrie

As I stood in my place in the Chamber delivering my speech and thinking of the media comments about possible failure of the Bill, I was a little nervous. The Members opposed to the Bill had their chance to speak against the Bill. The stage was reached when it seemed pressure for a Joint Committee of both Houses was likely to win the day. I made a number of interventions into Opposition speeches as a result of inaccuracies in the debate, knowing that the representatives from Peterhead Harbour Board were following proceedings from the Gallery. I could see this was having a positive effect.

At nine o'clock the Speaker called me down to his seat. He said 'Albert, I do not think things are going well for you to get the Second Reading through. Do you not think a Joint Committee of both Houses would satisfy the objectors to the Bill as it stands?'

I replied 'Mr Speaker, the Chairman, Mr Tom Buchan with Captain Alex Auld, Mr Colin McCrae Solicitor and Mr David Buchan Chief Engineer of the Peterhead Harbour Board are in the Gallery. I would like to have their opinion on your comments'. He said 'That is a good idea. Just let me know their views'.

At the Gallery I brought the visitors to the area just outside the Strangers entrance. I told them the Speaker's remarks. After discussing the positives and the negatives of this proposal with the Trustees, Mr McCrae said 'No, Albert, we cannot accept this proposal – **we are going for Bust**' – prophetic words which were to be headlines in the press the following day when victory was achieved.

I returned to Mr Speaker, advised him the Trustees were not prepared to alter their earlier decision of not accepting a Joint Committee of both Houses and instructed me to tell him **they were going for bust**. Mr Speaker said 'it is a matter for them and all I can say for their sake is I hope they have made the correct decision'.

The decision taken by the Trustees placed a heavy burden on my shoulders. In accordance with Parliamentary Procedure where a Closure is moved by a Member of Parliament it has to be done when the chance of success is greatest. I knew there would only be one chance. I could not take 'my eye off the ball' in the ongoing debate as points were being raised which I had to clarify.

At 9.35 p.m. I saw my opportunity. I jumped to my feet and in a loud audible voice I claimed to move 'that the question be now put' (this meant that the Vote to give the Bill a Second Reading should take place at once).

The Speaker then said 'the question is that the Question be now put. As many of that view say "Aye" on the contrary say "No". There were shouts to both at which stage the Speaker said 'I think the Ayes have it – Division'.

Members trooped out of the Chamber to the Voting Lobby. Mr Speaker announced 'Tellers for the Ayes Mr Albert McQuarrie and Mr Bill Walker. Tellers for the Noes Mr Robert Hughes and Mr Gerald Malone.' After eight minutes Mr Speaker shouted 'lock the doors'. This meant the Division Lobbies were closed and no one else could enter to vote. As one of the tellers, I remained in the Division Lobby until the Clerks had completed the count. When the Chief Clerk approached me I was filled with delight as it signalled the vote had gone in our favour. I could have jumped with joy. As I made my way to the Chamber and took up the right hand position in the line-up with the Tellers, there were shouts of success from our supporters in the knowledge the battle was won. I realised at that stage the Peterhead Harbour Representatives would not be aware of the outcome of the vote. Soon they were as happy as I was when the Speaker announced 'the Ayes to the right 119, the Noes to the left 53, so the Ayes have it, the Ayes have it'.

While this was a massive victory there was one further vote to be taken before we were sure the Bill could be sent to the Lords as is the custom. This vote was on the Motion of Objective to the Bill for the proposal to be sent to a Joint Committee of the House of Lords. If we failed to secure a majority on this vote it would mean the long procedure of taking the Bill through the Committee stages again which would take many months.

Mr Speaker, following the same procedure, then read out the Motion and put the Question. A division was called. He announced the Tellers for the Ayes would be Mr Gordon Wilson and Mr Malcolm Bruce; the Tellers for the Noes Mr Bill Walker and Mr Christopher Murphy. I sat tensely in my place waiting for the Tellers to appear. When they entered the Chamber and Bill Walker walked to the right hand side of the tellers I knew victory was ours. I looked to the Gallery where I saw a group of very happy men waving jubilantly. Mr Speaker announced the Vote for the Ayes was 69 and for the Noes (which was us) was 87. I was not concerned the vote was lower. It was now 10.30 p.m. and many Members had gone from the Chamber rather than wait to record their vote for the Second Reading of the Bill.

I left the Chamber as quickly as I could to meet up with the Trustees and Officials. There was great jubilation on meeting. I took them to the Pugin Room where the champagne flowed well into the night as we talked of the victory which had been achieved.

While there was great jubilation we were mindful of the fact the Bill had to have the approval of the House of Lords and then to be returned to the House of Commons for the Third Reading. I promised the Trustees my efforts to see this through the Lords would continue and I would also lobby Members to support the Third Reading in the Chamber.

The Bill was presented to the House of Lords on 24th March 1986. A number of Lords on the Labour benches of the House were critical of the Bill principally as they were of the opinion the development at Peterhead would damage the Port of Aberdeen. Lord Campbell of Croy delivered a stirring speech in defence of the Trustees and assured the Lords the development would have no adverse impact on Aberdeen Harbour activity. At the end of the debate the Motion to give approval to the Bill on Second Reading was given without a Division. The following day the Bill received its Third Reading in the Lords and sent back to the Commons where it was passed without Division. Notification was made to the Commons that the Bill had been approved by the Lords with the statement read out by Mr Speaker the following day.

At last all hurdles were over and the Bill became a reality bringing tremendous satisfaction to the Peterhead Harbour Trustees. On 26th March 1986 the Peterhead Harbours (South Bay Development) Order Confirmation Bill received the Royal Assent from Her Majesty The Queen. This was the culmination of the most ferocious debate I had witnessed in the House of Commons.

Once more the headlines in the media reflected the interest this Bill had generated:

Harbour Bill Approval thanks to Albert MP
Delighted responses to Harbour victory
The Final Battle Won
Peterhead Harbour Bill Passed – Triumph for McQuarrie

The *Buchan Observer* carried a headline reading 'Boothby pays tribute' in which it records a telephone call from Lord Boothby the former MP for

East Aberdeenshire when he said:

> I would like to pay tribute to the splendid job Albert McQuarrie has done in successfully guiding the passage through the House of Commons of the Peterhead Harbours Bill. There is one word he does not seem to know – and that is **defeat.** He never gave up despite all the opposition and won through in the end. The congratulations being heaped upon him now are well earned.

On 2nd May 1986 the Harbour Trustees held a Dinner. They invited me as Guest of Honour for the work I had done in successfully piloting the Bill through the House of Commons. Mr Tom Buchan (now deceased) Chairman in his address said:

> Mr McQuarrie did far and above what was expected of him as our MP. It was wrong of us not to have brought him into the picture before we did. He spent an enormous amount of time and energy getting the Bill approved. We are deeply indebted to him and hold this Dinner in his honour. As a mark of our appreciation I am presenting this crystal decanter with an appropriate silver plate to Mr McQuarrie.

The inscription reads:

Go for Bust
Presented by the Trustees of
The Harbours of Peterhead
To Albert McQuarrie Esq MP
At a Dinner in his honour
2nd May 1986

I was deeply touched by this gesture and also those memorable words I had spoken to Mr Speaker when I told him the Trustees were prepared to take the risk and **Go for Bust** when the Vote was called.

I watched the South Bay Development over the years. Two quays were constructed on either side of the water forming a basin to be named 'The Boothby Basin' in honour of Lord Boothby a Member of Parliament for East Aberdeenshire for thirty-four years. One quay was built projecting into the sea the other was built on the land side. It was this quay on which the new state of the art fishmarket was built and which has been greatly appreciated by the fishing industry.

Six years on, the Development was complete. I was delighted to receive an invitation from the Harbour Trustees to the official opening on 6th August 1992 by Rt Hon Douglas Hurd CH, CBE, PC, MP, the Foreign and Commonwealth Secretary. This was a very special day for all the people involved in the development – the Trustees, the Engineers, Tradesmen, Politicians and many others including myself. There was praise from a number of the Trustees on my steering of the Bill to its final approval in the House of Commons resulting in the approval of the Development. During the course of his speech to the assembled gathering on the seaside quay Mr Tom Buchan made reference to the quay where the new fishmarket stands and which is to be called The Merchant Quay. He further announced the quay on which we had gathered for the official opening was to be known as The Albert Quay. I was very pleased at this recognition of my efforts on behalf of the people of Peterhead and the Trustees in particular, but perhaps tinged with a little disappointment the quay was not named the Sir Albert Quay to take account of the Knighthood Her Majesty The Queen had conferred on me in July 1986. I looked proudly at the plaque bearing the words 'The Albert Quay'.

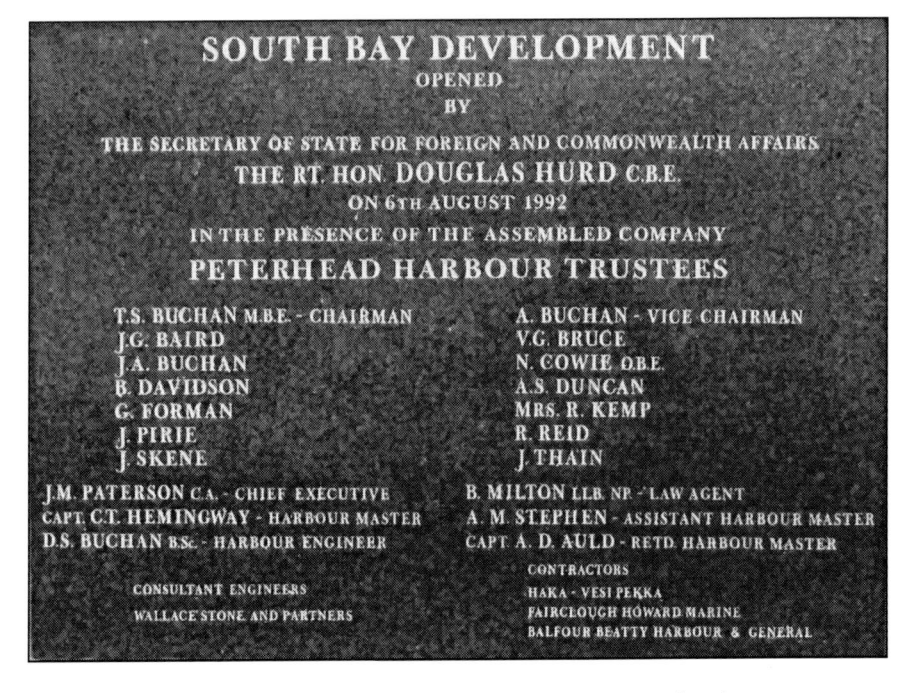

SOUTH BAY DEVELOPMENT
OPENED
BY
THE SECRETARY OF STATE FOR FOREIGN AND COMMONWEALTH AFFAIRS
THE RT. HON. DOUGLAS HURD C.B.E.
ON 6TH AUGUST 1992
IN THE PRESENCE OF THE ASSEMBLED COMPANY
PETERHEAD HARBOUR TRUSTEES

T.S. BUCHAN M.B.E. - CHAIRMAN
J.G. BAIRD
J.A. BUCHAN
B. DAVIDSON
G. FORMAN
J. PIRIE
J. SKENE

A. BUCHAN - VICE CHAIRMAN
V.G. BRUCE
N. COWIE O.B.E.
A.S. DUNCAN
MRS. R. KEMP
R. REID
J. THAIN

J.M. PATERSON C.A. - CHIEF EXECUTIVE
CAPT. C.T. HEMINGWAY - HARBOUR MASTER
D.S. BUCHAN B.Sc. - HARBOUR ENGINEER

B. MILTON LLB. NP. - LAW AGENT
A. M. STEPHEN - ASSISTANT HARBOUR MASTER
CAPT. A. D. AULD - RETD. HARBOUR MASTER

CONSULTANT ENGINEERS
WALLACE STONE AND PARTNERS

CONTRACTORS
HAKA - VESI PEKKA
FAIRCLOUGH HOWARD MARINE
BALFOUR BEATTY HARBOUR & GENERAL

75. Unveiling of South Bay Development, Peterhead

A later Honour from Peterhead Port Authority

On 22nd May 2012 I received a letter from Mr John E. Wallace Chief Executive of the Peterhead Port Authority, now incorporating Peterhead Harbour Trustees. In the letter Mr Wallace stated the Board members had unanimously agreed the Albert Quay should be renamed the 'Sir Albert Quay' and asked for my agreement to the proposed change. As 6th August 2012 would be the 20th Anniversary of the Opening of the Quay, a Ceremony was being arranged to mark the occasion and recognise the considerable development the Port of Peterhead had experienced. At the same time the quay would be renamed in respect of the Honour I received from Her Majesty. I assured Mr Wallace I would be delighted to attend the Ceremony.

76. Unveiling of the Sir Albert Quay Peterhead

On a bright but windy day a large company gathered at the quay with Mr Bill Mackie, Chairman of the Port Authority, who presided over the Ceremony. Mr Mackie was accompanied by present and former Trustees, advisers and officials who had been involved with the passage of the Bill through Parliament. Mr Mackie and Mr Wallace addressed the company. I was invited to formally unveil the plaque which I did with great pride. In one of my shorter speeches I did say how wonderful it was to have the quay renamed. I thanked the Board members and Mr Wallace for their kindness

Peterhead
PORT AUTHORITY

Sir Albert McQuarrie Kt KMLJ
20th Anniversary of the South Bay Development and the Re-naming and Dedication of the Sir Albert Quay
6th of August 2012

On this the 6th of August 2012, representing the 20th Anniversary of the South Bay Development and the Re-naming and Dedication of the Sir Albert Quay, the Board of Peterhead Port Authority in rightful recognition of the stalwart works of Sir Albert McQuarrie Kt KMLJ in securing the Passing in the House of Commons the Peterhead Harbour (South Bay Development) Confirmation Bill which received Royal Assent from Her Majesty The Queen on 26th March 1986, express their most humble and grateful thanks.

Let the record show that as evidenced in Hansard and physically in the infrastructural development of the port that the South Bay Development which benefited from the plans and toils of many parties, may never have 'seen the light of day', but for the efforts of Sir Albert McQuarrie in closing out the detractors and delivering the most necessary permissions.

During his time and service as MP for Banff and Buchan he championed many honourable and worthwhile causes, not least the Safety at Sea Bill for which many lives have been spared as continues to be the case. However, it was his tacit and tactical understanding of the Common Fisheries Policy and his unyielding efforts in that 'Great House' to derive maximum value from the flawed policy for his constituents, time and time again that demands enduring memory. We, the benefactors of all of these achievements, today honour, commemorate and recognise Sir Albert McQuarrie as a most loyal servant, guardian and champion of the Port of Peterhead for which we bestow this honour and offer our deepest eternal gratitude.

WJMR MACKIE, CONVENOR

J E WALLACE, CHIEF EXECUTIVE

77. Citation presented to me by the Board of Directors at Peterhead Harbour Authority and told the company I would never forget the battle in the Commons after the Trustees told me they would **Go for Bust** in an effort to secure the passing of the Bill. Mr Wallace presented me with a Citation, a copy of which I have included in the book. I expressed my grateful thanks to all for the wonderful expressions contained within the Citation which touched me greatly. The company then attended the Celebratory Luncheon where Mr Wallace again read the Citation. It was too windy to be heard at the Sir Albert Quay in Peterhead Harbour!

When we have visitors, and the grandchildren, to our home I never fail to drive them to Peterhead Harbour to have their photograph taken at the Sir Albert Quay.

Today Peterhead Harbours are extremely busy. The large fishing vessels are able to berth at both the Sir Albert Quay and the Merchant Quay while the smaller vessels can access the old harbour for berthing after off-loading their catch for sale at the new fishmarket. The continual use of supply ships servicing the North Sea Oil and Gas Industry have found Peterhead with its extensive quays of huge benefit. The farming and forestry industry make use of the excellent facilities.

As I wander round the harbours I still feel a sense of satisfaction that, as a Member of Parliament, I was able to achieve success for the Trustees of Peterhead Harbour who put their trust in me when they made the statement **Go for Bust** all those years ago, creating what is now one of the best range of quays within a harbour in the United Kingdom.

CHAPTER EIGHTEEN

Safety at Sea Bill, 1986

THE SAFETY AT SEA BILL was piloted through the House of Commons in 1986 by me as a Private Member's Bill. I would like to explain what a Private Member's Bill is, how it is dealt with in the House of Commons and how it came to be I was promoting one.

A Private Member's Bill is generally on a subject a Member of Parliament would wish to see passed into legislation. The Member provides the House of Commons' Clerks with details requesting a date when the Member can present the Bill in the Chamber. Unless there is substantial backing from all sides of the House and tacit Government approval there is little chance of a Bill succeeding. If by 2.30 p.m., on the day the Bill is discussed, it has not made progress to the next stage it is 'talked out', and has little possibility of success.

Once a year, there is a Ballot for Private Member's Bills. It is held in a Committee Room at the House of Commons. A Member who wishes to promote a Bill enters his/her name for the ballot. It is generally accepted the first six names have a good chance of success. While I was aware of the opportunity it was of little interest to me at the time as I had no subject matters given to me by any constituent which would justify me promoting a Private Members Bill.

This all changed in October 1985 when a fishing vessel from Banffshire was sunk at sea with the loss of four lives. As I stood at the graveside my heart ached for the widows and children devastated by the loss of their loved ones. The widows approached me and begged for something to be done to prevent further tragedies at sea. I gave my assurance to do my level best and would approach Ministers of the Government. I did, and found little enthusiasm from Ministers who told me there were no vacant slots in the proposed legislation for the next year.

While I accepted this from the Ministers I was determined to find some way of introducing a Bill to secure the safety of fishermen while at sea. I learned there would be a Ballot for Private Members Bills in the first week of November. I decided this was a route I could take to introduce a Bill and submitted my name to the House of Commons Clerks.

On the day of the ballot I made my way to the Committee Room. There was a picture in my mind of the widows at the graveside and my promise to them. The public area was packed with members of charities hoping 'their' Member would be successful in the Ballot to introduce a Bill beneficial to their particular charity. I sat in the area reserved for Members, closed my eyes and said 'Please God, let me have one of the early numbers as I wish to introduce a Safety at Sea Bill in an effort to save the lives of fishermen from stricken vessels at sea'.

To my great joy my name came fourth in the Ballot. I knew my Bill would have a good chance of being placed on the Statute Book as Legislation, provided I could gather sufficient support from members of other Parties in the House of Commons. I would also have to obtain the backing of the Government in order to see the Bill through its stages.

As I left the Committee Room I was approached by a number of charity representatives asking me to promote a particular cause. To all I replied I was sorry to disappoint them as it was my intention to promote a Safety at Sea Bill to save the lives of fishermen at sea.

The following day, I was most encouraged by the number of Members of Parliament from all Parties in the House welcoming my intention and offering support. From then on I realised the huge undertaking which faced me in the preparation of the Bill for presentation to the Commons. Unlike Government Bills, there was no official backing or support from Civil Servants during the preparation. I was determined to succeed. Nothing was going to deter me trying to get the Bill through the House of Commons and the House of Lords.

Preparing the Bill

I set about seeking information on existing safety measures on board vessels and what action fishermen were taking at present to prevent disasters happening. I was aware how important it was to have the fishermen and their organisations on my side. I expected there would be some reservation to a few of the proposed Clauses which I hoped could be overcome by personal contact with the objectors prior to the Clause being written into the Bill.

In gathering information I sought to ascertain the number of vessels lost at sea resulting in the loss of fishermen. I established in the period from 1972 to 1984 a total of 464 fishing vessels were lost at sea with the deaths of 246 fishermen. From 1977 to 1985, in the north east of Scotland seventy-four fishermen, mainly from my constituency, were lost at sea leaving widows and many children without a father. Receiving this information made me even more determined to do whatever could be done in an effort to halt the multiple tragedies. Gradually I assembled the main items for the Clauses in the Bill.

It became clear the location of stricken vessels could not always be pinpointed quickly to prevent loss of life. What I was required to do was to ascertain what equipment was available for skippers to carry on their boats to enable the Rescue Services locate a stricken vessel. I made contact with a number of businesses dealing in electronics, for discussions about a radio beacon. The support and the information I received was of great value.

On 7th February 1986 I presented my Safety at Sea Bill to the House of Commons for its Second Reading. In my opening address I highlighted the fact the Bill had wide all Party support and general approval from Her Majesty's Government. I paid tribute to all who had helped me reach this stage before proceeding to explain the content of the Clauses. I announced it was my intention to leave Clause 3 to the end as it was the most important, necessitating considerable discussion.

Clause 1 - Emergency Position Indicating Radio Beacon (EPIRB)
This clause relates to the fitting of a float-free emergency radio beacon which would increase safety at sea by automatically transmitting a vessel's position on aircraft frequencies prepared for satellite honing. The emergency beacon would float free and activate automatically should a vessel sink. Seldom is there time to broadcast a mayday message for long enough to provide a reliable radio location for search and rescue agencies if the vessel sinks. Even if there is time, such a radio location would indicate only the point where the vessel was lost.

By attaching a Hydrostatic Release Unit to the radio beacon the system can be activated by water pressure as soon as the vessel sinks. The action releases the lashings which hold the beacon canister securely in the deck-mounted cradle. Once the lashings are loosened the two halves of the spring loaded canister breaks open allowing the self-buoyant canister to float free from the sinking vessel at the same time the operation activated the beacon transmitter which then broadcasts on the civil and military air distress frequencies.

I went on to explain that if fishing vessels were fitted with emergency position indicating radio beacons, it would follow that the maritime and aircraft rescue services would be able to locate a sinking vessel quickly. This is an important factor, as on many occasions the vessel goes down with no indication of the position making the rescue services search hundreds of square miles to find the vessel. Signals with this type of EPIRB can be identified at distances up to 100 miles. Aircraft would not be constrained by the prevailing conditions or the size of the vessel in distress. Signals of distress from the beacon can be transmitted for at least seventy-two hours – an extremely important factor for the civil and military aircraft to reach the scene and also to alert fishing and other vessels in the disaster area to assist in the rescue.

78. Emergency Position Indicator Radio Beacon. EPIRB
Photograph by courtesy of Woodsons of Aberdeen

This Bill seeks to compel the use of approved distress beacons on all fishing vessels. It is to be hoped the Department of Transport which is the body responsible for shipping would ensure all vessels are required to fit the beacon if the Bill received the approval of both Houses and became legislation.

A number of Members raised the matter of cost for the EPIRB. I advised I had obtained a figure from a manufacturer of £800 for the EPIRB and £20 for the Hydrostatic Release valve. The costs would be apportioned for each share fisherman. The Scottish Fishermen's Federation did not consider £820 to be extortionate if it was to save lives. I stated the Sea Fish

Industry Authority would award a 25 per cent discount for all purchases of the EPIRB and release valve. Tax relief would also be granted as it would be a business charge.

Clause 2 – Fitting of Life Rafts

This Clause would require owners of fishing vessels of between 30 ft and 300 ft to have on board sufficient life rafts for the crew and any passengers. It would also require that life rafts should have Hydrostatic Release Units fitted so that the life raft would inflate automatically and float free if the vessel was to sink. Most vessels carry life rafts but not all would have Hydrostatic Release mechanism. If lives are to be saved it is vital the fitting of those units becomes compulsory.

There may be no opportunity to free a life raft if it had been stored on the deck or on top of the wheelhouse. If the Hydrostatic Release Unit is used it is guaranteed the life raft would come to the surface. A life raft with a unit attached has a pointer made fast to the weak link system of the Hydrostatic Release Unit. The location of the HRU is such it is readily accessible and is located on the seaward side of the vessel. When submerged to a depth of 1.5 m to 3.7 m the Hydrostatic Release Unit operates automatically. Freed of the lashings the container rises to the surface paying out the inflation painter line as it goes but retaining it to the HRU by means of the weak link. It is the combination of the rising container and the sinking vessel which provides the painter tensions which activates the gas cylinder and starts inflation once the free painter line is paid out. As the vessel sinks the weak line will break releasing the life raft from the vessel. The weak link breaking strength is such the raft is not dragged under the sinking vessel, thus ensuring the crew have another chance of being saved at sea. Without this essential piece of equipment the chances of survival at sea are slim. To throw more weight on the need for vessels to have life rafts with Hydrostatic Release Units a Report by the Department of Transport into a vessel lot at sea resulting in the deaths of five fishermen had a paragraph which read 'Lives might have been saved had the vessel's life rafts been fitted with Hydrostatic Automatic Release Units so they would have floated free when the vessel sank'. Maritime Shipping Notice M1173 recommends that such units are fitted in fishing vessels and the loss of the vessel in the Report underlines this advice.

I explained to the House this Notice is only a recommendation - many vessels do not have the units fitted. It is the aim of the Bill to make it mandatory for all fishing vessels to be fitted with the Hydrostatic Release Valves on the life rafts.

At this stage of my address I took a number of questions on life rafts from Members on both sides of the House. All were supportive of mandatory legislation. Issues such as costs of the units, number of vessels not carrying them at present were answered to their satisfaction and it was clear that these Clauses would receive approval on a vote when All Clauses had been discussed. I intimated my intention again to leave Clause 3 – one of the most important parts of the Bill - dealing with life jackets - to later and would proceed to consider the other minor Clauses.

Further Clauses
Clauses 4, 5, 6, 7, 8, 9, 10, 11 dealing with power to prescribe further requirements - Enforcement; Offences; Training in safety matters; Exemptions; Regulations; Drunkenness of Skipper of Fishing Vessel; Extension of powers to make safety regulations were all discussed. Some Clauses were withdrawn and others modified before going to Committee, then back to the House of Commons for Third Reading and finally to the House of Lords for approval.

Clause 3 – Life Jackets
I addressed the House on Clause 3 dealing with the wearing of life jackets while the vessel was at sea. My recommendation in the Bill dealt with the compulsory wearing of a life jacket on deck by crew members at all times. I was well aware when I announced the Bill, fishermen would resent the proposal. The fishermen were unaware the life jacket I was proposing was not the traditional type which did handicap a crew member when working on deck. The new model was neither cumbersome nor a problem to work in. It was of a harness design and was manufactured by Dunlop Beaufort after a number of discussions with the company. I explained the new design had been developed specifically with fishermen in mind and stressed too many fishermen had been lost due to not wearing life jackets. In many cases when a man falls overboard he strikes his head and is knocked unconscious. Wearing a life jacket, of the design I recommended, would result in the jacket inflating when it hit the sea triggering the automatic release action. I told the House the life jacket would also turn over to bring the man to face up position, preventing him from drowning even if he was unconscious.

I said fishermen should get into the habit of wearing a life jacket at sea. I accepted it would be difficult to legislate as it was 'up to the fishermen'. 'Would they be prepared to take the risk of not wearing one with the danger of being thrown overboard. Surely it is better to take preventative action rather than be drowned at sea. How many more widows and fatherless children must there be before the message gets home that fishermen working in hazardous conditions are loved and wanted at home? If they drown at sea they leave sad memories and dashed hopes'.

79. Dressed in a Safety at Sea Life Jacket

Many Members took part in the Debate on Clause 3. All were in favour of some measure to increase the use of life jackets. In an effort to allow Members see what the new life jacket looked like I had worn one under my jacket before entering the Chamber. At an appropriate moment I slipped off my jacket to display the life jacket. At once Mr Speaker rose and said:

> Order, Order, the Hon Gentleman should know things like this cannot be done in the House.

I apologised, but I made my point. Soon afterwards, Mr David Mitchell (now Sir David), Minister of State at the Department of Transport who was the Minister from the Government monitoring my Bill, in responding to a question about the life jackets from a Member said:

My Hon Friend the Member for Banff and Buchan (Mr McQuarrie) gave us a demonstration in the Chamber of the life jacket which is probably the only occasion such a demonstration has ever taken place in the House of Commons!

After further explanation was given on some of the non-controversial parts of the Bill the Question was put to approve the new Clause 3 which I had inserted into the Bill and to report the Bill as amended to the House. This was done and the Safety at Sea Bill was sent to a Committee of the House for scrutiny. It would then be sent back to the House of Commons for the Third Reading.

On 9th May 1986 the Third Reading of the Bill was debated. Account was taken of several amendments to the Bill arising from discussions I had with Ministers at the Department of Transport. Having clarified matters raised by other Members, the passage of the Bill seemed certain which gave me great hope. At this stage a number of Members on all sides of the House made complimentary remarks about the Bill. I was pleased and greatly appreciated the praises made about my presentation of such a worthwhile Bill.

Readers may be interested in some of the extracts from Hansard of the comments made by Honourable Members praising the passing of the Bill and the way I handled it in the House of Commons.

Rt Hon Donald Stewart (SNP)

I wish to congratulate the Hon Member for Banff and Buchan (Mr McQuarrie) on his Bill reaching Third Reading. The Hon Member for Banff and Buchan (Mr McQuarrie) has rendered a service to the fishing industry and to the fishermen themselves. Those of us who can stand back and who know something about the industry realise he has performed a signal service. I am certain he will have the thanks of the fishermen and their dependents in the years which lie ahead.

Dr Norman Godman (Lab)

I want to congratulate the Hon Member for Banff and Buchan as I am very grateful to him coming as I do from a fishing family. These measures to improve the safety at sea are welcomed by everyone.

Mr Austin Mitchell (Lab)

I enthusiastically join in congratulating the Hon Member for Banff and Buchan on his Bill. It represents a very real achievement. I hope it will become known as 'The McQuarrie Bill' as it is an important measure. The Bill provides for a safer existence for many hundreds of my constituents. There can be no greater achievement than that.

Mr Alexander Pollock (Conservative & Unionist)
I add my congratulations to my Hon Friend the Member for Banff and Buchan on his choice of subject which is dear to his heart. As a neighbour of his in Moray I can understand why. Like him I have had the harrowing experience during my years in Parliament of visiting the bereaved and attending memorial services after the loss of vessels at sea with the loss of lives and being conscious of the tragic heartache borne by the widows and children. I join with other Members in wishing this Bill a smooth passage through the House.

Mr Archy Kirkwood (Lib) (now Lord Kirkwood)
I pay my tribute to the Hon Gentleman for the way he has introduced this Bill. The House should rightly pay tribute to his continuing and general interest in a subject that affects not just his constituents but all other parts of Scotland. It is right this House should take a close interest on all aspects of Safety at Sea. At the end of the day Hon Members have a responsibility for ensuring there is adequate legislation to deal with the safety of our fishermen who go to sea to earn a living.

Mr Gerald Malone (Conservative & Unionist)
I should like to add to the congratulations being heaped on my Hon Friend the Member for Banff and Buchan. This is an extremely worthwhile Bill. The House's only regret at its passing into law is we shall be deprived of the sight of my Hon Friend (Mr McQuarrie) walking the Corridors of the House dressed in a variety of interesting life jackets and bearing a Distress beacon! I congratulate my Hon Friend in presenting the Bill in one of the most able and comprehensive Second Reading speeches I have heard. I congratulate him and wish the Bill every success.

Mr Robert Hughes (Lab) (now Lord Hughes)
I join Hon Members in all quarters of the House who have congratulated the Hon Member for Banff and Buchan on his choice of subject. It is no pun when I say we will give the Bill a fair wind! The new life jackets are easy to wear and are compact. It will not affect people's movements or agility. The Bill deserves support to prevent accidents and loss of life in fishing vessels. I give it my whole hearted support. *(I was grateful to Bob Hughes who led for Labour during the Debates in the House and made a number of helpful suggestions which were incorporated into the Bill.)*

Mr David Mitchell (Member of State, Department of Transport) (now Sir David)
I am happy to join those who have wished the Bill a successful and rapid passage on to the Statute Book. All Hon Members, as representative of the consumer, owe a debt to the fishermen. My Hon Friend for Banff and Buchan

through his initiative and determination has given us an opportunity to help make the role of fishermen less dangerous. The House, the fishing industry and the Government have every reason to be grateful to my Hon Friend (Mr McQuarrie).

Following these tributes which filled me with pride the question was put for the Bill to be read a Third Time which was done without the need for a vote. The Bill was sent to the House of Lords for approval.

On 4th June 1986 the Bill was presented in the House of Lords by my good friend the Earl of Lauderdale (now deceased) who made an impressive presentation. He set out all the Clauses and highlighted the great benefit the Bill would be to save fishermen's lives. On the Labour side of the House Lord Underhill said 'he was in total agreement with the Earl of Lauderdale in expressing thanks to Mr Albert McQuarrie the Member for Banff and Buchan who brought the Bill forward in the House of Commons'. Lord Underhill concluded by expressing the hope the Bill will have a speedy passage in the House of Commons. The debate in the Lords was wound up by Viscount Davidson. In his remarks he said 'I should like to add my congratulations to those already expressed by my Noble Friend Lord Lauderdale and to the Noble Lord Underhill, to my Honourable Friend Mr Albert McQuarrie who so ably piloted this Bill through another place. This Bill is an admirable measure and we feel it deserves your Lordships full support'. In response, before putting the Question for approval, Lord Lauderdale said 'Thank you to the Government side of this House, thank you to the Opposition for their support and thank you above all to Mr Albert McQuarrie'. The Bill was sent to a Committee of the whole House for Consideration.

On 17th June 1986 Lord Lauderdale reported to the House of Lords no amendment had been received and no Noble Lord had indicated a wish to move a manuscripted amendment or to speak in Committee. He then made a Motion for the Order of Commitment to be discharged. On the Question being put it was agreed without a vote and the Bill returned to the Commons.

The following day the decision of the House of Lords to approve the Safety at Sea Bill without a division was reported to the House of Commons at its Sitting and the Bill was granted formal approval. All that remained was Her Majesty's Royal Assent which was granted on 26th June 1986 as the Safety at Sea Act 1986 bringing it into legislation with the passing of the Act to the Statute Book. It was with much pleasure that I had successfully piloted this Act through the House of Commons in the knowledge it would be of immeasurable help to all fishermen in the United Kingdom and particularly in my own constituency of Banff and Buchan.

Over the twenty-seven years since the Bill became law many fishermen lives have been saved largely due to the use of the EPIRB and a much greater use of lifejackets by fishermen working on deck. It was a hard fight to get the Bill through the Chamber as I wanted. I am proud of my success which has given wives and children of the fishermen comfort in the knowledge there are considerable safety measures now in place to prevent, if at all possible, further tragedies to fishermen while working at sea.

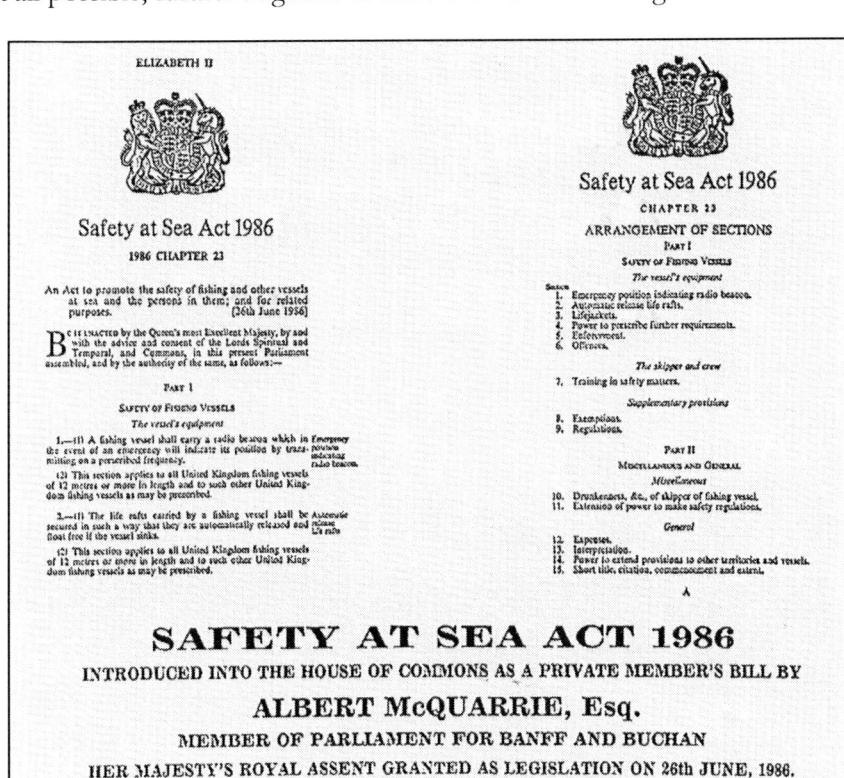

80. The Safety at Sea Act 1986 promoted by me

CHAPTER NINETEEN

The Sudden Passing of Roseleen

ON THE 10TH JUNE 1986 I suffered a terrible blow when Roseleen, my wife of forty-one years, died very suddenly in our London home.

81. Roseleen at our Teuchar Lodge Home, 1985

It was Roseleen's birthday and on my way to our London home from the House of Commons at lunchtime, I purchased two pots of roses to place in a bowl our grandchildren had given as a present for her birthday when we visited them in Rutherglen the previous weekend. When Roseleen saw the roses she said 'how nice they will look in the bowl'. After lunch when I was about to leave for the Commons I said to Roseleen 'Put on something nice for the evening. I am taking you out to dinner'. I had reserved a table at the Ritz, I told Roseleen I would be back by 7.30 p.m. as there was no vote that night. Roseleen was bright and cheerful as she told me of her shopping in Oxford Street during the morning, purchasing food to entertain our niece Monica who lived in Kingston-on-Thames and was bringing her newborn daughter, Clara, to see Roseleen.

At 7.15 that evening I returned home. I entered the sitting room and saw Roseleen lying on the settee sleeping, as I thought, with the same clothes on as she had when I left earlier. I said 'are you not going out tonight?' There was no reply so I said it again and lifted Roseleen's arm which fell limply to her body. I thought she must have fainted and quickly phoned our good friend Dr Roger Docherty and his wife Helen who lived near us. They both came at once. When Roger examined Roseleen he said 'I am afraid she is dead'. This was a terrible shock. Roger telephoned the Coroner, a friend of his. He came to the house right away and confirmed she was dead. I contacted John Ward, a friend and Member of Parliament and his wife Jean who lived a few doors away. They joined Roger and Helen and supported me in this awful situation. John telephoned the Prime Minister's office at 10 Downing Street to give the news to Margaret Thatcher. As Roseleen's death was so sudden there had to be a Coroner's Report. The Report indicated Roseleen died from an aneurism which acts suddenly with fatal results.

The news had to be broken to our son Dermot who at the time was with Scottish Television in Glasgow. Roger spoke to Dermot who boarded a flight to London and arrived late in the evening. It was a huge comfort to have him with me. I called my sister Margaret and arranged for her to travel to London.

In the morning I received a handwritten letter from the Prime Minister. She wrote from Denis and herself 'To lose one's partner in life is to lose a part of yourself. Your sorrow will be very difficult for you and we pray God will give you the strength to bear this tragic loss. To submerge yourself in work will perhaps help a little with the comfort of friends and your marvellous constituents whose help and affection will see you through these difficult months. We are all so anxious to help. With our deepest sympathy. Yours sincerely Margaret'.

THE SUDDEN PASSING OF ROSELEEN

In his letter Mr Speaker Weatherall said 'I have just been told of your tragic loss and I share your grief at the loss of your dear wife Roseleen which must have been devastating for you. I send you my heart-felt sympathy. Please be assured Lyn and I will support you in our prayers. If there is anything I can do, you have only to let me know. With my most sincere condolences - Jack.'

I received a message from Sir Joshua Hassan, Chief Minister of Gibraltar which read 'On behalf of all Members of the House of Assembly and of the people of Gibraltar I send you our most sincere condolences on your very sad loss. Roseleen was a good friend and popular with everyone here – she will be sadly missed'.

I was deeply touched, and found it hard to cope, by the many calls and visits from colleagues in the House and from Roseleen's friends at the Dulwich Golf Club where she played and where she enjoyed weekly Bridge sessions.

With the media reporting on her passing, tributes were being paid. The *Gibraltar Democrat* carried the heading 'Gibraltar loses a good friend'. The *Johnstone Gazette*, from Roseleen's home town in Scotland, had the heading 'A Birthday Tragedy' and wrote of Roseleen kindly. Most of the National and Local newspapers reported on the tragic loss I had suffered along with Dermot and his family. We were devastated.

Dermot stayed for a few days to help with the arrangements for Roseleen's funeral. We decided her burial would be in Johnstone after a Service in St Margaret's Church, Johnstone. I received a call from the Rt Rev Mario Conti, Bishop of Aberdeen, offering to preside at the Funeral Service and at the graveside. I accepted his offer knowing Roseleen had a great respect for Bishop Conti.

The Funeral Service took place on 16th June 1986. The majority of Scottish Members of Parliament including the Secretary of State for Scotland, Rt Hon Malcolm Rifkind, and his Ministers were present. Bishop Conti led the Service assisted by Rev Canon John Boyle and Canon Gerald Mungavin, and the Rev Fathers Connolly, Murphy, Sheehan, McLaughlan and New. Following the Service, the cortege proceeded through the streets lined with people to the Cemetery where Bishop Conti made the committal prayers as my darling wife and mother of my son Dermot was laid to rest.

Many people in the constituency, in London and Gibraltar had expressed their sorrow at Roseleen's passing. Dermot and I decided to arrange for three Memorial Services for Roseleen's life. The first Service was held in St Mary's Church, Cadogan Street, London on 25th June 1986 attended by Members of Parliament, their wives known to Roseleen and Roseleen's friends in London. The Service was conducted by Reverend J. Michael Hendry whose address was phrased around words from the Epistle to the Philippians 'I thank my God for every remembrance I have of you'.

In his address he said 'I, like everyone of you, have had the privilege of knowing Roseleen McQuarrie, her family, her husband and their son Dermot, and so I know we all have much to remember, and much for which to give thanks.

'Even though it may be, never be tempted to ask the question Why has God done this? God knows what He is doing. Do not complain because she who has gone was kind and good. Do not complain she was still in the full bloom of life. For that too, we should give thanks to God because he has called her to a better life, a happier life than she could ever have known, or had in this world.

'Consider rather to whom the loved one has gone and take comfort. She has gone where the whole company of Saints have gone. She has gone to God which she prayed for and that is cause for thanks indeed.

'Roseleen McQuarrie believed fervently in God, she lived with God in everything she did and said. She looked forward without fear, to a time of supreme happiness when she would be with the God she loved. He took her in a moment. She did not suffer nor did she know pain. God stretched out and His hand touched her, and she slept'.

82. Roseleen and me with the grandchildren at Teuchar Lodge, Cuminestown in summer, 1985

THE SUDDEN PASSING OF ROSELEEN

Rev Father Hendry ended his address with the words 'Roseleen McQuarrie, loyal wife, devoted mother and grandmother, beloved friend, I thank my God for every remembrance I have of you. May you Rest in Peace'.

The second Memorial Service was held in Our Lady of Mount Carmel Church in Banff where we worshipped whenever we were in the constituency. This moving Service was held on 29th June 1986 attended by many people from the Banff and Buchan Constituency and from the north east of Scotland. The grandchildren who were greatly affected by the loss of their dear grandmother attended this Service.

As a tribute to Roseleen I arranged for a brass plaque with an inscription to be fitted on the wall inside the Church of Our Lady of Mount Carmel as a lasting memorial to an exceptional lady who befriended everyone with whom she came into contact and was much loved by all.

The third Memorial Service for Roseleen's life took place on 4th July 1986 in the Cathedral Church of St Mary The Crowned in Gibraltar, a place dear to Roseleen during the years we lived in Gibraltar. The Service was conducted by the Bishop of Gibraltar accompanied by Clergy from other churches in Gibraltar. The Chief Minister Sir Joshua Hassan, the Leader of the Opposition Mr Joseph Bossano, the Mayor of Gibraltar the Hon Abraham Serfaty and Mr Peter Isola, Leader of the Democratic Progressive Party in the House of Assembly attended. There were Members of the House of Assembly present and our many friends, and even those whom we did not know but mourned her passing.

It was a beautiful Service with a most touching address, by His Lordship the Bishop in which he expressed his deepest sympathy to me and the family in our loss. He recounted the many occasions when he had discussions with Roseleen and the deep faith she had in God. The other Clergy taking part also offered their condolences at Roseleen's sudden passing.

This, like the other Services, was a very sad one as the people of Gibraltar said farewell to Roseleen. Many tears were shed.

These Services brought much comfort to me and the family, helping us to bear the terrible loss at Roseleen's passing so suddenly. I am forever grateful for all the help and support I received at the time from so many parts of the world by people who had known Roseleen and shared a deep and lasting friendship with her. May she Rest in Peace. I thank God for the forty-one years of our marriage and the lovely times we had together.

I end this Chapter with 'A Message of Friendship' Roseleen quoted on a number of occasions during our time together:

My dear friend, if we should be parted by my death please think on it thus.
Death happens to us all; to every being on earth.
In God's great design for each one of us it is only a transition.
Be not afraid, because, as we understand it death happens only to our mortal being;
Our support or soul lives on.

I, am, as I always was, in spirit, possibly greatly improved.
What we felt for each other, surely we must still feel.
The only change is that, in spirit, we are now closer than ever before.

When you think of me, please do not feel sorrow, for I am now closer to God and therefore happier. Feel sorrow rather for those I have left behind; pray for their happiness.
Please talk about me in the course of your days as you always did.
Speak of me with good cheer and without sadness or remorse.

Now that I am out of mortal sight, please do not leave me out of mind.
Remember the good times we had together, the laughs and above all the most beautiful and tender times.

Remember that good thoughts are of God, the Holy Spirit.
Good thoughts will bring us closer together than ever before possible.
Think positively of us both.
Finally, remember that I am well.
Be happy and strive yourself to remain well and cheerful.
That will please me greatly.

CHAPTER TWENTY

Visiting the Homeless in the Streets of London

AS A MEMBER OF PARLIAMENT I had taken part in a Debate in the House of Commons on the problems of homeless people living in doorways or sleeping on the footpaths in cardboard boxes in the streets of London following a campaign by a number of office and street cleaners who wished to see a solution to the problem. It had been reported there was a vast increase in the number of men and women who were bedding down each night in these cardboard boxes and other forms of shelter. During the Debate I spoke out strongly at the lack of Government activity in seeking a solution and urged early action to rid the streets of London from these unacceptable scenes in the streets and doorways of shops.

The year 1987 had been nominated as the International Year of Shelter for the Homeless. I had been involved in highlighting the problems in the cities and towns of the United Kingdom and particularly in the City of London. I had meetings with a number of electors and built up a host of evidence that action was urgently necessary to solve the problem otherwise the entire situation would escalate to the degree there would possibly be violence in the streets against the homeless.

Shortly after the Debate in the House of Commons I was contacted by Major Booth, a Salvation Army Officer based in London. He was leader of a group within the Salvation Army who each night toured the London areas where the homeless set up their cardboard shelters. The group distributed food and drinks to the homeless men and women. Major Booth invited me to make a tour of the areas with him to see just how serious the problem was. I readily accepted. Arrangements to meet the group from the Salvation Army were made to accompany them in the Inner London area. I had learned Dr Roger Docherty, a good friend from my time in Gibraltar was coming on the tour as a representative of the British Medical Association. I arranged to meet with him and travel together for the first of several locations on the tour. With the experiences of that extraordinary night so vivid in my mind I wrote an article which was published in the *Aberdeen*

Evening News on 13th February 1987. *The House Magazine*, the weekly journal of the Houses of Parliament, reproduced it and now I wish the readers of the book to share my experience in the 'Cardboard City'. I am grateful to *Aberdeen Journals* for permission to use it in my Memoirs.

It is 10.30 p.m. in a bleak and cold City of London. The snow lies at least eight inches deep on the footpaths and is still on the roadways as we set out to visit the 'Cardboard City', the name given to the places where men and women, young and old, sleep in cardboard boxes out in the open.

We meet Major Booth, of the Salvation Army, who tells us he has a surprise. General Eva Burrows, leader of the Salvation Army, is to accompany us on the tour of the sites. We were delighted such a distinguished member of the Salvation Army would be with us.

The first stop was the bandstand of Lincoln's Inn Fields. We departed in a blue van filled with new blankets and sleeping bags and a red van loaded with sandwiches, pork pies and a huge container of hot soup. We walked over the grass into the bandstand. I was staggered. There, all around us were large cardboard boxes, big enough to house a person. Alongside the boxes were people just lying in blankets.

83. The homeless in London's Cardboard City

The three Army Officers started handing out the food while I walked with General Burrows around the bandstand. She spoke to everyone and was well received.

To one of the men, she said 'Is your name Tom?' He replied 'No, it is John.' She spoke to him for a time and then said 'John, I will be praying for you'. We then stepped outside and to my amazement we saw more of the large cardboard boxes covered with polythene sheeting. We could see that men were sleeping inside these boxes. We walked over and the General said 'Is your name Tom?' He replied 'No, it's George'. She said 'How long have you been sleeping in this box, George?' 'For a good number of years' was the reply. The General said 'Would you not like to go to the hostel where it would be warm?'

He told her he did not like the hostel and would rather stay where he was until he got a house of his own. Having satisfied their needs with food and warmth, we set off for the Embankment. It was the same picture there. The General walked among them, asking the now familiar question 'Is your name Tom?' Again came back the reply 'No, my name is Peter.' Once more the sleeping bags, blankets and food were distributed. My heart ached for these people with no home or room to sleep in – just the cold footpath, not even the cover of a bandstand or a park bench.

Off again, this time to Waterloo and under the Arches. This was a sight never to be forgotten. Dozens and dozens of people, mainly young girls and boys, not even helped this time by cardboard boxes, only the covering of blankets. They were huddled together to keep warm. The General and I moved among them, speaking to as many as we could, asking about their lives and where they came from. We approached one man and again, the General asked the question, to which he replied 'No, it's Johnstone. Who are you?' The General said 'I am the leader of the Salvation Army. We have come here this evening to help you and give you food.'

While they talked, I walked over to another car from which young people were handing out tea and sandwiches. They told me they were Baptists and Anglicans who came to the Arches every Friday. I returned to the General's side. Before leaving Johnstone, the General said a little prayer and gave him a kiss on the cheek. We never did learn Johnstone's Christian name.

It is 2 a.m. and bitterly cold. We only have enough time and food, blankets and sleeping bags for one more visit. The vans and car drive into an open area – under the Festival Hall. I am astounded. I alight from the van and join the General. We look around us and all we can see are the cardboard boxes. Some even have guard rails in front of the boxes for protection from intrusion by others. The General said 'Albert, this is the Festival Hall where people come with their evening gowns and dresswear – something has to done about what we have seen this evening – how can we help?' I am overcome at the sight of it all.

While the others are seeing to the needs of the people, the General and I walk about speaking to them. Suddenly, a man on blankets with his head against the concrete shouted 'Eva, Eva, do you not recognise me? I am Ernie'. The General looked startled at this recognition in such circumstances. Then Ernie said 'I met you at the college in Dulwich where I worked for a time'. The

General walked toward him saying 'I do remember you. What are you doing here?' He told her that vandals had smashed up his house and he had nowhere to go. The General dropped on her knees beside him and I withdrew to let them have a private talk. Then I saw her kiss him on the cheek and get up.

When she returned to me there were tears in her eyes. She said 'We must do something about these people. Does the Prime Minister know what goes on in these places? I know she cannot come as we have tonight because of security problems, but someone like you must tell her what you have seen and just how bad it is'. I promised I would most surely tell the Prime Minister as soon as possible. It is now 2.45 a.m. and the General looks tired and cold. We gather round and she says a prayer. I thanked her for coming out on such a cold night to give succour to these unfortunate people, and for her obvious deep compassion. I repeated to her something must be done, not only in London, but in the other towns and cities throughout the UK and I would do my utmost to set the wheels in motion.

In my own constituency as in all others, there are homeless people. Homes must be found for these people in their own environment and not have them come to London to sleep in a Cardboard City. It is not only the Government but Local Authorities, Churches and Education Authorities who must dissuade them from going off to London. We must all play our part and offer support.
It is not enough to speak – action speaks louder than words – and action must be taken to rid ourselves of this scandalous situation especially in this International Year of Shelter for the Homeless.

Despite the General's question on meeting the homeless, **we never did find Tom!**
I returned to my London home at 3.30 a.m. and thanked God I had somewhere to sleep under cover and warm. I was determined to ensure this great problem was not allowed to go without immediate action by the Government. Within hours I gave an account to the Prime Minister in her Commons office giving her an account of what I had seen along with General Eva Burrows and other Officers of the Salvation Army. The Prime Minster was moved and assured me the matter would be taken up, not only with the Housing Minister but with other Ministers who had jurisdiction over the allocation of funding for Social Housing.

For my part I pursued the matter with the Local Authorities in my constituency meeting Senior elected Members and Chief Officers making them aware of the problems of homelessness and seeking reports from the Authorities on steps taken to reduce the problem of homelessness in the areas. To their credit the Authorities in my constituency, bearing in mind this was the International Year of the Homeless, had positive plans for more social housing.

VISITING THE HOMELESS IN THE STREETS OF LONDON

I will never forget my visit to the Homeless on the streets of London along with General Eva Burrows, and the impact it had on me. I thank God it has been possible for me to help those unfortunate people who have been forced into this terrible situation of homelessness. Sadly this problem is not solely in the London area. It is all around us and something has to be done to rid ourselves of these pathetic sights on the streets and doorways.

Great credit must be given to the Salvation Army and other charities who tour the streets of our cities and towns providing food, blankets and drink to the Homeless. They seek no reward – only our help and support to allow them continue the good work they carry out every night.

CHAPTER TWENTY-ONE

The Chairman's Panel

THE NUMBER OF MEMBERS OF PARLIAMENT who reach Ministerial Office is limited. People like me who regularly took the Government to task are not likely to be in line for a Ministerial appointment. The Chief Whip does not look too kindly on those Members as recommendations are made to the Prime Minister for consideration. This was not a concern of mine as I was perfectly happy fighting for my constituents and I much preferred not to have my hands tied behind my back.

There are a number of alternative appointments which a Member of Parliament may be invited to take up. One of these is to be nominated by Mr Speaker to serve on the Chairman's Panel (the Chairman is Mr Speaker). At any one time there are only twenty Members of Parliament serving on the Chairman's Panel and appointments are made at the sole discretion of Mr Speaker. A member of the Chairman's Panel acts as the representative of Mr Speaker on all deliberations in the Committee Rooms or in the Chamber of the Commons when business discussed is a Committee of the whole House.

In January 1986 I had the honour of being appointed to the Chairman's Panel. It was a most unexpected appointment and I was thrilled at my appointment to the Office by Mr Speaker for the Office. During the following days many newspapers commented upon my appointment. One newspaper had the headline 'Accolade for MP' and comment 'Banff and Buchan MP Mr Albert McQuarrie has achieved a major honour in the House of Commons. The local MP has been personally selected by Mr Speaker to serve on the Chairman's Panel. This prestigious appointment is in recognition of the work carried out by Mr McQuarrie in Parliament'. A Parliamentary spokesman said 'It is a great honour for Mr McQuarrie to be selected by Mr Speaker for the appointment'.

Within days I was appointed along with six other Members of Parliament and representatives from the House of Lords to a Special Select Committee to examine the process of enacting private legislation. This subject was

THE CHAIRMAN'S PANEL

causing concern in both Houses of Parliament. Government had decided the processes had to be altered as much of the existing legislation goes back to Disraeli. The work was completed with considerable satisfaction to the Government.

The media indicated I had been selected because of my considerable experience in the matter of private legislation. It was highlighted I had been responsible for the Peterhead Harbour Bill and Safety at Sea Act, the Registered Establishments (Scotland) Act 1987 and the Harwich and Parkeston Quay Bill. It was also noted I had served with other Members of the Commons and the Lords on the Edinburgh Western Relief Road Private Legislation.

One other appointment I was given, pleased me immensely. It was the Office of Chairman of the Scottish Grand Committee which met at the old Royal High School in Edinburgh. The Grand Committee comprised of all Members of Parliament representing a Scottish Constituency. I enjoyed the Grand Committee sitting in the historical building and often wondered why the High School was not taken over as the Scottish Parliament Headquarters rather than the building where the Parliament meets today. What the Government could have done with a saving of £450 million!

84. Chairman of Scottish MPs meeting in Edinburgh 1986

239

All was not rosy when carrying out the duties of Chairman. I had an extremely difficult experience when sitting as Chairman during the Debates on the Abolition of Domestic Rates (Scotland) Bill which was carried out by the First Scottish Standing Committee. The legislation was bitterly opposed by many in Scotland. Domestic Rates were to be abolished and in place a Personal Community Charge was to be introduced. The Debate commenced on 16th December 1986. As I was presiding over chairing other Committees I had no involvement in the early stages of the Debate. The Committee was chaired by either Mr Hugh McCartney MP or Mr Ian Campbell MP, both Members of the Chairman's Panel.

On the evening of 18th December 1986, events began to happen. The Committee had been sitting that afternoon under the Chairmanship of Mr Hugh McCartney. At 7.00 p.m. he said 'I am now, as Chairman, exercising my right to suspend the business of the Committee until half past ten o'clock on Tuesday 13th January 1987'. This was a total surprise to Committee members as it was expected to continue the Debate after the dinner break. Worse was to follow. The Government Chief Whip was rushing around in great anger as arrangements had been agreed between the Government and the Opposition that the Committee would sit again at 8.00 p.m. The Chief Whip had a meeting with Mr Speaker requesting him to have the Committee re-convened at 9.00 p.m. The Speaker sent for me requesting I should take up the position of Chairman at the 9.00 p.m. session. I accepted. At the appointed hour I took up my place as Chairman of the Committee. The Committee Room was a large room on the first floor of the House of Commons. It has a section set apart from the Members' area where the public can watch the proceedings.

As I called 'Order, Order' denoting the session had commenced Mr John Maxton MP for Glasgow Cathcart rose and said:

> On a point of order, Mr McQuarrie, may I ask on what basis you are reconvening the sitting at this time. At 7 o'clock the Chairman suspended the sitting until 10.30 a.m. on Tuesday 13th January 1987. I would like to know by what power you have the right to reconvene the Committee. I advise you Mr McQuarrie that while I accept that it was neither the fault of the Government nor the Opposition, the Chairman suspended that sitting. I do not believe that you know whether the Hon Members who left the Committee on the understanding that we had finished for the night have been properly informed by officials of the House that the Committee has been reconvened. Whether that was an accident does not matter. The fact is that we cannot have a sitting when Members of the Committee have not been informed that it is taking place. I know that some of my Hon Friends were aware of the fact but others have not been informed and they are unaware of it.

THE CHAIRMAN'S PANEL

Therefore, I request that you, Mr McQuarrie, seek information about whether we may continue the sitting at this time.

At this there was an interruption by a Member of Parliament in the Public Gallery. I rose from my seat and said:

Order, persons in the Public Gallery must not interrupt the Committee deliberations. I have a statement to make to the Committee in response to the comments made by the Hon Member for Glasgow Cathcart. I have been appointed by Mr Speaker as a Chairman of this Committee.

There was a further interruption from the Public Gallery. I rose from my seat and said:

If the Member of Parliament in the Public Gallery persists in these interruptions I will have the Constable remove him.

I proceeded with my statement.

The Chairman of a Standing Committee may for the Committee convenience suspend the Committee informally. He has no power to adjourn the Committee. The understanding was that the Committee would break for Dinner between 7.00 p.m. and 9.00 p.m.

Mr Maxton responded by saying:

I do not think that that is good enough Mr McQuarrie. I can find nothing in the Standing Orders that says that a Chairman cannot suspend a Committee as he wishes informally. I will quote what is said in 'Erskine May' on page 619 about the suspension of sittings of a Standing Committee. It states 'The sitting of a Standing Committee may be suspended *informally* by the Chairman in which case he will announce to the Committee that the sitting is suspended and that he will resume the chair at a certain hour.'

He went on:

As far as I am aware 'Erskine May' does not state that the hour cannot be three weeks, four weeks, or five weeks hence. It merely states that a Chairman may suspend a Committee sitting and states he will resume the chair at a certain hour, informally or formally.

Mr Maxton continued:

Therefore I do not understand by what power, Mr McQuarrie, you are attempting to take the Chair of the Committee at this time. Members of Parliament who have been appointed to the Committee left it at 7 o'clock believing in good faith that they had finished for the night and could go away. I accept that some of these Hon Members have been contacted and asked to return at 9 o'clock. Others however have not been contacted and we have been unable to contact all of our Hon Friends. Therefore we do not believe that the Committee can be reconvened when Hon Members who are legitimate

Members of it have not been requested to be present at 9 o'clock.

There was a further interruption from the Public Gallery but Mr Maxton continued:
> It is up to the Government to get us out of what I accept is a difficult situation and to be reasonable about it. The agreement was for an hour. Why on earth are we going on like this for an hour? The Minister or his Whip should ask for the Committee to be adjourned until Tuesday. That will let all of us out of a difficult and embarrassing situation. Anything other than that will cause a continuation of points of order and of difficulties. There has been an embarrassment to you, Mr McQuarrie, to me and to the Government. It would be better if the Government were to move for an adjournment so that we could suspend the sitting.

At this point there was a very voluble noise of shouting from a Member of Parliament who was seated in the Public Gallery, and not a member of the Committee. I rose and said:
> Order. I must ask the Member of Parliament in the Public Gallery not to respond. It is most undignified to have such behaviour in the House. Members of Parliament in particular should respect the dignity of the House and not persist in interrupting with comments made by Committee members.

I then stated:
> In response to the Hon Member for Glasgow Cathcart I should say I have been appointed by Mr Speaker. I trust the Hon Gentleman is not questioning Mr Speaker's reasons for appointing me to the Committee.

To which Mr Maxton responded:
> I have never done so.

I proceeded:
> I am grateful for that. As I pointed out there was no authority to suspend the Committee until 10.30 a.m. on Tuesday 13th January 1987. The Committee could have gone on until one o'clock on Friday afternoon when there would have been an automatic adjournment.

I was about to continue when there was a further interruption. The Member of Parliament who kept interrupting from the Public Gallery had seated himself on one of the Committee room seats which can only be occupied by members of the Committee. I said:
> Will the Hon Member remove himself from the Committee. He is not a member of the Committee and should remove himself from the Committee area. As the Hon Gentleman will not withdraw I suspend the Committee for five minutes. Sitting suspended.

THE CHAIRMAN'S PANEL

When the Committee resumed the Member of Parliament had again taken a seat in the Committee section of the room and not the Public Gallery which by this time was full of other Members of Parliament including Mr Malcolm Rifkind, Secretary of State for Scotland, and Mr Donald Dewar, Shadow Secretary of State for Scotland and Lord James Douglas Hamilton a Conservative Whip. Once more I made the request to the Member occupying a Committee seat and said:

> I ask the Hon Member to remove himself from the precincts of the Committee's deliberations.

This brought more shouting from the Member. I said:

> I appeal to the Hon Member to leave. He is placing his colleagues in considerable difficulty if he does not leave.

More shouting from the Hon Member. I said:

> The Hon Member refuses to leave.

(more shouting from him) – I said:

> Order, I suspend the sitting until half past ten o'clock.

On resuming at 10.30 p.m., I once again asked the Member to leave the Committee section of the room. He refused to do so. I suspended the sitting for a further five minutes. During the suspension I had a short meeting with the Labour Whip. I told him as this situation was reaching the farcical stage I would accept a Motion to adjourn the Debate. At 10.37 p.m. this was done and the sitting ended. The anger was great on all sides against the Member who had continually disrupted the proceedings.

For me it was the end of a very nasty experience brought on by the unruly Member of Parliament who should have known better.

The media reported the incident in full the next day. One newspaper had a heading 'Baptism of Fire for Buchan MP'. The article referred to Commons Committee Chairmen tending to lead a quiet life as they sit hour after hour expecting little trouble while the Committee discuss the matters on hand and how it is considered an honour to be chosen a member of the Chairman's Panel. The writer states that:

> no-one was more "chuffed" about being chosen than Mr Albert McQuarrie the Banff and Buchan MP.

The article goes on to say:

> No-one could have expected the truly bizarre experience he had to endure when he was responsible for a Standing Committee Bill going through the

Commons. Within living memory no such Committee had been suspended for rowdy behaviour yet within 90 minutes of finding himself in the hot seat, Mr McQuarrie had to suspend business three times. Far from being blamed for calling the suspensions, most observers were full of praise for Mr McQuarrie's handling of a very difficult situation'. In the writer's words he continued by saying 'Such a sudden and unexpected change of Chairman was always bound, especially pre-Christmas, to lead to some fun and games. Had it been only that, it would not have mattered but the appearance of a Labour Member of Parliament with a little too much of the Christmas spirit turned the Standing Committee into a highly emotional one.

What impressed MPs and observers was the firmness with which Mr McQuarrie handled the situation and the way he also kept calm in circumstances which would have tried the patience of a far more experienced Chairman.

For some time Mr McQuarrie has enjoyed the nickname of the Buchan Bulldog - the tenacity he showed in Chairing the Committee under such circumstances showed it was justified.

Over my time as a member of the Chairman's Panel it was my privilege to be Chairman on many Standing Committees. I never had to face up to another situation like that of the Abolition of Domestic Rates, nor did I have a Committee where the rowdy Member of Parliament was a member of the Labour Group discussing a Bill – maybe just as well as I might have found a reason to suspend him rather than the whole Committee!

My thanks to all mentioned in this Chapter particularly John (now Lord) Maxton and Peter Woodifield of *Aberdeen Journals*. My thanks also to the use of extracts in the Official Report, and other media of the Committee's deliberations when the incident was recorded.

CHAPTER TWENTY-TWO

Margaret Thatcher

Author's note

I wish to include this Chapter as it is a memory which will live with me for the rest of my days. It relates to the late Baroness Thatcher of Kesteven LG, OM, PC, FRS, MA, BSc the former Prime Minister who died in London on Monday 8th April 2013 at the age of 87 years.

THE DEATH OF BARONESS THATCHER ON 8th April 2013 was very sad news to me. I express my condolences to her two children, Sir Mark and Carol, and also to her grandchildren who she adored. They can be assured the name of Margaret Thatcher will never be forgotten as one of the most famous Prime Ministers of all time.

I put on record my condemnation of the street parties and other joyous activities organised by those who celebrated with joy the death of this wonderful woman. Most of the disgraceful conduct, sadly, was carried out by young people who never knew Margaret Thatcher or the role she played in saving this country from economic disaster, and how she saved the people of the Falklands against the military forces of Argentina.

Margaret Thatcher may not have been acceptable to all because her policies did not suit, but she led this country with a firm determination believing the people would benefit. It is very sad that Baroness Thatcher was castigated by some mindless individuals after her death. Fortunately they were few and they will be ignored. In the minds of most people Margaret Thatcher will be held in the highest esteem as the Prime Minster who transformed this country to advantage for its people.

I first became acquainted with Margaret Thatcher at the Conservative Party Conference in 1976 when I was the Westminster Parliamentary Candidate for East Aberdeenshire. Margaret attended the reception party of the Scottish delegates when she spoke to many in an uninhibited way. I was fortunate to have a conversation with her and asked if she would visit East Aberdeenshire. She said it would be placed in her dairy. True to her word

245

the first of several visits to East Aberdeenshire was enthusiastically received when she visited Peterhead, Fraserburgh, Turriff, Strichen and the Party Headquarters in Mintlaw. I could sense her visit was doing my campaign good as crowds of people cheered her at every town and village she visited.

85. Margaret Thatcher in Dundee 1978

It was on her first visit I learned one of Margaret Thatcher's practices. Her driver at the time was Colonel Dalziel, a Scottish Conservative Central Office-Bearer. I was invited to join them in the Colonel's Jaguar while driving in the constituency. As we drove through the country roads I noticed Margaret dropped her head, closed her eyes and made no conversation for a while. The Colonel signalled to me not to speak. After a time, Margaret broke into voice asking questions about East Aberdeenshire, the fishing and the farming industries.

During the afternoon while travelling from place to place Margaret 'dropped off' again. I spoke to Colonel Dalziel about it. He told me Margaret had this habit of 'cat naps' to relax her mind. In later years when Margaret visited my constituency I made sure she was not disturbed from her 'cat naps' wherever she travelled.

On visits around the country Margaret relaxed not only by 'cat naps' but in the evenings when the day's work was done. In hotels where she stayed, and it happened in my constituency, a small private room was made available

86. Margaret Thatcher in East Aberdeenshire 1979

for her to meet my Office-Bearers, constituents and myself before dinner when plans for the following day were confirmed. Margaret made no hesitation in asking for a pre-dinner drink saying 'I will have a large malt'. I recall, before retiring for the night. Margaret would enjoy another of her favourite malts knowing she was due at the fish market in Peterhead for the sale which began at 7.00 p.m. She was up with the lark and first off her mark to the fish sale.

After the 1979 General Election when our party became the Government and Margaret Thatcher was elected Prime Minister she kept her word to visit Scotland where we had reduced the SNP from eleven seats to two, leaving Rt Hon Donald Stewart and Gordon Wilson the only two representatives in the House of Commons. A very early visit after becoming Prime Minister was to the Scottish Conservative and Unionist Conference in Perth where the crowds were in rapturous mood. The Station Hotel in Perth was packed to capacity, as were other hotels. At the City Hall she gave an inspiring address which at the end was received with a long standing ovation. I spoke to her that afternoon taking the opportunity of thanking her for her visits to East Aberdeenshire in the run-up to the General Election. I assured her these visits had been vital to me in securing the seat for the Conservative and Unionist Party in Scotland from the Nationalists and electing me as Member of Parliament for East Aberdeenshire.

When I first entered the Chamber at the House of Commons I recall asking a Policeman exactly where the Prime Minister sat when she was in the Commons. Directly behind the Despatch Box was the reply. He also told me the seats behind the Prime Minister were reserved for the Prime Minister's Private Parliamentary Secretary and other Ministers' Private Secretaries. Having received this information I made my way to the third row selecting a seat in line with the Prime Minister. I decided this was to be 'my seat' in the House of Commons from then on where I would be able to support the Prime Minister. For the next eight years, I used the little green card to reserve 'my seat'. Many a time I barracked against the Opposition Benches when Members sitting there were attacking the Prime Minister. I was told by Ian Gow MP, her PPS, that Margaret appreciated the support as I could do what was impossible for her to do from the Despatch Box.

I remember on one occasion Ian Gow was sitting in his place at Prime Minister's Questions. It was a Thursday. Ian turned to me and said 'where were you on Tuesday?' I told him I had been in Northern Ireland with a delegation on the matter of security. He said on returning to the Prime Minister's room behind the Chamber after Prime Minister's Questions on the Tuesday, Margaret said to him 'Where was Albert today? I badly needed him with so much noise against me from Labour Members'. We laughed but Ian later said to her 'we must keep Albert off these delegations – you need him all the time in the Chamber during Prime Minister's Questions!'

During my time as a Member of Parliament I had the privilege of meeting the Prime Minister on a one-to-one basis in her room at the House of Commons. I always found her kind and considerate. She was a good listener and if the subject discussed required any impact by her she was never found wanting. On one occasion the meeting was about the very difficult situation of Domestic Rates when increases were made by the Local Authorities, including Banff and Buchan District Council in my constituency. After the discussions with Margaret she followed it by a letter from her 10 Downing Street office in which she wrote:

> Thank you for coming to see me to talk about the problems of rates which your constituents are facing. I can understand only too well the deep anxiety felt throughout Scotland on this matter. I found it especially helpful to talk to you about it because you were able to spell out in more personal terms the many examples in your constituency of the particular increases in rates which face both domestic ratepayers and businesses and the difficulties being caused.
>
> As you know, the Secretary of State for Scotland has allocated an extra £38.5 million to help ease domestic rates; and I have also asked him to see what can be done to speed up the appeals procedure on the revaluations.

The problem does go deeper than this. Like you, I believe that these rate increases emphasise the weaknesses in the present system of local government finance. I have therefore set up a review into this whole subject, including rates, and one of its main objectives is to bring about improvements to help ratepayers. Work on this is taking place as a matter of urgency. Once it has been completed and decisions taken, we will then be in a position to make an announcement.

On a personal note, can I say again how helpful it was to see you and hear at first-hand about the problems faced by your constituents. I want you to know I have their interests very much at heart.

I was pleased with the letter as it showed she cared for the concerns of the people who were suffering due to these increases.

There were other occasions when her interests and concerns were made known to me. Two of them were the Peterhead Harbours (South Bay) Development Bill and my Safety at Sea Bill when she assured me that as neither were Government Bills her support for them was total and if her vote was necessary for the passing of the Bills I could be assured she would be in the right Lobby.

Margaret Thatcher was a courageous lady. Her decision to send troops, vessels and aircraft in defence of the people in the Falkland Islands against the Argentine armed forces was an outstanding example. The recent poll in the Falklands where ninety-nine of the people voted to remain as part of the British Commonwealth clearly indicated the debt those people felt for the former British Prime Minister who had secured their future as British subjects.

Margaret Thatcher was the target of the IRA. The death of Airey Neave and Ian Gow caused her great distress. Both men had been outstanding Members of Parliament and personal aides in the Commons. The worst attack on her by the IRA was on 12th October 1984 when a bomb exploded in the Brighton Grand Hotel at the time of the Conservative party Conference. This was a direct attack on Margaret Thatcher by the IRA in an attempt to kill her. They failed – but a number of people were killed and others severely injured. She was devastated yet determined to carry on.

I have personal recollections of that night. I was staying at the hotel where earlier in the evening I had drinks with colleagues. Later in the evening I travelled to London along with the Member for Brent North, Mr Rhodes Boyson MP to deal with urgent Parliamentary business. The following morning I took an early train to Brighton intending to make my way to the hotel for breakfast. Arriving at Brighton I called a taxi and asked to be taken to the Grand Hotel. The driver told me about the bomb. I was shattered. The area where we had drinks a few hours previously was completely demolished. Some of my colleagues had been killed, and wives of others killed or severely injured. I spoke to Margaret Thatcher in the hotel when she said nothing was going to divert her from attending the Conference. She said 'We are going on. The IRA and nobody else will defeat us'.

These were the words of a Prime Minister who displayed a determination in adversity giving a message to the world she was indeed 'The Iron Lady'.

Margaret Thatcher suffered a huge loss when her husband Sir Denis died. I doubt if Margaret recovered from his passing. He was her lifeline – the one who kept a steadying influence on her and always at her side. He was the one, when attending functions and mingling with lots of people who would stand behind her during conversations. He seldom took part, and at an appropriate moment when he thought she had talked long enough to a particular person, he would gently nudge her in the back indicating it was time to move on!

On 10th April 2013 Parliament was recalled from its Easter Recess. Members in the House of Commons and the House of Lords paid tribute to Baroness Thatcher. Sadly from the Labour benches of the Commons there were uncomplimentary remarks from a few Members. These were dismissed as disgraceful by other Members. In the Commons Rt Hon Sir Malcolm Rifkind who had been Secretary of State for Scotland amongst other high offices he held, made an exceptional speech while in the Lords, Members, who had known Margaret Thatcher well, gave tributes in praise of all she had accomplished during her term as Prime Minister. Notable among the speeches delivered was Michael Forsyth's, now Lord Forsyth of Drumlean and former Secretary of State for Scotland, who took special care of Margaret Thatcher in her final years for which he received admiration from Members of the Lords.

On the eve of the funeral which was to be held at St Paul's Cathedral on Wednesday 17th April 2013, the coffin was received into the Chapel of St Mary Undercroft in the Palace of Westminster where a short service was attended by family, senior Parliamentary figures and staff of Baroness Thatcher. A vigil was kept overnight. On the morning of the funeral, watched by millions of people worldwide, the coffin was moved from the Chapel by hearse to the Church of St Clements Danes – Church of the Royal Air Force. From there it was transferred to a gun carriage drawn by the King's Troop Royal Horse Artillery for the procession through the streets lined with people to St Paul's Cathedral. Her Majesty The Queen and His Royal Highness Prince Philip attended the service, as did the Prime

Minister and all Cabinet Ministers. The Speakers of both Houses and many dignitaries from all over the world were in St Paul's to pay their respects to this most famous political lady.

On arrival at the Cathedral, the West steps were lined with Service Personnel and Uniformed Pensioners from Royal Hospital Chelsea where the ashes of Margaret Thatcher would be interred alongside those of her husband Sir Denis.

The service was led by The Very Reverend David Ison, Dean of St Paul's. Amanda Thatcher, daughter of Sir Mark Thatcher gave the first reading from Ephesians 6: 10-18. She read it beautifully and with deep sincerity. The second reading from John 14: 1-6 was read by Prime Minister David Cameron with equal sincerity. The address was given by the Right Reverend and Right Honourable Richard Chartres KCVO, Bishop of London and the Blessing was given by The Most Reverend and Right Honourable Justin Welby, Archbishop of Canterbury, Primate of All England and Metropolitan.

> Lord, now lettest thou thy servant depart in peace: according to thy word.
> For mine eyes have seen: thy salvation,
> Which thou hast prepared: before the face of all people;
> To be a light to lighten the Gentiles: and to be the glory of thy people Israel.

Fitting words for a great lady sung by the choirs as The Recessional took place.

Thank you Margaret for all you brought to this country and the world during your years as Prime Minister. May you Rest in Peace.

CHAPTER TWENTY-THREE

Special Events, 1986

ON 16TH JULY 1986 Lord Boothby of Buchan and Rattray Head died in a London Hospital after a short illness. This caused me great sadness.

Robert Boothby, affectionately known as 'Bob', was born in Edinburgh on 12th February 1900. At the age of 24 he was elected a Unionist Member of Parliament for East Aberdeenshire with a majority of 2,683 votes. He

87. With Lord and Lady Boothby signing Fishing Petition

held the Seat for thirty-four years before receiving a Life Peerage. He was succeeded by Mr Patrick Wolrige-Gordon who held the Seat for the Conservative and Unionist Party with a majority of over 12,000 votes. In the House of Commons Bob Boothby's ability was quickly noticed by Winston Churchill who appointed him to the role of Parliamentary Private Secretary and later to the Office of Minister for Food.

It was my pleasure to enjoy a good relationship with Bob Boothby. He referred to me as his successor strongly supporting the work I undertook in the constituency, particularly for the fishermen and the farmers. The last speech Bob made in the House of Lords was to move the adoption of my Safety At Sea Bill by the Lords when he congratulated me for bringing forward a Bill which would help save lives of fishermen at sea.

Lord Boothby's funeral service took place on 25th July 1986 in London. I gave the Eulogy at the request of Lady (Wanda) Boothby. The final farewell to this exceptional and well loved man was when his ashes were scattered at sea one mile off Rattray Head - one of the names he took when elevated to the House of Lords. This was a touching ceremony. Sailing out of Peterhead Harbour on a wet and windy August morning were a fleet of fishing vessels with, among other mourners, Lady Boothby, the Rt Rev Bishop Fred Darwent and myself on board the lead vessel. When the convoy reached the point off Rattray Head, Lady Boothby scattered the ashes of Lord Boothby into the sea. Bishop Darwent said prayers following which a number of wreaths were cast into the sea. The convoy turned. We could see the floral tributes to a dear and true friend tossing in the waves.

In his time as Member of Parliament for East Aberdeenshire he built up a wonderful relationship with his constituents. During my campaign in the lead up to the 1979 General Election I spent many days knocking at doors asking for support. It amazed me the number of times I was told 'Sorry, Mr McQuarrie – I'm voting for Boothby', mainly from elderly ladies with an obvious respect for Bob Boothby who had by that time served sixteen years in the House of Lords. I am quite sure Patrick Wolrige-Gordon had the same experience when campaigning to follow Bob Boothby as the Member for East Aberdeenshire. He too made his mark, like Boothby, serving the people for twelve years – a shorter period than Bob but that is the way of politics. I speak from experience.

'No' to the Travellers

In November 1986 the Banff and Buchan District Council proposed to build an official site at Greenbanks in Banff for the travelling people at a cost of £250,000. There was an outcry from the Banff residents. In 'no time' over 120 objections were received by the Council. A petition against the proposal signed by 1688 people was lodged with the Director of Planning at the District Council offices. Many protesters contacted me. I decided to back them and advised the Council of my opposition to the proposal. I issued a Press Release in which I invited the people of Banff, and Macduff the neighbouring town, to speak their minds on the issue and make them known, in the strongest terms, to the District Council. In my article I indicated nothing I had heard since the District Council had decided to promote this proposal had changed my views. I expressed pity for the travellers but pointed out bluntly to them that the Greenbanks site was not suitable as a traveller's one. I requested the Council make a survey to source an alternative site which would neither cause offence to local people nor be too remote for the travelling people. My determination was that the strongest case possible would be made for not developing this site which, if it happened, would result in creating an unattractive approach to the historic town of Banff.

Despite intense activity to halt this development the District Councillors forced it through the planning process. In the course of time the new travellers' site was completed and occupied by its people. This battle I did not win. I was sorry for the people of Banff and Macduff who had voiced their real concerns so strongly against the Council's proposal.

Dire Prospects for Farmers

Early in 1987 I had a request from Ben Dalgarno, the Branch Secretary of the Buchan National Farmers Union for an urgent meeting. The agricultural industry was facing disastrous prospects with the beef industry particularly badly hit. According to the members of the Union whom I met, farm borrowings made by beef producers had increased dramatically as a result of the market price set at 26p per kilo less than the target price. The situation had reached the stage where Continental imports into intervention and a grossly overvalued green pound had combined to depress end prices to below the cost of production. I undertook to raise matters with Ministers:

a) To demand the devaluation of the pound to remove damaging MCSs and allow farmers to operate in fair competition with European Practice.

b) To press for the introduction of measures to remove cull cow beef from the market.

c) To make contact with the Chancellor of the Exchequer to seek lower interest rates.

d) To advise the Secretary of State for Agriculture of the farmer's opposition to any proposed cereal control measures which will discriminate against Scottish growers.

e) To ascertain from Ministers whether there is a possibility of the Government providing a discussion document on rural policy.

On returning to the House of Commons I set about dealing with all of these matters. Some of the responses I received were encouraging, others were not so. The Union was kept informed and I was thanked for my efforts. Unfortunately the event six months later meant I was no longer able to do my bit for the farmers. It was up to another to take on the role.

Fishermen in Crisis

Early in 1987 brought another crisis in the fishing industry. The House of Commons was debating European Commission proposals brought before it by the Secretary of State for Agriculture Fisheries and Food. Forming the major part of the proposals was the Total Allowable Catch and Quotas for the year 1987.

I had received countless complaints from the fishing industry in my constituency suggesting the scientists had got their calculations of fish stock in the seas wrong and that their findings were a distortion of the true facts. It was obvious to the fishermen the proposals would do immeasurable damage to their livelihood and have an adverse effect on the on-shore processing industry.

I attended the Debate and was lucky enough to be called by Mr Speaker to address the House when I made the following comments:

> Members of the House should be aware of the deep concern in the Scottish Fishing Industry at these proposals. When this Government successfully secured a Common Fisheries Policy in 1983 it was backed by the industry as the 'greatest step forward for many years'. As a result of it the industry had gone from strength to strength. The proposals before the House are taking a backward step which is deplorable. Cod and haddock quotas are being drastically cut while other nations' fishermen plunder our waters. There is no way the Scottish Fishing Industry can accept a 50 per cent cut in the Total Allowable Catch of these species.
>
> Instead of cuts in the quotas the procedure followed last year should be carried out again this year. At the eleventh hour at the December 1986 discussions Ministers were able to obtain an increase of 10,000 tonnes to the previously fixed quotas. This would be acceptable to our fishermen allowing them to earn a living.

I would urge the Minister to use the system of last year as a weapon against the European Commission Officials and insist upon an increase in the Total Allowable Catches for haddock and cod.

In his reply the Minister agreed with the recommendation I had made and assured the House he would do his utmost to secure the extra 10,000 tonnes between the two species. The good news was he succeeded and 1987 was a brighter year for the industry but not so bright for me as despite all my hard work in the Commons for many constituents in the fishing industry I lost my Seat.

CHAPTER TWENTY-FOUR

1987 General Election

WITH A CONSIDERABLE NUMBER OF matters referred to me by Constituents and Organisations, 1987 started off with a heavy workload. Suddenly the Prime Minister sprang a surprise on us all by calling a General Election. For a second time, the term was a four year one rather than five years as was normal. I was disappointed the Prime Minister had taken this step. My concern was our Party in Scotland was facing attacks due to the threatened Poll Tax imposition.

I sought out the Prime Minister at the Commons and told her the fears I had for the future of a number of the Scottish Conservative and Unionist Members holding their Seats. I recalled how I had warned her of the dangers we faced in Scotland when the 'Poll Tax' was first proposed and suggested to her the problems had not gone away. Ever the optimist she said 'Oh, no Albert dear, it will not happen. I am confident we will come back with a working majority'. I could do nothing more to convince her. With fears in my mind I left her office.

For the next month legislation moving through the House of Commons was dealt with speedily. At the same time I had to devote my attention to the election campaign. On both counts things went well until Parliament was dissolved and the campaign started in earnest. I had a great team of workers who did their utmost to secure votes for me as our Party's candidate. I thought my standing would help me when taking into consideration the work done for constituents over the previous four years. The opposition from other candidates was strong. This was particularly so of one Party who brought in students from all over Scotland. The conduct of many of them was despicable. Like any other Party at an Election time, bills and boards were used widely around the constituency in support of my candidacy. Bills were ripped; paint was thrown at business premises in Banff where the owner displayed his support for me. Boards placed in farmers fields were damaged beyond repair with some never to be seen again. At no time did the candidate from the offending party condemn the vicious acts of students and others. Never in all my political life had I been subjected to such disgusting activities. I made sure none of my workers stooped to acts like those directed at my Party and me as the candidate.

Election Day dawned. Although I believed we had fought a good campaign, there were too many occasions when the matter of the 'Tory Poll Tax' was raised. It was difficult to combat especially when all opposition Parties were using it as a weapon against us. During the course of the day I visited all Polling Stations where I received reports of good support but there were the areas where it was not good. These bothered me. The count took place late that evening and into morning. There were areas where we had done well but when it came to the areas we knew our support was thin, the main opposition Party gained. I lost the seat by 2,441 votes despite having increased the vote I had in 1983 by 950. I polled 17,021 against 19,462 votes in favour of the winner of the Seat. Tactical voting happened then as it happens now. In the run up to the election there had been a strong campaign inducing people to tactically vote SNP to get rid of 'the Thatcher man', and it succeeded. It was a sad day for me to lose my Seat. I was so sorry for all the hard work the Party workers gave in their efforts to have me re-elected. I left the hall with my Agent, Miss Rhoda Gall. As we reached the exit we were subjected to torrents of abuse by a group of SNP supporters. Two words describe the scene – absolutely disgraceful.

So ended my time as the Member of Parliament for Banff and Buchan. It had been a great honour to represent the Constituency of East Aberdeenshire from 1979-1983 and Banff and Buchan from 1983-1987. I served the constituents to the best of my ability over the years and look back with pride on the major achievements I obtained for my constituents during my time as 'their Member'.

Messages of regret came pouring in. Many thanking me for the first class service I had given to Banff and Buchan and previously East Aberdeenshire and hoping I would return as the Member of Parliament! There was one particular letter written by Mr K.R. Donovan to whom I am grateful for making the sincere tribute. It was printed in the *Buchan Observer*. He wrote:

Goodbye Albert
A newspaper billboard outside a newspaper shop in Peterhead said it all, 'Buchan Dumps Bulldog', because that is what the voters of Banff and Buchan did to Albert McQuarrie. Whilst our new MP attempts to cut off Scotland from the rest of the UK without the help of anybody else, I hope that the people of Peterhead, at least, will remember what Mr McQuarrie did for us.

Don't forget that the price of fuel is lower because of Mr McQuarrie putting his foot down a couple of Budgets ago. Because he stuck up for his constituents in the more remote parts of Scotland a planned rise in duty was slashed by 50%. Don't forget, that if the life of one fisherman is saved due to the implementation of Mr McQuarrie's 'Safety At Sea' Bill, then he will feel his work was not in vain.

Don't forget, that when the new Search and Rescue Helicopter swoops down to rescue the crew of a stricken vessel or winches a badly injured person off a cliff top, you can thank our ex-MP for the time and effort and bullying it took to get this badly needed service on the West Coast.

There is much more, but one final example will, I hope, show what a fine MP we have lost.

Don't forget, that when the new Harbour extension is finished, it will, and will continue to, bring prosperity and jobs into Peterhead. It has only come about because Mr McQuarrie fought off opposition from all sides and put his political future on the line by forcing his Bill through Parliament (the Peterhead Harbour Bill).

It would be fitting if, when the 'Boothby Basin' is completed a part of it could be called 'Albert's Quay' in recognition of the work done by Mr McQuarrie.

Finally, to Mr Salmond: it is to be pointed out that after the 1983 election the SNP tried to make political capital out of how many people voted against Mr McQuarrie. Well for your information, Mr Salmond, 24,513 voters did not vote you as their MP.

Goodbye Albert and thank you. You will be missed.

The days following my defeat I spent at my home dealing with correspondence. I flew to London on the Sunday, picked up my London car and drove to the House of Commons. There was no difficulty in entering the House of Commons as the office which I occupied had to be cleared of my files, mostly political but some personal. I was fortunate to have the services of a most helpful Security Officer who helped me load my car. These files remained in Sancroft Street until the furniture removers shipped them to Teuchar Lodge in Aberdeenshire. As I left the Palace Yard I have to confess to having tears in my eyes in the realisation I was no longer a Member of Parliament. The reality was there were many more in the same position reflecting on a political career which was suddenly brought to a close. My memories of serving in the Palace of Westminster are many, but in particular the legislation which I helped to bring about for the betterment of the lives of my constituents and the people of Scotland. The future beckoned me – I would not sit back and retire.

Some months after the Election, I had a dental appointment in Kilwinning, Ayrshire. The assistant dealing with me said 'Are you Albert McQuarrie who was the Member of Parliament for Banff and Buchan?' I said 'Yes, why do you ask?' She responded 'Well I was one of the students recruited to defeat you'. Needless to say the conversation ended. It proved what I had been told. I had no further visits to that Dental Surgery!

On returning to Teuchar Lodge I spent my days sorting out papers, discarding those which were of no further use and assessing my future on what to do to fill in my weekdays. It was then I had a call from Alan Chisholm of Bredero, which I refer to in an earlier Chapter, asking me to take up a consultancy role in the firm but this time in Paisley. I accepted and soon commenced a working life again but this time away from active politics. I retained an interest in the Banff and Buchan Conservative and Unionist Association where I was made Honorary Life President and maintained contact with Miss Rhoda Gall who had been my Agent at the General Election and had helped me in many ways.

The Knighthood

On 18th July 1987 I received a letter from the Prime Minister in which she advised me, in strict confidence, she had it in mind, on the occasion of the Dissolution Honours List, to submit my name to Her Majesty The Queen with a recommendation that Her Majesty may be graciously pleased to approve that the Honour of Knighthood be conferred upon me. The Prime Minister went on to write that before doing so she would be glad to be assured this would be agreeable to me.

Suddenly all thoughts of my defeat were wiped away at this wonderful news. I was delighted. A Knight of the Realm. There was I, born in Greenock of humble parents, living a normal life, serving in the war, setting up a number of successful companies before a life as a Member of Parliament. Bearing in mind the letter from the Prime Minister was sent in strict confidence I had to tell someone who would share my joy. Who better than my son Dermot, and my Agent Miss Rhoda Gall. They were delighted for me and promised to tell no one, as the Dissolution Honours List would not be published until the end of July. Dermot and his family were holidaying at Teuchar Lodge. The house was full as his parents-in-law had travelled from Gibraltar to be with their daughter Libby and grandchildren, and a sister of Libby's with her family were there also. Far too many for me so I decided to spend a few days with my brother-in-law Vincent McCaffery and Mary his wife at Kildary near Tain in Ross-shire. I took my golf clubs with me for a bit of relaxation.

10 DOWNING STREET

THE PRIME MINISTER

IN CONFIDENCE   17 July 1987

Dear Albert,

    I am writing to let you know, in strict confidence, that I have it in mind, on the occasion of the forthcoming list of Dissolution honours, to submit your name to The Queen with a recommendation that Her Majesty may be graciously pleased to approve that the honour of knighthood be conferred upon you.

    Before doing so, I should be glad to be assured that this would be agreeable to you.

Yours sincerely,
Margaret

88. Prime Minister's letter 17th July 1987

The day the Dissolution Honours list was published Vincent and I enjoyed a game of golf at Fortrose and Rosemarkie Club. On the 18th green we were met by a man who said 'Are you Sir Albert McQuarrie?' I responded by saying 'I must be if you say so. You are obviously a journalist'. He said 'I am George Macdonald from the *Glasgow Herald* and I want to offer you my congratulations'. He interviewed me. His report was published in the *Glasgow Herald* on 31st July 1987 with the headline 'A reward for the Buchan Bulldog'. On driving through Tain later I found many of the daily newspapers with headings like 'Now it is Sir Albert': 'Well deserved Honour for Sir Albert': 'Knighthood for defeated Banff & Buchan MP': 'A delighted Sir Albert on his Knighthood'. Vincent and Mary opened their home the following evening for a splendid celebration party.

At home at Teuchar Lodge, Dermot was fully occupied taking telephone calls from well-wishers, and from radio and television wishing to arrange an interview with me. It was all very exciting and more so when I arrived home to find the bundles of congratulatory letters and cards, and the plans Dermot had made for a Champagne Party.

Early in September 1987 I received the notification from the Office of the Lord Chamberlain at Buckingham Palace intimating the date when Her Majesty The Queen would confer a Knighthood upon me. It was 10th November 1987. The notice gave information that I could have two guests and a driver.

I invited Dermot and his wife Libby. I also invited Edward McCaffery, my late wife's brother and my nephew Kevin, Edward's son, to accompany me. Both were thrilled to be part of this special day. Kevin arranged a Mercedes car for the day. We arrived at the gates of the Palace, I sat in the back with Dermot and Libby, Edward sat in front with Kevin. I showed my invitation to the Police Officer – he looked in and said 'Sorry you are only permitted to have two guests and a driver'. I very much wanted Edward to see the Ceremony too. Quickly I said to the Officer 'This man is my bodyguard'. He looked at me and said 'That is in order Sir'. He moved to the side to allow the car access to the courtyard. I was delighted. All of us were allowed in.

On entering the Palace, I was directed to the room where I and others were told the procedure and how to approach Her Majesty. We lined up in the order of being called. My name was called first. I walked forward and knelt on the stool. I received the Accolade from Her Majesty who hung the Insignia of a Knight Bachelor round my neck. I rose facing Her Majesty. Her remarks were fitting. I responded suitably, bowed and turned to take my seat in the room. At the close of the Ceremony my party gathered in the

Courtyard for photographs which are a wonderful memento of a memorable day at Buckingham Palace. We lunched and flew back to Scotland later in the day.

Prior to the visit to Buckingham Palace the Banff and Buchan Conservative and Unionist Association had invited me to a function in my honour, later in November. I was to be presented with gifts in recognition of my service as Member of Parliament for the constituency. It was a splendid occasion attended not only by Party members but constituents who had felt they wished to contribute to the success of the evening and to the gifts which had been bought from their contributions.

89. At Buckingham Palace with Knight Bachelor Insignia

I have treasured the inscribed silver salver over the years and proudly display the Elizabethan silver dish in our home, constant reminders of a wonderful evening among friends.

The inscription on the silver salver reads:

> Presented to Sir Albert McQuarrie KB
> for
> Outstanding Service to the Community
> as
> Member of Parliament
> for
> East Aberdeenshire Constituency 1979-1983
> Banff and Buchan Constituency 1983-1987

I was deeply honoured and extremely grateful to those who wished my efforts as Member of Parliament to be recognised in this manner. It was a fitting close to the celebrations of the Honour conferred upon me by Her Majesty The Queen on the recommendation of Prime Minister Margaret Thatcher.

90. With my son Dermot at Buckingham Palace, 1987

CHAPTER TWENTY-FIVE

Elections!

IN 1988 I WAS INVITED BY THE Scottish Conservative and Unionist Party to put my name forward as a candidate for the 1989 European Parliamentary Election. I responded by saying I would consider it and would make my decision known.

Over the months since the General Election I had kept contact with Miss Rhoda Gall, my former Agent. I decided to discuss with her the approach made for nomination as a candidate for the European Parliament. I felt I could face another challenge, my health was good and after discussing the possibility with Rhoda I decided to accept the invitation from the Party. Selection meetings were held in Paisley for the Strathclyde West Seat and in Inverness for the Highlands and Islands Seat. In the event I was selected for both. I decided to go for the Highlands and Islands which, as it turned out, was an error as I would have found running a campaign in the west of Scotland which included my home town of Greenock, perhaps, more productive. However, the decision was made. I started a positive campaign knowing the SNP Candidate was the sitting Member.

The Party had an established office in Elgin with Alan Dean as Agent. Although he was very much my Agent for the European Election, I found I was discussing more and more matters with Rhoda. Our relationship had grown and we decided to get married. A quiet wedding was planned at a church in London on 19th April 1989 where a good friend of mine was the Minister – only weeks before Election Day.

On returning to Scotland and to my office in Paisley I was told an Alastair Bisset wished to speak with me. Immediately I recognised the name of a journalist with *Aberdeen Journals* in the Elgin area and assumed the call would be in connection with the Election. I called him. He had one question 'Have you married Rhoda Gall?' I replied 'You must be talking nonsense'. He again said he had learned we had married in London. I said 'Somebody must have been kidding you'. My reason was to allow a few days for all our families to be informed. The immediate families knew of the 'quiet' planning of the occasion. Alastair then said, 'OK Albert I will print the denial in the paper tomorrow'. At that I had to accept defeat. Next day the *Press & Journal* printed a photograph of Rhoda and me with the caption 'Buchan Bulldog weds in secret' with a story of our wedding. The following day all the north east of Scotland papers carried the story. We were showered with messages of congratulations and good wishes. Our secret was well and truly out.

With an Election to be fought the campaign was foremost in our minds. We rented a house at Ballindalloch which was used for campaign meetings and regular briefings with my Agent. I was so pleased Rhoda was sharing with me this extremely challenging venture.

91. Election Campaign House at Ballindalloch

The Highlands and Islands Constituency for the European Parliament is vast, stretching from the Shetlands, through the north of Scotland, the Western Isles and into Argyll. We covered several thousands of miles by car, aircraft and ferry. I adopted the slogan 'Keep Britain United – Say No to Separation'. Then as now the SNP was promoting a campaign of Independence. We canvassed extensively. I addressed countless meetings

ELECTIONS!

92. On the campaign by helicopter - European Election 1989

supported on one occasion in Inverness by the Rt Hon Edward Heath MP former Prime Minister. The hall was packed for this most senior politician.

All my efforts, and those of many workers from the Northern Isles to the tip of Argyll, were not enough to win the Seat. What I had achieved was to bring the Party vote from a poor third in the previous European Election to second place with a much increased vote. The hard fact was the electorate did not support my Party. I was disappointed. Rhoda and I returned to our home in Troon to lead a normal life. We joined the Troon Branch of the Ayr Conservative & Unionist Association and took an active interest in local affairs.

By 1992, the year of a General Election, I was Deputy Chairman of the Ayr Association. Our candidate was Phil Gallie, a hard worker with the determination to win, sadly now deceased. Two weeks into the campaign when driving into Ayr, I was struck by Labour Posters on practically every lamp standard but not one for my Party. I drove to the office of Phil Gallie's Agent Pat McPhee who told me she had neither posters nor cardboard. I telephoned a friend of mine who supplied cardboard for packaging and ordered 100 boards to a particular size. I approached a local printer and asked him to print 100 posters urgently. Within two days I was in possession of both. I borrowed a pick-up truck from a farmer to hold the ladders I needed to climb the lamp standard. I pasted the posters on to the cardboard and fixed string for tying onto lamp standard.

The pick-up was loaded and I set out heading for the main roads and approaches to the towns and villages making sure the posters were fixed at a height where they would not be easily torn down. The operation took me two days but the impact on the Party workers was immense. There was a new enthusiasm. Phil Gallie was thrilled. I received only one complaint. It was from a woman in Bentinck Drive, Troon. As I was fixing the poster on the opposite side of the Drive she asked me what I was doing. I said to her it was obvious what I was doing. She told me I could not fix a poster on the column opposite her home. I looked across and saw a Labour poster displayed from her window. I said 'Madam, I am putting up this poster and you cannot stop me. If you interfere in any way with this poster, I will return each day and double the number of posters on the lamp standard'. I continued my 'work'. She retreated defeated. Phil Gallie won the Seat for our Party and was forever appreciative of my actions with the posters which he said had won him the day. I attended the Count. It was there I saw the same lady after the result was declared with a group of dejected Labour supporters. I was delighted at the victory for our Party in Ayr Constituency and the part I played. When the dust had settled I decided to take a rest from active politics other than retain my contact with the local Association.

It was time to relax a little more, enjoy playing golf on the wonderful Links courses in Ayrshire, even a day at the Races at the Ayr Western Club. Mingled in with the pleasures of a semi-retired life I obtained commissions for Planning Development throughout the west of Scotland, something which occupied a lot of my time, but it interesting and rewarding work.

Rhoda and I thoroughly enjoyed living in Troon and made many friends but in 1998 the decision was taken to move from Troon to Aberdeenshire and to the village of Mintlaw, an area well known to us both. After a period of re-establishing ourselves I became involved in activities within the local Community. There were a number of organisations in which I played a part one of them as a Trustee of the Public Halls and Playing Fields which many years ago had been gifted to the village for all time. I became Vice Chairman with a remit to secure funding for a new Children's Play Park within the Playing Fields. This was a challenge as the cost of the work and the provision of equipment amounted to £90,000.

After some 300 pieces of correspondence, many meetings and telephone calls over a two year period the funds were identified for the Play Park to be constructed. Rhoda played a large part in the preparation of applications for funds and letters of correspondence resulting in 90 per cent of the total funds being secured by myself and Rhoda with the balance from the Trustees and other sources. The Children's Play Park was opened in April 2012. It has been an outstanding success, giving pleasure to hundreds of children from Mintlaw, the surrounding area and to visitors. Shortly after the opening I tendered my resignation and at the same time wished the Trustees every success in their future activities and fund-raising.

Order of St John of Jerusalem, Knights Hospitaller

In September 1991 I was Invested as a Knight of Honour in the Order of St John of Jerusalem, Knights Hospitaller, a Christian Chivalric Order operating under the Royal Charter and Constitution decreed by His late Majesty King Peter II of Yugoslavia. The International Order has Grand Priories, Priories and Commanderies in many parts of the world. Although the Decrees by His Majesty only date from 1963 and 1964, the Order of St John has been in existence since 1099 when a Hospice was opened in Jerusalem by a band of Brothers who, during the Crusades, were designated Knights. There are a number of Orders of St John of Jerusalem, Knights Hospitaller operating throughout the world.

As there was no Priory in Scotland I was attached to the Priory of England within the Grand Priory of the United Kingdom and Eire. In 1995 I was requested to promote a Commandery in Scotland and in 1997 a new Commandery was established. The membership increased considerably. In 1999 the Commandery was elevated to a Priory and I was appointed the first Prior. During the year 2,000, a change took place when the Priory attached itself to the Sovereign Order of St John of Jerusalem, Knights Hospitaller whose Head Office was in Vancouver. A Grand Priory of the United Kingdom and Ireland was created. I was elected Grand Prior and also elevated to the rank of Knight Grand Cross of Justice and made a Bailiff of the Order. A few years later I was elected as a Conventual Bailiff of the Order holding the Office of Grand Counsellor.

In 2007 a considerable number of members aligned themselves to the Order of St John of Jerusalem, Knights Hospitaller, whose Headquarters are in the United Kingdom, and has as its Grand Master His Royal Highness Prince Karl Vladimir Karadjordjevic of Yugoslavia GCSJ, nephew of His late Majesty King Peter II. His wife HRH Princess Brigitta Karadjordjevic of Yugoslavia is a Grand Dame in the Order. In the same year the Priory changed its name to the Priory of St Margaret of Scotland.

It was now time for me to step back. I had spent a large amount of time and energy working for the Order. My successor was Knight Commander of Justice Nicholas Larkin who only after a year in Office resigned due to pressure of business. His successor was Lady Rhoda who still holds the Office and was elevated to the rank of Bailiff in March 2010.

93. Rhoda and me in Order of St John of Jerusalem Robes

---

port of the House of Commons debates.
lisher had to be found. Some years earlier The Memoir Club to write a book which it would publish. I did nothing about it. In tacted the Managing Director of The Memoir Club and in a short and conditions were agreed. Rhoda and I set to work. I wrote – s scribbled – the information for each Chapter. Rhoda laboriously d my writing as each Chapter landed on her desk before sending to ir Club for the compilation of the book.

94. Rhoda and me attending grandson Robert's Wedding

cise has been in many ways a satisfying one. When permission w use an extract from a newspaper or to publish a photograph, the en with pleasure. On making the decision to write my memoir o cover the many different parts of my life and in doing so b many happy memories of years past. Little did I realise when this journey that I would write 100,000 words with n phs as illustrations taking twelve months to complete the chap wrote each Chapter there were many moments of reflection

It is pleasing to record that in the years since 1997 over £150,000 has been raised by members of the Priory in Scotland for charitable purposes. A large proportion of these funds have been distributed to deserving causes in Scotland, with areas of great distress throughout the world receiving financial aid from the efforts of this Order of St John of Jerusalem, Knights Hospitaller.

Now it will be up to those younger members to carry on the fine ceremonial traditions handed down over the years as well as continuing to help those less fortunate than ourselves in the United Kingdom and Overseas.

CHAPTER TWENTY-SIX

The Conclusion

AFTER MANY MONTHS OF RESEARCH formulation, the concluding Chapter was rea experience then it has been a most fascinatin information for each Chapter - a proportion of proportion from records gathered over the years. U documents which would have been so valuable h which can happen to us all. It is hoped fami Parliamentary colleagues who read the book will find

For many years people asked me why I had n straight and simple answer is I have been so occupie put pen to paper. Now at the age of 95+ the book i compiling the Chapters of *A Lifetime of Memories* sinc glad to share them with so many who in some contributed to the book.

Over the years I have written many articles but decided to write one, I considered a 'Ghost Writer'. been David Torrance whom I knew had written bo when sourcing material which David had no means reminded about the sealed boxes containing my Par private files having been thrown into a tip by a relat this loss as deeply felt again. The relative was transporting the boxes which included personal ar from Teuchar Lodge to my home in the West of Sc the boxes was a Nebuchadnezzar of Champagne, equ had won at a Tory Ball in London. It was not to be. was broken open and those who drank it threw the bottle into the tip – lost forever.

After much thought I advised David Torrance I Ghost Writer realising the only way to proceed was by which would be heavily taxed, but also in the kn information, photographs, Press Releases and Recor with one exception, were of happiness and satisfaction. On travelling the road from my childhood to manhood, through the war years, to running successful businesses, embarking on a political career representing the Constituency of East Aberdeenshire and later Banff and Buchan, a boyhood ambition was achieved. The honour of a Knighthood conferred upon me in July 1987 by Her Majesty The Queen.

My interest in politics whether it be National or Local has never waned. My unbroken membership of the Conservative and Unionist Party spans seventy-nine years. I have kept my political interest alive and have heavily supported candidates at all levels of politics over the years. More recently my endeavours, along with those of Rhoda, have been geared towards charitable fund-raising which included a large proportion of funds raised for the Mintlaw Children's Play Park, as well as charitable works within the Order of St John of Jerusalem, Knights Hospitaller.

95. Rhoda and me attending Prime Minister's Reception

When the Association of Former Members of Parliament was formed I became a member. Joe Ashton, a former Labour Member of Parliament, and a few other 'retired' Members of Parliament he gathered around him, set up the Association which received wholehearted support of the Rt Hon Michael

THE CONCLUSION

Martin MP (now Lord Martin) who was Mr Speaker at the time. Since then successive Governments have supported the Association. Meetings are held in the House of Commons where the Association members are most appreciative of access to the Palace of Westminster by being able to show their Pass and walk up to the Central Lobby, the meeting place of many Members of Parliament past and present. A newsletter is published entitled **Order, Order!** – An interesting read for members, and non-members, of the Association and for serving Members of Parliament who in future years will make up the membership.

I am the fourth oldest former Member of Parliament from a total of 880 former Members living at this time. I am also the oldest former Conservative and Unionist Member of Parliament and the oldest member of the Association of Former Members of Parliament. It is always a pleasure to meet with former colleagues on special occasions when Mr Speaker hosts a Reception for the Association at Mr Speaker's House or when the Prime Minister issues an invitation to Association members to a Reception at his official residence 10 Downing Street.

Taking a holiday has never been uppermost in our minds. Over the years, I have had some wonderful holidays and am glad I was able to 'travel' the world when travelling was not quite as easy as it is today. Rhoda and I have had memorable holidays and have been fortunate in that Dermot and his wife, June, have a very nice home in Rancho Mirage near Palm Springs in California. Each time we have been there it has been in the months of January and February when the weather is around 75° with the swimming pool at a constant 83°. Since my childhood I have taken every opportunity available to me to swim in the sea or a swimming pool. There is nothing more I enjoy than exercising in the pool. I recall the days when I swam from Gourock across the River Clyde to Kilcreggan – I'm afraid I am no longer able to carry out that kind of activity and restrict myself to a swimming pool rather than the open sea!

As I pen the last lines of my book I do so with tremendous satisfaction. Rhoda's contribution has been magnificent. I am the first to admit her task was not an easy one. Without a doubt she succeeded, with a smile on her face, to do what no one else could do – and never a cross word!

Now the waiting game will commence when I anxiously await receipt of the first copy of my book on my desk. Completing this book follows the pattern my life has taken recognising the potential of situations as they arose and using the capabilities I was blessed with to help others not so fortunate as myself. It reveals a secret Rhoda and I have shared for some time. For both of us it has been interesting and rewarding.

I have always borne in mind the fine words of Simon Grellet in all I have tried to do and will continue to do. The words are:

> I shall pass through this world but once
> Any good I can do or any kindness I can show
> to anyone, let me do it now;
> Let me not defer or neglect it
> For I may not pass this way again.

It is with considerable satisfaction having recalled much of my life, I have finally completed *A Lifetime of Memories.*

Index

Aberdeen, Lord 12
Abraham, Walter 173
Anderson, Barry 105
Anderson, Commandant Major 20, 92
Anderson, John xiv
Ashton, Joe 275
Auld, Captain Alex 208
Aunt Dora 21
Azzopardi, Michael 76
Baroness Thatcher, Margaret, LG, OM, PC, FRS, MA, BSc 107-109, 112, 128, 129, 133, 136, 137, 164, 186, 229, 246-52, 259, 265
Benady, Pat 146
Benady, Samuel M, CBE, QC 146
Bethell, Lord Nicholas 144, 150, 154, 155
Bisset, Alastair 266
Bolton, James 14
Booth, Major 234, 235
Boothby, Lady Wanda 253, 254
Boothby, Robert (Lord Boothby of Buchan and Rattray Head) 96, 100, 101, 135, 136, 163, 184, 210, 211, 253
Borbidge, Robert 177
Bossano, Joe 145, 232
Botha, Mr P. 201
Bowie, Reverend Alan 9
Boyd, Viscount 150
Boyd-Carpenter, Lord 150
Boyle, Janet 3
Boyle, Rev Canon John 230
Boyson, Rhodes, MP 250
Braden, Bernard 44
Brant, Mr C.T. 195
Brown, Miss 7
Brown, Ronald, MP 206
Bruce, Malcolm 209
Buchan, Alan xiv
Buchan, David xiii, 208
Buchan, Tom 208, 211, 212
Buchanan, Richard 63, 64
Buchanan-Smith, Alick, MP 100, 132, 180, 190
Burniston, Norman xiii
Burrows, General Eva 235, 237, 238
Calder, Vincent 92
Callaghan, James 106
Callander, William 14
Cameron, David 252
Campbell, Ian, MP 241
Campbell, Rt Hon Gordon 95
Campbell-Savours, Dale 169
Canavan, Mr 146
Capurro, Mr 71
Champion, Don 176, 178
Champion, Maurine 176, 178

Charles, H.R.H. Prince 83, 86, 87, 114
Chartres, Rt Reverend Richard, KCVO 252
Chisholm, Alan 102, 103, 105, 106, 261
Churchill, Winston 87, 111, 254
Clarke, Kenneth 129
Clark, Major 24, 25
Clark, Professor Manning 173
Cleary, Hon, M.A. MP 178
Connolly, Rev Father 230
Constable, Robert 9
Conti, Rt Rev Mario 230
Cook, Sandy 102, 103, 105, 106
Coppleton, Charles 53
Cutler, Sir Roden, VC, LCMG, KCVO, CBE 175
Daley, Pa 10
Dalgarno, Ben 255
Dalziel, Colonel 247
Damanski, Maria 183
Darwent, Rt Rev Bishop Fred 254
Davies, Rt Hon Denzil, MP 155
Davidson, Ian, MP 61, 62
Davidson, Lynn xiii
Davidson, Viscount 225
Dean, Alan 266
Dempster, Mr 90
Dewar, Donald 244
Dingwall-Fordyce, J Alexander 96
Dingwall-Fordyce, Mary 97
Dingwall-Fordyce, Sandy 101
Docherty, Dr Roger 229, 234
Docherty, Helen 229
Donald, Dr John 36
Donovan, Mr K.R. 259
Doult, Bill xiii
Dron, John xiii
Duncan, Ken xiii

Dunn, James, MP 171
Fairgrieve, Sir Russell, MP 100, 132, 133
Fleming, Roger 54
Foot, Rt Hon Michael, MP 136
Forsyth, Michael (Lord Forsyth of Drumlean) 251
Frampton, Miss 111
Franco, General 63, 64, 66, 134
Fraser, Rt Hon Malcolm, CH, MP 177
Gaggero, Joseph 65
Gall, Rhoda xiv, 195, 258, 260, 265-70, 273-75
Gallie, Phil 268, 269
Gareze, Colonel Pepe 72
Gareze, Elizabeth (Libby) 72
Gareze, Mrs 72
Gay, Andrew 195, 203
Gifford, Audrey 19
Gifford, Lorna 19
Gifford, Mr & Mrs 19
Godman, Dr Norman 223
Gordon, David xiii
Gow, Ian, MP 187, 249
Grellet, Simon 277
Grocott, Lady Sally xiv
Hailsham, Lord 150
Hakim, Professor Nadey 73, 74
Hamilton, Lord James Douglas 244
Hamilton, Reverend Thomas 46
Hannah, Provost Thomas 65
Hart, James 12, 13
Hassan, Sir Joshua 78, 141, 145, 155, 157-60, 230, 232
Heath, Rt Hon Edward, MP 87, 101, 102, 268
Henderson, Douglas 102, 107, 133, 186

INDEX

Henderson, Mr 120
Hendry, Reverend J. Michael 231, 232
Her Majesty The Queen 39, 47, 73, 74, 87, 112, 119, 138, 160, 173, 176, 179, 188, 210, 212, 250, 260, 262, 264, 274
Hinchcliffe, Colonel 16, 17
Hodge, Mitchell 9
Hooker, Sapper James 33
Howe, Geoffrey 161, 166
Howell, Rt Hon Denis, MP 171, 178, 179
Hudson, Arthur 9
Hughes, Lord 150, 155, 206
Hughes, Bob MP (now Lord Hughes) 209, 224
Hurd, Rt Hon Douglas, CH, CBE, PC, MP (now Lord) 212
Hutchison, William 8
Isola, Peter 145, 232
Ison, Reverend David 252
Jackson, Wheatley 31, 32
Johnson, John, MLC 177
Johnston, Lord Provost 54
Joseph, Sir Keith 138
Karadjordjevic, His Royal Highness Prince Karl Vladimir, GCSJ 270
Karadjordjevic, HRH Princess Brigitta 270
Kelly, Barbara 44
Kelly, Lawrie, MP 177
Kirkwood, Archy (Lord Kirkwood) 224
Langford-Holt, Sir John 171
Larkin, Knight Commander of Justice Nicholas 271
Latham, Sir Michael, MP 155
Lloyd, Ian 186

Lovie, Jimmy 100, 106
Mabon, Dr J. Dickson, MP 54, 55, 57
Macdonald, George 263
MacDonald, Ian 56
Mackie, Bill xiii, 213
MacLay, Viscount John S, MP 43, 45
McCrae, Colin 208
MacRobert, Lady 12, 13
MacRobert, Sir Alexander 12
Maitland, Patrick (Earl of Lauderdale) 94
Malone, Gerald 209, 224
Mara, Ratu Sir Kamisese 84-87
Martin, Lloyd 177
Martin, Rt Hon Michael MP (Lord Martin) 276
Mason, David 61
Mather, E.H., MBE 175
Mathie, Jimmy 14
Mati, Lieutenant Colonel G 83
Mati, Mrs 83
Maxton, John, MP (now Lord) 241-243, 245
McAusland, Hugh 14
McCaffery, Dermot 48
McCaffery, Eddie 48
McCaffery, Edward 261
McCaffery, Hugh 49
McCaffery, Kevin 261
McCaffery, Mary 261
McCaffery, Vincent 48, 261
McCarthy, Mr & Mrs 201
McCartney, Hugh, MP 241
McCloy, Rachel 5
McClumpha, Robert 61, 64-66, 68, 69, 80
McColl, Roddy 100
McDonald, Mr 59

McKirdy, Miss 6
McLaren, Captain 32, 33
McLaughlan, Rev Father 230
Mclennan, Robert (Lord Mclennan of Rogart) 94
McNaughton, George 49
McPhail, Alice 35
McPhail, Samuel Forbes 5, 39
McPhee, Pat 268
McQuarrie, Algernon Stewart (Algy) 1, 2, 3, 5, 9
McQuarrie, Catherine Mary 73
McQuarrie, Charles 3, 5, 6, 9, 13, 39
McQuarrie, Dermot H H 36, 48, 51, 61, 63-66, 68-73, 79-82, 84, 87, 94-97, 108, 130, 134, 195, 204, 229-231, 261, 263, 265, 276
McQuarrie, Dermot Junior 73
McQuarrie, Elizabeth 73
McQuarrie, Jonathan 73
McQuarrie, June 276
McQuarrie, Lachlan 118, 171, 175, 176
McQuarrie, Louise 73
McQuarrie, Margaret Hastings 3-6, 9, 72, 228
McQuarrie, Robert (Grandson) 73
McQuarrie, Robert Sharman 3, 9, 10, 41, 44
McQuarrie, Roseleen 24, 33-36, 43, 48, 49, 51, 61, 63-65, 69, 70-72, 79, 82, 84, 87-90, 94, 96-98, 106, 108, 110, 113, 114, 123, 126, 134, 157, 159, 185, 186, 189, 195, 201, 203, 204, 228-233
McQuarrie, Roseleen (Granddaughter) 73
McQuarrie, Stephanie 73
Merrivale, Lord 150

Miller, Stuart 24
Milne, Stewart 103
Mitchell, Austin 224
Mitchell, David (Sir David) 223, 225
Mitchell, Joe 100-02
Mitchell, John 92, 93
Mungavin, Canon Gerald 97, 230
Mungavin, Margaret 97, 98
Murdoch, John 52
Murphy, Christopher 209
Murphy, Rev Father 230
Murray, George 105
Naughtie, James xiii, 135, 137
New, Rev Father 230
Nicol, Rev. W.J. 8, 16, 17
Orr, Depute Provost William 105
Park, Sandy 7
Paterson, Chris 130
Paterson, Peggy 130
Pearson, Sandy 7
Peliza, Major Sir Robert 155
Peralta, Louis xiii
Peters, Clara (daughter of Monica) 229
Peters, Monica 229
Peters, Sergeant Major 25, 29, 30
Pittendrigh, Alexander 101
Poggio, Albert CBE xiii
Pollock, Alexander 224
Pragnell, Donald 177
Prato, Da 22
Raison, Timothy 149
Raynor, William xiii, 132, 135
Reid, Flight Lieutenant 'Willie', VC 13
Renouard, Dominic 189
Richardson, Pipe Major 10
Rifkind, Sir Malcolm, KCMG, PC, QC, MP 191, 203, 230, 244, 251

INDEX

Rollo, Alex 44
Ross, Rt Hon William, MP (Lord) 92, 134, 171
Russell, Hector G. 11, 12, 13, 14, 17
Salmond, Mr 260
Sartin, Barbara 119
Scarff, Charles 69
Searle, Dominique xiv
Serfaty, Abraham 156, 232
Sempill, Lady 206
Sharman, Alice Maude 1
Sharman, Bob 5
Sharman, Grandfather 5
Sharman, Granny 5, 19, 21, 33
Shaw, David W. xiv
Shaw, W.L. Ramsay xiv
Sheehan, Rev Father 230
Sim, Harry 97
Soames, Lord 150, 154
Soames, Rt Hon Nicholas, MP 87
Stewart, Rt Hon Michael (Lord) 63-65, 134
Stewart, Rt Hon Donald 223, 248
Stonehouse, John 114
Strachan, Peter xiii
Stratton, William 14
Sturrock, Hon F.C. 202
Sutherland, Christine 100
Sutherland, Douglas 178
Taylor, J.E. 174
Thatcher, Amanda 252
Thatcher, Carol 246
Thatcher, Sir Mark 246
Thatcher, Sir Denis 229, 251, 252
Thomas, Rt Hon George (Viscount) 112, 116
Toomey, Dr 69, 70
Torrance, David 273
Underhill, Lord 225

Walker, Bill 117, 209
Walker, Peter 132, 180
Wallace, John E. xiii, 213, 215
Wallace, Sybil 130
Walter, Corporal 70
Walters, Charles 75
Ward, Jean 229
Ward, Sir John 229
Watt, Michael xiv
Watti Tagilala, Mr 83, 84
Watti Tagilala, Mrs 83, 84
Weatherall, Jack (Lord) 230
Webb, Professor Edwin C. 173
Welby, The Most Reverend Archbishop Justin 252
Wheeler, D.L 176
Whitelaw, Rt Hon William (Lord) 140, 141, 148, 150-152, 154
Whyte, Dr John 176, 178
Whyte, Flora 176
Wigoder, Lord, QC 155
Wilson, Gordon 209, 248
Wilson, Rt Hon Brian 62
Wolrige-Gordon, Patrick 96, 101, 135, 184, 254
Woodifield, Peter xiii, 245
Wran, Neville Kenneth, QC, MP 176, 177
Wren, Sammy 11,
Wright, Professor Esmond 93
Younger, Diane 93
Younger, Hon George, MP (Viscount) 57, 93, 106, 122, 204, 207
Zyle, Mr & Mrs Van 200, 201